KINGSTHC

A Royal Manor

TONY HORNER

Léonie Press

ISBN
1 901253 51 1
First published November 2005
Reprinted November 2005

© Tony Horner 2005

British Library Cataloguing in Publication Data.
A catalogue record for this book is
available from the British Library.

Published by:
Léonie Press an imprint of
Anne Loader Publications
13 Vale Road, Hartford,
Northwich, Cheshire CW8 1PL Gt Britain
Tel: 01606 75660   Fax: 01606 77609
e-mail: anne@leoniepress.com
Website: www.anneloaderpublications.co.uk
www.leoniepress.com

Design and layout by:
Anne Loader Publications

Printed by: Antony Rowe Ltd
Bumper's Farm Industrial Estate
Chippenham Wiltshire SN14 6LH

ABOUT THE AUTHOR

TONY Horner's maternal ancestors came to Kingsthorpe in 1774. He was born in 1932, when his parents kept the *King William IV* on the Green, and he lived there for the first seven years of his life. Then, just before the Second World War, his parents took on the licence of the *Bantam Cock* on Abington Square, Northampton; but contact was maintained with friends in Kingsthorpe for a number of years afterwards. He began his primary education in Kingsthorpe, continued it at St Giles's School, and then went to the Grammar School for boys (as it then was) on the Billing Road. Work at the old Borough Engineer & Surveyor's Department, in Dychurch Lane, was interrupted by two years' National Service in the RAF. He was then employed by the Northampton Town & County Building Society (which eventually became part of Nationwide), where he remained until obtaining early retirement in 1987. He worked as a cashier, as a mortgage advisor, and then as one of the first members of the department set up to introduce computer technology to the Society.

He married Teresa (a Kingsthorpe girl) in 1956, and they lived in Kingsway for five years before moving to Northampton for the next thirty years. In 1991 they moved back to Kingsthorpe, having produced a family of three boys and a girl – who in their turn have produced a range of grandchildren. Like so many people in recent years, retirement gave time to become involved in family history research; this revealed the wealth of historical documents possessed by the Northamptonshire Record Office, and Tony began the process of researching the history of his birthplace. He also has a variety of other interests, such as gardening and visiting other people's gardens, reading (and writing) about the spirituality of Christianity, Judaism, Buddhism and several other faiths. He and his wife are members of St Aidan's Catholic Church in Kingsthorpe.

CONTENTS

KINGSTHORPE: A ROYAL MANOR EXPLORED

CONTENTS

INTRODUCTION

THIS history of Kingsthorpe is necessarily based on the surviving documents, many of which once resided in the Parish Chest. As might be expected, the 19th century is well represented; but there are also some records from the late 17th century that throw light on the lives of the inhabitants at that time. Earlier documentation is more generalised, but useful inferences can be drawn from it. I have gone as far back into the past as possible, but have not brought the story right up to the present time. The beginning of the 20th century, when Kingsthorpe ceased to be an independent self-governing entity, is my approximate cut-off point; but where a subject requires rounding off I have extended it by a few decades into that century. It is the sort of history that I wanted to read, but since it had not been written I had to write it myself.

I have based much of the text on research at the Northamptonshire Record Office, where there is a wealth of material. I have also made use of the work of others who have studied the history of this parish, and whose dissertations are to be found in the Northamptonshire Studies Collection at Northampton Public Library. I am particularly grateful for the work of the late Alec Brooking, whose widow kindly gave permission for me to make copies of portions of his documents, and for the unpublished theses of G R Bispham and Suzanne Wright. My thanks are also due to Geoffrey Starmer for the use of his research of the Kingsthorpe mills, and to Leo Bell who provided information relating to the more recent history of St David's. Sources of information, as well as quotations, have been referenced to the *Bibliography* or to documents at Northamptonshire Record Office; see the section entitled *Sources*. I have avoided direct quotations from such material as far as possible, preferring to state the facts recorded or my own interpretations of the records; but where the material is of sufficient interest I have provided a transcription. Some of the interpretations or assumptions that I have made will be incorrect, and I shall be pleased to receive corrections from any reader who has better knowledge of the facts.

The older history of a community such as this is always centred on the parish church. This is not simply because most of the inhabitants were churchgoers, but because it was the Parish Vestry Meeting that was the instrument of Local Government until the end of the 19th century. This was especially so from the 16th century onwards, when the powers of the manors were gradually returned to the parishes. In the case of Kingsthorpe, which had almost always been self-governing, it was more a question of a change in the name of the meetings rather than any change in the people who were appointed as Parish Officers.

I have used, and often listed, the names of pieces of land wherever they occur; the names of Closes, Fields and Furlongs are often attractive and imaginative. However, it is not usually possible to relate such names to the modern topography – though I have tried to do so in certain instances. Readers may wish to build on the foundation I have laid, in this and other respects. There are some very good old buildings in the village, many of them 'Listed', and I have traced some of them as far back as the available documentation allows.

My sincere thanks are here expressed to the people who assisted me in the compilation of this history: the archivists and staff of the Northamptonshire Record Office, who were always most helpful in answering my many queries; Ron Greenall, the Hon. General Editor of the Northamptonshire Record Society, for his invaluable advice; and Jill Mitchell and John Parbery, who read drafts of the text.

Tony Horner
January 2005

CURRENCY, MEASUREMENTS & ABBREVIATIONS

Currency

Until 1971 English currency was expressed in **pounds, shillings,** and **pence**. Twelve pence made one shilling (1s.0d or 1/-), and twenty shillings made a pound (£1 = 240 pence). The symbols used to denote these units, **£** (a form of L) **s** and **d**, are derived from the Latin names *librae, solidii* and *denarii*. A pound was originally that weight (i.e. 16 ounces) of silver, from which 240 pennies could be minted. A **farthing** was a quarter of a penny and until 1279 was produced, like the half-penny, by cutting up a penny. A gold **Sovereign** was issued in 1489, and it was worth 30/- by the reign of Elizabeth I. James I replaced it with the **Unite**, named after the union of England and Scotland, which was worth £1. The Sovereign was reintroduced from 1817 until 1917. It was common for many centuries to use fractions of a pound: starting with 10d, this can be doubled to 1/8d, doubled again to 3/4d, and again to 6/8 – which is one third of a pound. A gold coin of this value was minted in 1344; known as a **Noble**, it was superseded in 1464/5 by the **Angel** – so called because it had a depiction of the Archangel Michael on its obverse. Two thirds of a pound, 13/4d, was referred to as a **Mark**, though this was never an actual coin in England. A **Florin**, when minted in silver in 1849, was worth 2/-, but a gold coin of this name was minted in 1344 and was worth 3/-; its name was derived from Florence, the city that minted Europe's first gold coin. One pound and one shilling was known as a **guinea**, although originally this was a gold coin worth £1; it was first minted in 1663, and named after the place where the gold was found: Guinea in West Africa. In 1717 it was given a value of 21 shillings, and discontinued as a coin in 1813.

Further details about coins and tokens can be found in Section Q of Richardson's book; see the *Bibliography*.

Land measurement

Beginning with the linear measure of a **rod**, this originated as a long **rod** or **pole** used as an ox goad; it needed to be long in order to reach to the front of a team of oxen. It was eventually standardised at 5½ **yards** = 16½ **feet**, there being 3 feet (36 inches) to one yard. When multiplied by 4 we have 66 feet = 22 yards = 1 **chain**, the standard length of a cricket pitch. (The actual chain used by a surveyor had 100 links, and distances would be specified, in decimal form, in chains and links.) 10 chains = 220 yards = 40 poles = 1/8 **mile**, also known as a **furlong** (furrow-long). One mile is 1760 yards = 5280 feet; this was standardised in 1593. Now moving into area measurements, an **acre** is 40 poles multiplied by 4 poles, or 220 x 22 = 4840 square yards. Think of it as a piece of land a furlong in length and four poles in width. A **rood** is 40 square poles – a quarter of an acre, and sometimes referred to as a quartern or quarteron. So the area described as one rod, pole or **perch** is 5½ x 5½ = 30¼ square yards in extent. Land area measurements were expressed in acres, roods and poles (or perches), abbreviated as a. r. & p.

More ancient measurements, such as those used in the Domesday Survey, were usually based on the **Hide**, which was defined as the amount of land needed to support one peasant family throughout the year. Its actual size would thus vary, depending upon the quality of the land under cultivation. One **Hide, Carucate** or **Ploughland** = 4 **Virgates** or **Yardlands**, and one Virgate or Yardland = 2 **Bovates** or **Oxgangs**. But these were extremely variable in extent, and one Virgate or Yardland could represent anything between 10 and 20 acres. Further information will be found in Richardson, Section A1.

Weight measurement

16 ounces (ozs) = one pound (1 lb).

14 lbs = one stone. (The Romans used an actual stone for weight measurement, and the Latin for stone is *calculus*).

112 lbs = one hundredweight (1 cwt).

20 cwts = one ton = 2240 lbs.

Dates

In the Middle Ages one frequently finds the year designated by the regnal year of the monarch; for instance 12 Henry VIII would be 1520 AD (though, strictly speaking, only after 22 April, the date of his coronation). A table of regnal years is necessary in order to convert such dates into years AD. The actual day upon which an event occurred was often designated as so many days before or after a particular feast day or fast, so a table of such days is necessary in order to translate such dates into modern civil terms.

Caution is needed when AD dates are quoted in old documents, since the beginning of the civil year was often designated differently in different places; it might be 1 January, 25 March, or even 25 December. The first *Book of Common Prayer* stated that the year should begin on 25 March, and it gave as the reason for this the belief that this was the day on which the world was created, and it was the date of the conception of Christ – usually referred to as the Annunciation to the Blessed Virgin Mary. As a result, the majority (but not all) of parish records changed the year on this date. This means that the first three months of our (new style) year were the last three months of their (old style) year, which can cause the unwary genealogist or historian to trip. When transcribing dates in those months, it is good practice to give both old style and new style years in the form 20 March 1520/21. Note also that the numbers of the months in what we would call the previous year also reflect the old style format: the names September, October, November, and December actually mean the 7th, 8th, 9th and 10th months – March being considered to be the first. Since some parish records use such abbreviations, this potential ambiguity can also cause confusion.

The calendar used in England was changed in September 1752. Until that time, the Julian calendar had been in use, although many continental countries had changed to the more accurate Gregorian system introduced by Pope Gregory XIII in 1582. But since England was then a protestant country it was decided not to use this popish system. The inaccuracy of the Julian calendar meant that the two systems gradually drifted apart, and by 1752 there was a difference of 11 days between them. In order to lose that number of days, it was decided that the day following 2 September in that year would be 14 September. No wonder that the cry was heard "Give us back our eleven days!" At the same time, the civil and ecclesiastical year began on 1 January in that year, 1752. Some people introduced this change prior to its official inception, so care is needed in this respect when examining documents of the period.

Abbreviations used in the text
NRO Northamptonshire Record Office
PR   Parish Register
PRO Public Record Office

SITUATION AND TOPOGRAPHY

KINGSTHORPE is now a suburb of the town of Northampton, but was once a village two miles northwards from the centre of that town. It was also a Royal Manor, which the inhabitants held at Fee Farm from the Crown; see *The Manor of Kingsthorpe* below for details. It formed part of the administrative area known as the Hundred of Spelhoe. A Hundred was an administrative division of a Shire, and is a term that probably dates back to the 10th century. Some areas of the country used other terms for these divisions, such as Wapentake, Leet, Ward or Liberty.

The church, dedicated to St John the Baptist, was, along with that at Upton, a chapel of ease to St Peter's in Northampton; it was established as a full parish in 1850. There were connections with St Andrew's Priory, from which the original impetus for the building of a church in Kingsthorpe probably originated some time in the reign of the Saxon King Edward (1042-1066). The original parish was bounded on the north by Boughton; on the east by Moulton Park and Abington; on the south by Northampton; and on the west by the river Nene, which separated it from Dallington, Church Brampton and Chapel Brampton. The original ecclesiastical parish was gradually divided up amongst new parishes following the development of housing estates in the 19th and 20th centuries: St Paul's in Semilong (1877); St Matthew's in Kingsley Park (1891); Holy Trinity in Queens Park (1899); St David's on the estate of that name (1967); and St Mark's in White Hills (1980).

In 1900 Kingsthorpe's independent status came to an end when it became part of the borough of Northampton.

Situation

Alec Brooking well describes the early village as forming an L-

1

shape, with the church and the Green at the elbow. It was sited at the junction of the permeable Northampton Sands and the Upper Lias Clay, which accounts for the numerous springs and man-made wells that supplied the inhabitants with water. Being built on the Northampton Sands gave the houses a dry situation with local supplies of limestone, ironstone (or ferruginous limestone), and sandstone for building purposes. The highest point in the original parish was about 400 feet (125 metres) above sea level, on the Great Oolite Limestone Belt. The soil in the surrounding area has always been very suitable for farming. At the east end of the village there was an important trackway (now the A5199) running from Northampton to Leicester via Welford. The road to Market Harborough only became important after the Norman Conquest, since that town was not established until the 12th century. Not surprisingly, there were early connections with the nearby town of Northampton. The Domesday Survey of 1086 makes it clear that there was a settled community here during Edward's reign, probably consisting of 130 or so persons.

The Mills

Kingsthorpe had three water mills, which were known as the North or Farre Mill (being furthest from the village), the Nether Mill in the village, and the South Mill nearer to Northampton. The latter was also called St Andrew's Mill, due to its connection with the priory of that name. It was also the origin of the name Semilong, which is a contraction of South Mill Wong: the meadow of the South Mill. These mills are mentioned in the Domesday survey of 1086, at which time they produced a rental of £2.3s.4d per annum. In 1822 they belonged to Sir George Robinson, bart., and were subject to a fee farm rent of £12.12s.4d per annum: £2.10s.0d for the North Mill, £4.4s.0d for the Nether Mill and £5.18s.4d for the South Mill. In the late 19th century they were sold off to different purchasers.

A Journey around the Manor Boundaries

To travel around the old boundaries of Kingsthorpe Manor, in approximate terms only, one would have to start at the northern end of Meadow View on the Welford Road. The boundary started at the river, crossed the road here, and continued towards the Harborough Road, which it crossed at a point just north of the *White Hills* public house. It then continued through 'Kingsthorpe Heath', just north of where the Cemetery now is, curving round somewhat towards the southern edge of Moulton Park, roughly where Yardley Drive joins Boughton Green Road. Moulton Park, or King's Park, was extra-parochial and described as a Royal Peculiar. It had been a royal hunting estate from at least the mid 12th century, and was used on the occasions of the king's visits to Northampton Castle. Suzanne Wright says (p.13) that in 1380 Richard II stayed at Moulton hunting lodge rather than at the Castle.

The boundary then ran along the south of Moulton Park and around the Old Inclosures known as Edmunds's Farm until it reached the Kettering Road at the bottom of Spinney Hill. From Yardley Drive, south along Boughton Green Road for a short distance, there is a foot-path off to the left that runs in a south-easterly direction towards the Kettering Road. Some of the land to the north of this path was in the parish; first there were two allotments made to Thomas Powys in 1767, bordering his farm at Moulton Park, and then about a third of the old inclosure known as Edmunds's Farm. The path can be traced across that farm on the draft Inclosure map of 1767, when it was awarded as a private road. To the right of the path is the area once known as the 'Park Field', and then, nearer to the Kettering Road, the 'Brook Field'. On reaching the Kettering Road the boundary turned right, with 'The Dry Close' in Abington parish to the left, and then it went along Park Avenue North. 'Swarbidge Head Furlong' used to lie to the right, between Park Avenue North and Kettering road. The boundary continued as far as Cedar Road (approximately), where it turned west as far as Collingwood Road. It then turned south again towards Abington Avenue, and west again to Abington Grove; it followed this to the junction with the Kettering Road, where the gallows stood. The area roughly bounded by Park Avenue North, Abington Avenue, and Abington Grove was the 'Manhill (also known as Mannings, Manwell or Manuel) Field'.

Its course continued along Kingsley Road, turning left into St George's Avenue, with 'Northampton Heath', now The Racecourse

3

Park, on the left. About half way along the Avenue the boundary went off to the right, curving round the area which, according to Speed's map of 1610, contained brick kilns, until it reached the main road at Kingsthorpe Hollow roughly where Monarch Road is now. From there it went towards Kingsthorpe, but only as far as Burleigh Road where it turned left and left again into Semilong Road – once known as 'Cut Throat Lane'. The 'Simmeylong Field' was to the right here, extending down to the river. It continued along Semilong Road until it came to Mill Road, where it turned right and continued down Mill Lane into St Andrew's Road to a point just south of the South Mill, or St Andrew's Mill. The remaining, western portion of the boundary consisted of the river northwards to the starting point of this journey.

The Stream known as Walbeck

Among the laws and customs of Kingsthorpe set out in 1547, as recorded by the Rev Glover (p.93), was one which forbade anyone who was not of the Town of Kingsthorpe from digging, damming or fishing in Walbeck Brook, which ran from "Swarbrong Hedd to Walbecke". Defaulters were to be fined 3/4d. Baker says that the stream rose at "Swavey Head near the new road to Kettering," where it had a strong petrifying quality; it then ran along the hollow way between Kingsthorpe and Northampton, now known as Kingsthorpe Hollow, and into the river Nene. Bridges says this rivulet was fed by nine springs in a row, all within half a mile of each other.

The Rev J C Fox refers to the source of this rivulet in a record of 1656, relating to a water supply for Northampton, where it was named as 'Swarbutts Head.' Then there is a furlong named 'Swarbidge Head' in the Robinson Survey of 1727, also mentioned in the Inclosure Award of 1767, at the east end of the Brook Field, between what is now Kettering Road and Park Avenue North. Swarbrong Head, Swavey Head, Swarbutts Head and Swarbidge Head are all variations in the name of the same source of water; and no doubt it was this stream that was the origin of the name of the Brook Field, which stretched across to the Semilong Field.

This brook, anciently known as Walbeck, but sometimes as

Wallbank, had its rising, (to judge by the contours) near to the present Brookland Road. From here it made its way northwards along what is now Brookfield Road and flowed along the valley between Fairway and Kingsthorpe Golf Course. Here it used to cross the road (Gipsy Lane), and in December 1857 the Surveyors of the Highways were instructed to construct a footbridge over it; this bridge is mentioned in George James de Wilde's 1863 walk to Kingsthorpe, described in the chapter *Rambles Roundabout*. Suzanne Wright (p.72) says that it was known as Sourlands Brook where it crossed Gipsy Lane; no doubt it took this name from Sourlands Furlong, which must therefore have been in this area. It then flowed between Balfour Road and Stanhope Road and eventually into the river. There is an old specification which mentions a bridge in connection with some works in Kingsthorpe Hollow "for lowering the hill on the north side of Wallbank and for raising the Hollow between the Hills, for making the road over the new surface and for building the requisite drains, bridge, fences and field gates." There are very few visible traces of this stream remaining today. The land that was its catchment area has long been built upon, and the rainwater diverted into drains.

Near to the point at which this stream entered the river, there were some enclosed parcels of land that took their names from it. They were known as Walbeck Close, Great Walbeck Close and Little Walbeck Close. According to Speed's map of 1610, the stream clearly marks the boundary between Walbeck Close and Little Walbeck Close.

The Leper Hospital

It is perhaps not well known that a Lazar or Leper Hospital once functioned at Kingsthorpe Hollow. This hospital was first mentioned in The Victoria County History of the Counties of England (VCH ii, 162) under the heading *The Hospital of Walbek, Northampton*. The Rev R M Serjeantson (1915, p.25) gives more details in his article about the leper hospitals of the town, under the heading *The Hospital at Walbeck, Northampton*. He says that very little is known of its history and it appears to have had only a short existence. He found it mentioned twice in the Episcopal Registers at Lincoln. Both entries relate to the early years of the 14th century and to the granting of indulgences to "all benefactors of the sick men in the Hospital of Walebek" and to "all who...contributed to the sustentation of the poor lepers of the house of Walbek without the North Gate of Northampton".

Serjeantson discovered another reference to this long forgotten Hospital in one of the Coroner's Rolls for Northamptonshire (1344-1362; No.113, M.11), in which a tragedy is recorded as having happened "at Walbeck, in the parish of Kingsthorpe." In April 1347 two lepers, Richard de Wynwyck and Roger of Aylesbury, were found dead in the hospital. According to the evidence, one of the servants of the hospital, Henry of "Ashebourne in le Peke" (what a nice descriptive name!), had struck Richard on the head with a hatchet and had also killed Roger.

Rambles Roundabout

The author (G.J.) of a piece in William Hone's Year Book of 1832 (Page 1167, or 584-5 in some editions) began by saying that there was not a prettier village near Northampton than Kingsthorpe; half an hour's leisurely stroll along a rural route was sufficient to get him there. He began his walk along Sheep Street, then along the main road as far as the Racecourse. There he went through a gate on his left, down a path to a picturesque lane (now Semilong Road) where he turned right and so came back to the main road. He then stepped over a stile on the left and walked along a footpath, separated from the main road by a row of fine elm trees, with a lovely view to his left. Crossing one or two more stiles, he came into the Park (now Thornton Park) with a pretty view of the stone mansion; the Park contained some fine forest trees. He then crossed another stile back into the main road, on the right of which stood a charming cluster of thatched stone cottages that had been formed from the remains of St David's chapel. (Today there is a row of shops, terminating with the *White Horse*; the major portion of St David's Hospital had been on the other side of what is now Kingsthorpe Grove.) Taking the first turn on the left, down Mill Lane, he saw on his right some enclosed grounds, stables and an "antique looking" farmhouse. Following the lane further he came to the village of Kingsthorpe proper, "famous

Late 19th century view from 'The Bank' looking towards the church. This is very much as it would have looked to the writer in William Hone's Year Book of 1832. (Picture courtesy of Robert Hounslow).

for its beautiful springs", beside one of which, the King's Well, he proceeded to sketch the view of the church. (A few decades later those beautiful springs would be seriously polluted – but that is a matter for a later chapter: *The disposal of sewage.*)

In 1863 George James de Wilde, the Editor of the Northampton Mercury, also came this way, but varied his route when he got to the *White Horse* (which has, of course, been rebuilt since his time). By 1863 this was no longer an inn, but he indulged in reminiscences about its past, with its beautiful bowling green and its open prospect of trees, undulating fields and rustic roofs. He said that, had he come this way in 1831, like the writer in Hone's Year Book, he could have sat at a little round table outside the *White Horse* in the evening sunshine and enjoyed a cheesecake – for which it had a reputation – and "a glass of amber home-brewed". He reminisced further about the fashionable aristocrats who might have frequented the bowling green in the past. (Perhaps he knew something of the Kingsthorpe

Bowling Green Club, whose members met there from 1771 until 1852.)

But then his enthusiasm turned to *The Cock*, "an inn to glad the rambler's eye", that he likened to the inns in Hogarth's pictures. He describes the vine growing across its front, its ample bay windows and its balcony with seats over the front door. He then crossed the wide main road to the Blacksmith's shop, part of which consisted of some remains of the Hospital of St David (or The Holy Trinity): "one large arch and two Decorated niches, one blocked up." He quotes Baker on the Hospital of the Holy Trinity at some length, before following the main road and taking the left fork towards Welford. The last building on his right was *Court Farm*, which had an impressive entrance gateway of stone, and a side doorway that he ascribes to the transition period between Gothic and Renaissance. (This building may have been the venue for the Manorial Courts prior to the building of the Town House; it later became *The Court House* and then *Wardington Court*.)

Present day view from 'The Bank' looking towards the church. (Photo by the author).

He suggests several routes by which one could get to the heart of the village: by streets of quaint cottages and old stone houses, or by narrow lanes running between stone walls that enclose gardens and orchards. He is clearly referring here to High Street and to Danes Backside footpath or The Leys. The village Green is the next object of his admiration, and he describes the scene there as eminently rural. He mentions the Town House, which once served as a Workhouse, and goes on to describe the church. He says that it had once been the custom, when a grave was opened in the churchyard, to shovel the bones of its previous occupier through the window at the east end of the crypt, which thus became a charnel house. It had since been cleared, and the bones buried in a pit at the north-east end of the churchyard.

Describing the Morgan mansion, which used to stand east of the church, he says that the stone casing of a doorway, the pediment above and an alcove on either side "can still be seen". He then quotes from an advertisement in the Northampton Mercury of 1721, which

The Cock Inn before 1893, with its balcony over the front door, so enthusiastically described by G J de Wilde. (Picture courtesy of Alan J Clarke).

Welford Road, Kingsthorpe at around 1900, looking north; the cart is outside the Rose & Crown public house at the junction with High Street. This view would have changed little since G J de Wilde walked this way in 1863. (Picture courtesy of Alan J Clarke).

described it as "a very handsome, large, pleasant house, with a very good close, gardens, stables, coach-house, dove-house, brew-house, and other outhouses and conveniences thereunto adjoining, being late the dwelling house of John Morgan, esq., deceased." The Morgan family, he tells us, can be traced back to Judge Morgan in 1558; and he goes on to mention the other major families who resided in Kingsthorpe.

The return journey was by a rural lane (now Kingsthorpe Grove) that was bordered by hedges, overhung with trees, and surrounded by "long fields of barley and of rye". At the bottom of the hill he crossed a footbridge over a stream and returned to the town across the Racecourse.

THE MANOR OF KINGSTHORPE

THE elements of the name Kingsthorpe tell us two important things. First, its earliest known name, Torp, which comes directly from the Danish and means a small outlying settlement. (Alec Brooking lists some of the forms which the name took in early documents: Torp, 1086, 1174, 1175; Trop, 1195; Thorp, 12th century; Kingestorp, 1190; Kinestrop, 1202; Throp, 13th century; Kyngesthorp, 14th & 15th centuries.) So there was certainly a settlement here during the 9th century, when this part of the country was under Danish rule. But there was in all likelihood a Saxon village here at an early date, and probably a church – even if it was only a wooden structure. Second, the name tells us that this was a manor that belonged to the King. This is confirmed by the Domesday survey of 1086, which says that Torp had been in the King's hands at least since the time of Edward the Confessor (1042-1066). During King Edward's time, as at the time of the Domesday survey, it produced a rent of £15 per annum together with a rent of £2.3s.4d. for the three mills. This rental increased somewhat during subsequent centuries. During the reign of Henry VI (1422-1461) it was £60 until, in 1437, it was reduced to £50 owing to the great poverty of the inhabitants. A rent of £50 was confirmed by Henry VII in 1489, again by Henry VIII in 1519, and from time to time until 1594.

Kingsthorpe manor was not important enough to become a corporate borough, but it was fortunate enough to escape having either a bailiff appointed by the King, or the rent collected by a third party – who could have charged an excessive amount in order to make a profit. Instead, and quite unusually, the inhabitants were granted a lease direct from the Crown, under which they held the manor at 'Fee Farm.' This historical term means that tenure was held from the King at a fixed rent without any other services being required. Records show that this method of tenure for Kingsthorpe dates back at least to the reign of King John (1199-1216). The annual rental was paid through the Trustees of the Manor (or Town) Lands; and there was a bailiff, who was chosen by a majority of the freeholders. They had their own seal, dating from the 14th century, which portrayed a crowned head between two *fleurs de lys*.

A wax impression of the Seal of Kingsthorpe. The seal itself dates from the late 14th century. (Picture from the late Alec Brooking's collection).

The head has the two-pointed beard that was characteristic of Richard II (1377-1399); it also appears on his monument in Westminster Abbey. The *fleur de lys* symbol relates to the royal house of France, so the seal probably dates from just after the marriage in 1396 of Richard II and Isabella of France, and may indicate that Queen Isabella held the manor; Richard's first wife, Anne of Bohemia, had previously held it. Just beneath each *fleur de lys* appears a sprig of common broom, *planta genista*, which appears in the crest of the House of Plantagenet. The Latin inscription around the seal reads *Sigillum Comune de Kyngesthorp* (the Common Seal of Kingsthorpe).

In 1616 the manor was granted by King James I to Francis Morgan and 31 other gentlemen and yeomen as trustees for the other freeholders. An indenture of 1 May 1617 refers to the Letters Patent of 13 April 1616 which granted to these trustees the 'Towne and village of Kingsthorpe' at an annual rental of £40. The number of these trustees would be reduced with the passage of years, but the survivors were empowered to nominate new members. In 1705 Queen Anne appointed new trustees and regulated future appointments. This indenture, dated 29 September 1705, conveyed the manor *from*: John Morgan, Esq.; Henry Milward, gentleman; Wm. Atkins, gentleman; and John Billingham, yeoman, *to*: Francis Cooke, Edmund Morgan, Hatton Atkins, gentlemen; Wm. Green, junior; Wm. Morris, senior; Wm. Morris, junior; Richard Hollis, John Cooch, Samuel Crick, and Edward Atkins, yeomen, all of Kingsthorpe.

An example of the appointment of new trustees occurred in October 1752, when three freeholders of the 'Manor, Lordship, or Seigniory of Kingsthorpe', Sir John Robinson of Cranford St Andrew, bart.; Samuel Hartshorne of Northampton, Gent.; and Richard Greene of Kingsthorpe, yeoman, released the manor to nine new trustees: William Goodday of Strelling, Notts., Clerk (in Holy Orders); Luke Langdon of Southwark, Surrey, Gent.; Lucas Greene, Richard Wood, Henry Tibbs, Thomas Greene, and William Jaquest, (all yeomen of Kingsthorpe); William Treslar of Kingsthorpe, baker; and Thomas Cooch of Harlestone, yeoman.

A stone Town House was provided for the meetings of the trustees by Sarah, Lady Prichard (1637/8-1718). She was born Sarah Cooke, and her family held one of the large estates in Kingsthorpe.

Most fee farm rents were sold off during the Commonwealth period (1648-53), but those pertaining to Kingsthorpe were not sold until 1672 when Lord Chief Justice Rainsford purchased them. The annual rental of £40, together with £12.12s.4d. for the three mills, was paid to him and to his heirs from then onwards.

Following the Inclosure of Kingsthorpe in 1767 almost all the land was held by individuals, who could freely dispose of it thereafter as they wished. The Inclosure Commissioners allotted to the Trustees for the Manor and Town some land in the Park Field, subsequently known as the Town Land or Town Close. A further piece of land comprising 14a.0r.11p, known as Bush Close or the Poor's Close, was allotted to provide income for those poor people of the parish who had previously been able to collect furze from the common land.

The original manor and parish of Kingsthorpe was large, extending in Baker's time to 1850 acres. The Inclosure Act of 1767 referred to a total of 1743 acres, though the subsequent Award refers to only

1583a.1r.37p; this included the public and private roads and foot-ways. But this total excluded a considerable area of old inclosures, including the village itself.

KINGSTHORPE MANOR AND TOWN LANDS CHARITY

This appears to be the name eventually given to the group of Manor Trustees, perhaps following the Inquisition of Charities in 1682. But it only became a charity in the modern sense during the 19th century, following the inclosure of the common lands. A legal document dated 24 January 1708/9 appointed new trustees to the Kingsthorpe Town Charity: Wm Atkins & Henry Milward, Gents., appointed John Morgan Esq.; Hatton Atkins, Gent.; Wm Morris the elder, Yeoman; and Wm Greene, Yeoman.

When the land was inclosed in 1767, the Commissioners allotted 14a.2r.14p. to the feoffees (or trustees) of the Manor. The income from this land was applied to road repairs, rates and taxes and to other parochial purposes. From at least 1808 onwards the trustees leased it out every seven years to the highest bidder. The first meeting recorded in the earliest extant Vestry Book was held on 5 October 1808, and its purpose was stated as the letting of the Town Close, late in the occupation of Thomas Green and Charles Fitzhugh. It was agreed that one acre would be used for the digging of stone – meas-ured from the existing pit towards the hedge next the road (Pitchwell Hill, now known as Boughton Green Road) alongside the land of John Walton. The lease was granted to the highest bidder, John Wood, at £102.

By 1865 the surviving trustees of the charity were Abraham Abbott of Old in the County of Northampton, Farmer; Sir George Stamp Robinson of Cranford, baronet; Thos Green of Kingsthorpe, Farmer; and Wm Trasler of Kingsthorpe, Farmer. In 1870 the accounts were as shown overleaf.

It was reported to the Vestry Meeting on 30 October 1890 that Mrs Thornton had arranged for a large elm tree on the Green to be felled and sold off. The question was asked: "Do the Trustees of the Manor Lands have authority to do this sort of thing?" (Mrs Thornton's daughter, Mary Susan, records in her diary on 11 November 1890:

Income:	£	s	d
Balance in hand at the beginning of the year:	106	3	6¾
One year's rent of Town Close, let in allotments	34	3	8½
One year's rent of Town House due 21 December	10	0	0
Interest from Northamptonshire Banking Co.	1	15	6
Outgoings:			
Annual contribution to the National School	20	0	0
Mr Cumberpatch for repairs to watercourse	3	11	10
W Beardsmore for repairs to Kings Well	31	12	2
Mr Longland: refreshments for Allottees paying rents	1	11	6
R Fitzhugh for making list of Allottees		5	0
R Fitzhugh, one year's salary as Beadle	1	10	0
Poor Rates (Feb., Apl., June, Oct.)	4	17	6
New locks		15	0
Land Tax		15	0
Clerk's salary due 31 December	2	2	0
Postage		1	0
Balance in hand	85	1	9¼

Charity Accounts, 1870

"Disgraceful Vestry Meeting about the Tree &c.") On 13 November Mrs Thornton was requested to plant lime trees around the Green, 12 yards apart, as compensation for the loss of the elm tree. The Vestry minutes record: "The carelessness and neglect of the feoffees in not protecting the property of the Parish deserves the condemnation of the parishioners." But on 18 November it was reported that Mrs Thornton would not accept any claim for compensation for felling the tree. The parishioners demanded to know the powers of the Manor Land Trustees in relation to tree felling, and demanded a published balance sheet annually of the property under their control.

One month later the Vestry wished to know the right of Mrs Thornton to close the footpath from Kingsthorpe Road to Mill Lane. James Fremeaux, following an Inquisition in April 1773 in his favour, had originally closed this footpath. Although he did this quite legally, many people still intruded access from time to time. The legality of the closure was questioned in 1810 by the Rector, Rev. Baxter, following the erection of a wall by T R Thornton to prevent public access. But Letters Patent (King's Licence), which James Fremeaux had inadvertently omitted to obtain, were issued in April 1811 confirming the closure. A certified PRO copy of this Royal Licence was obtained on 20 December 1890, just after the matter of the footpath had once more been raised at the Vestry.

On 22 January 1891 Mr E M Browne, one of the trustees, was unable to give a positive opinion as to who were the owners or guardians of the Village Green. A motion was agreed that the people of Kingsthorpe collectively owned the Village Green; any alteration to this would have to be agreed by the Vestry. Subject to the Vestry, the Overseers for the time being of the Parish were to be the guardians of the Green. It was also agreed that the Trustees of the Manor Lands should transfer the money from the sale of the tree to the Overseers. It was reported that the Hardingstone Highways Board said that the footpath from Harborough Road to Mill Lane was not an awarded one. It does, however, appear on the 1767 Inclosure map. Mr E M Browne gave assurances that Mrs Thornton would close no other footpaths.

These exchanges relating to the village green and the footpath indicate that the men of Kingsthorpe were still capable of showing some of the spirit of their 14th and 15th century forebears in dealing with infringements of their rights: see the next section about problems with neighbours.

In April 1897 the Kingsthorpe Urban District Council appointed two Councillors, John Ball and James Sargeant, as Trustees for the Manor & Town Lands Charity. This charity is still in existence; its purpose now is to benefit the inhabitants of the ecclesiastical parishes of St John the Baptist and St David in areas not covered by rates, taxes or other public funds.

PROBLEMS WITH THE NEIGHBOURS
Fishing Rights
Problems in this area go back a long way, and led on at least one occasion to an affray. During the 15th century the South Mill of Kingsthorpe was leased to St Andrew's Priory, and the monks and servants therefore claimed the right to fish in the river between the Nether and South mills. In a Court Roll of 12 Henry IV (1410) Richard Napton, the prior of St Andrew's, and his monks and servants, were

accused of fishing in the 'shote' of the South Mill and of making a weir to the harm of the town of Kingsthorpe. The VCH (p.85) says that in 1413 the prior promised to abstain from fishing until the matter was legally settled; but clearly a lasting arrangement was not made, since in the 1440s the prior alleged that the bailiff of Kingsthorpe, along with other men, came armed to the mill and then to the gates of the monastery. Such were the relations between landlord and tenant at that period! Details of the legal proceedings can be found among documents relating to the Court of Chancery at the Public Record Office (C 1/15/106): *Prior and convent of St Andrew, Northampton versus Thomas Reeve, bailiff, of Kyngsthorpe and many others. Riotous attack on the monastery, and breaking up Thorp Mill and the monastery in the field of Northampton.*

Rights Of Warren

This was the subject of long controversy during the 16th century. The keepers of Moulton Park claimed free warren extending into the parishes of Boughton and Kingsthorpe, and caused holes to be made in the walls of the park so that the rabbits might run out into the fields. This proceeding was much resented by the inhabitants of Kingsthorpe, who said that 100 acres of grass and corn were destroyed, 80 acres of ground lay fallow, and that if there were no conies they would sow 40 more quarters of corn. They attempted to keep down the rabbits but were severely punished by the under-keepers, who placed them in the stocks kept in Moulton Lodge, took away their guns and ferrets, even beating and wounding the shepherds and killing their dogs. When Sir Nicholas Vaux was keeper of the park he withheld lands from the inhabitants of Kingsthorpe and occupied them as warrens for rabbits. Thereupon the men of Kingsthorpe "did plough up a whole clapper of conyes lying upon the flat beneath the foxholes, lying next the place called Whyte Hills" and brought a suit against Lord Vaux which was decided in their favour. However, on the condition that Lord Vaux "should be goode and lovying towards them for the sum of 13s.4d. yearly" (!), he was to occupy four 'clappers' of conies in Kingsthorpe Heath from year to year at the will of the bailiff and inhabitants. After the death of Lord

Vaux the inhabitants ploughed up the ground, meaning to sow it for the "relief of their poor churche there"; but the under-keeper Henry Maye, cut the plough gears of the parishioners.

The Rev Glover's calendar of documents lists the following item (no. 13):

A writing, by which certain Inhabitants and Tenants (named) of Thorpe, alias Kyngesthorpe, in co. Northants, appoint John Hopkyns, Peter Diconson, Thos. Reeve, and Simon Baker as their attornies to proceed against one Henry Maye, under-keeper of the Park of Moulton, for the recovery of certain arable and pasture lands in Kyngesthorpe, the fee farm of which had been recently confirmed to them by the King. Dated 12 October, anno 15 Hen. VIII [1523].

Serjeantson (1904; pp.169-170) records:

In 1547 matters reached a climax, and the good people of Kingsthorpe despatched three of their number to London to plead their cause in the Star Chamber. They were away for thirty-four days, and the journey cost the township £9.4s.5d...The delegates kept a minute account of their expenditure, setting down each day the exact amount expended on their dinner and 'sopper'; on their 'drynkynge before and after supper'; on their 'horse meyte'; on the bribes they gave to the officers of the Court for 'helpeyn them to fynyshe their mattr.' Occasionally a charge occurs for shoeing one of their horses; 'for a boytt [boat] to Westminster'; 'for ferrying over to Shene'; or for a 'botyl of secke and a faggot.' The whole account is printed in full in Mr. Glover's *Kingsthorpiana*, and is extremely interesting reading. Now, this expedition cost the township a sum equivalent to nearly £100 at the present [i.e. 1904] rate of money, and the question arises – how was this large amount raised in a small country parish? Apparently by the sale of the church plate. On the last page of the statement of the delegates' accounts occurs the following entry, which is certainly suggestive:

Item: Resevyd of ye Towne as hereafter folls.
Item: for iorn, [iron] brasse, latyn, [see below] and wyxe [wax] xls. [40/-]

Item: for wight plate	viij li	viijs[£8.8.0]
Item: for gilt plate	v li	vs [£5.5.0]
Sum	xv li	xiijs [£15.13.0].

('Latyn' or latten, is an alloy similar to brass.)

This must have been an unusual and perhaps exciting trip for these three Kingsthorpe men, but they seemed to have coped very well with life in the city. Robert Cooke, one of their number, was no doubt a man who was familiar with the ways of a world where bribery was necessary to get one's business completed.

Serjeantson says that selling the church plate would normally have been indefensible, but at the date in question there were rumours on all sides that King Henry was about to take away all chalices and other valuable items from the parish churches, leaving only the cheapest types of vessels for use thereafter. "One can hardly wonder" he continues "that the church officials sometimes turned their plate into money for the use of the parish, rather than that it should fall prey to the rapacity of the king's commissioners." Their fears were well founded, for in 1552 an inventory was taken of the goods of every church, and only the articles essential for the services were left. Everything else was taken to London or sold by the commissioners.

LAND AND ITS OWNERSHIP

IT SEEMS to have been forgotten by many people that the primary use of land is the production of food. Land is thus the source of life; but it can also be the source of wealth and power for those who own large areas of it. In the past, and certainly in Kingsthorpe's past, those persons who owned, or even leased, a little land had the ability to grow food for themselves and their families, thus gaining a measure of economic independence. Those who owned or leased more land could employ others to cultivate it; they could then sell the produce at a profit. When labour was cheap, as it often was in the past, then profits were high. Also, only those who owned land of a certain value had the right to vote and thus, at least in some measure, they had the ability to exercise control over the manner in which they were governed.

In order to understand the changes in ownership of the main estates in Kingsthorpe, it is necessary to appreciate something of the history of the families involved. Should there be no male heir following the death of the estate owner, then marriage to the heiress brought the whole estate into new hands. In this way the Morgan estates came into the possession of the Robinson family of Cranford, and the Cooke estates into the possession of the Fremeaux family and then the Thornton family. Details of these families will be found in the chapter *Family matters*.

The Open Field system, particularly as it existed in Kingsthorpe, is examined below. The memorable names given to the various pieces of land are listed; these were essential knowledge for everyone at a time when only estate owners possessed maps. There are some excellent records of the Robinson Estate in Kingsthorpe from the first half of the 18th century; and there is a 19th-century description of the estate that passed from the Cooke family to the Fremeaux family and

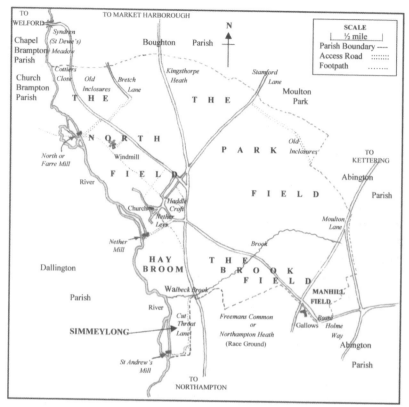

The parish of Kingsthorpe prior to Inclosure

then to the Thorntons of Brockhall.

Following the inclosure of the common lands in 1767 the pattern of land holding was greatly changed. With the exception of the Rector, whose tithes were commuted into a massive holding of land, those who owned the most land before the event received the largest allotments from the division of the commons and open fields. Those who owned little got little, and only then if they could afford to enclose it. The 1767 Land Tax assessment gives a good indication of the main landowners at that time: The Rev Mr Lockwood (the Rector); Sir George Robinson, bart.; James Fremeaux esq.; Mrs Deborah Atkins; Christopher Smith; John Danes; Rev Gooday.

The impact of the inclosure of the open fields and common lands

21

of the parish must not be underestimated. Its effect, inevitably, was to allow the rich to get richer and the poor to become poorer. Worthy of note is the fact that the Rector (on behalf of the church, but to his own personal benefit whilst he remained in office) was undoubtedly the greatest beneficiary of this operation; as noted elsewhere, he was already a rich man with his own estate. Inclosure also enabled the growth of Kingsthorpe in the later 19th century, when large profits were made from the sale of land for housing development – much of it for occupation by Northampton people who wished to live in a less urban environment.

THE OPEN FIELD SYSTEM

Prior to the inclosure of the common lands, the land was cultivated on an open field system that had been in place since Saxon times. The description 'common' applied to three kinds of land:

1. The unenclosed arable *fields*, of which there might be three or four, each consisting of a number of *furlongs*, each of which was subdivided into *strips*.

2. The meadowland, very often next to the river.

3. The common, strictly so called, often referred to as 'waste'.

The arable land, divided into strips, belonged to various owners, some owning many and some only a few. Those strips belonging to a particular owner were not all in one place, but scattered in groups among the furlongs and among the several fields. Strips were divided from each other by a balk (or baulk) – a band of grass – or a furrow. A balk at a right angle to the strips formed a common headland, and would serve as a grass access road. Strips were cultivated each year in a previously agreed uniform manner, but after the crops had been harvested they were thrown open as pasture. The meadowland was distributed among the owners of strips by lot, and then measured and pegged out. Once the hay had been carried, the meadows were also thrown open as pasture. The waste consisted of areas of land that we would today refer to as commons, but also of woodland, heath, or roadside verges. These areas were used as common pasture throughout the year.

David Hall (p.39) provides evidence to show that the ridge and furrow undulations that survive in modern pasture fields are of pre-inclosure origin. Each strip was ploughed in a clockwise direction from the centre outwards, so that the soil was moved to the right and thus built up towards the centre. The strips were aligned down the steepest gradient, so that the furrows provided drainage as well as demarcation. The sole remaining portion of the ancient open fields of Kingsthorpe can still be seen at the extreme end of Vicarage Lane.

Some areas of common land had been inclosed from time to time, a practice that was permitted by the Statute of Merton (1235) as long as there was still sufficient pasture remaining. These are usually referred to as 'old inclosures', even though such a piece of land might be known as 'New Inclosure'! For example, an Indenture Feoffment of 30 April 1674 refers to a piece of land "...next [to] land then of John Mewes upon the late inclosure in the North Field of Kingsthorpe." And a conveyance of 7 November 1728 refers to "two little closes...in the new inclosure in the North Field of Kingsthorpe and a Cow Common in Cottiers Close." So hedges and fences or walls were not unknown in earlier times; they would also be found marking parish boundaries.

In Kingsthorpe parish the meadows were particularly found near to the river, those next to the three mills being known as Mill Holmes. Bush land appears to have been important in this and neighbouring parishes – hence the names of modern streets such as Bush Hill and Bushland Road – probably because it was a source of firing and small game. The arable and ley land was where agriculture was concentrated. The original open field system involved, in many parishes, at least three large unenclosed areas known as fields, two of which would be under cultivation at any time, whilst the third lay fallow. Each field was divided into furlongs, which were further divided into strips that varied in size, perhaps from ¼ to ½ an acre. Each farmer had strips – in Kingsthorpe and elsewhere known as 'Lands' - scattered throughout the large fields. Although this practice had fallen into disuse in many areas by the Middle Ages, something very similar continued in Kingsthorpe until the common land was inclosed in 1767. Evidence for this is provided by the land survey of 1727, described in the chapter entitled *The Robinson Estate*. Although certain advantages were claimed for inclosure, and the consequent creation of large areas of land given to each owner in one, or perhaps two, allotments, the disadvantages of the open field system were often exaggerated or purposely overlooked. There must have been some important advantages that would explain why this apparently inconvenient form of farming persisted for so long in a number of areas, including Kingsthorpe. At least it meant that each owner got some good land, as well as some of the not so good, when his holdings were not concentrated in one place.

The above-mentioned Robinson survey gives the names of Meadows and Closes, and of the Furlongs within which various farmers held strips for cultivation. Since such names sometimes have historical associations, and are usually imaginative and attractive – which made them memorable – they are listed below, together with some indication of their situation in 1727; the list also contains names gleaned from other documents. Obvious parallels with names quoted from old Court Rolls in *Kingsthorpiana* (Glover, J.H. 1883) are also indicated. That source also quotes several mentions of arable lands in 'Woodfield' in conjunction with Brookfield and Northfield; however, Wood Field is quoted as an alternative name for the Park Field in the Glebe Terrier for 1685. There may well have been other Furlongs in which the Robinson estate had no holdings, so the following listing is not exhaustive. The importance of such names should not be under-estimated: we can find our way around by means of maps and street names, but at the time of the open field system everyone needed a mental map of the whole parish; these memorable names provided that.

Names of Furlongs in the Brook Field: [*Kingsthorpiana:* Brukfield]
Astill Hollow
Berry Locks
Between Slades
Conduit
Gorsbeard
Hillocks
Langlands
Moulton
Pease [*Kingsthorpiana:* Pese]
Potty, or Petty [*Kingsthorpiana:* Port wey?]

Shattelbridge [*Kingsthorpiana:* Shottylbridge]
Shrub Bank
Simmilong (The Common west) [*Kingsthorpiana:* Southmyllwonge]
Sindews Ash [Clearly this was once St Dewe's Ash, and by the late 18th
century had been further corrupted to Cinders Ash. In the
Glebe Terrier of 1685 it is St David's Ash.]
Souerlands [*Kingsthorpiana:* Sowrland]
Swarbridge (The Common south) [*Kingsthorpiana:* Swarlbridge way]
Swarbridge Head (Abington Hedge east, Kettering
Road west, Wm. Thursby north, and south of part)
Thistle Home [*Kingsthorpiana:* Thystylholme,
Fystylholme] (The Glebenorth).
Thomas Bank
Thro(a)vedale [*Kingsthorpiana:* Threfdale, Theavedale]
Tinkers Hedge
Walbank
Names of Furlongs in the Park Field:
Between Styles [Cf. Tween Stiles]
[Furlong] Butting into Miller's Gape
Claitlands
Deadmen's Irons [*Kingsthorpiana:* Deadman's irons]
    (The Glebe east. Butting to Moulton Park corner)
Elm Tree (The Glebe south. One Land on Wheat Hill)
Heay Broom [*Kingsthorpiana:* Heybrome] (Northampton Road east).
Ingles
Nether Heay Broom (The Common south)
Picko, or Picker [*Kingsthorpiana:* Pykkow]
Picko Corner (Boughton Moor east).
Pishwell Hole, or Pistlehill [*Kingsthorpiana:* Pywell hull?]
    (Elm Tree Furlong west. The Glebe east)
Rough Baulks (Town Common West)
Shortlands
Snellow [*Kingsthorpiana:* Smetho?]
Tween Stiles or Between Styles.
Names of Furlongs in Mannings Field: [*Kingsthorpiana:* Manuelfield,
    Manwellfield]
Middle
Monks Park (Wm. Thursby south)
Nether
Short (Wm. Thursby west)
Upper (Kettering Road west, Wm. Thursby east)
Names of Furlongs in the North Field:

Between Mill Ways
Boreman's Hole
Frost
Gravel Pit
Mill
Mill Brook Slade
Onion Piece
Parsons Town End
Short La[n]ds
Town Piece
White Hill (Bretch Hedge west) [*Kingsthorpiana*: Whithill]
Names of Meadows:
In the Thatch (Wallbank Ditch south)
North Meadow
South Meadow
St Andrew's Mill Holme
The Dam (River west, Road east)
Upper Mill Holme Meadow
Wooster's Holme [*Kingsthorpiana*: Wolsterholme, Worcesterholme]
Names of Closes:
Addlecroft [alias Haddlecroft, see below. Since it lay mainly on a north
     facing Slope, its name may be derived from the word 'addle' - barren
     or empty.]
Barnaby's Close [alias The Cock Close]
Barnaby's Garden
Bowling Green Close
Cock Close [alias Barnaby's Close]
Corner Close
Cott[i]er's (Cottager's) Close
Dovehouse Close
Elm Close
Great House Close
Haddle Croft [*Kingsthorpiana*: Hodell croftys]
Hollis Spinney Close
Knights Close
The Moore Close Leys
The Moors Close
Pike Close
The Road Close
Walbank [Walbeck] Closes.
Another useful source of information relating to the open field sys-

tem of Kingsthorpe is the collection of Glebe Terriers, which exist for the years 1685, 1726, 1730 and every few years up to 1758 prior to the 1767 Inclosure. The earliest of these reads as follows:

1685: A Terrar of the Glebe Lands of the Rectory of Kingsthorpe:
In the Brookfield:

Upon Thravedale 4 lands, Mr Cook east & west.

Upon Hopeing furlong 4 lands, Doct. Connant west, Mr Cooke east.

Upon Berrylocks 4 lands, Mr Morgan west, Mr Cannon east.

Upon Hillocks 4 lands, Mr Morgan east, Ric. Hollis west.

Upon St David's Ash furlong 4 lands, Mr Milward east, Mr Gooday west.

Upon Long Pease furlong 4 lands, Dorothy Jenaway south, the High Way north.

In the Parke or Wood Field:

Upon Shortland 3 lands, Mr Morgan west, Clement Darlow east.

One headland on ye same, Fran. Billingham west.

Upon Ingles 4 lands, Mr Atkins north, Mr Darlow south.

Upon Claytlands 4 lands, Edward Causby south & Mr Cannon north.

At the stone pitts 4 lands abutting against the Parke, Mr Cooke south & Mr Morgan north.

Upon Deadmans Irons 4 lands, Mr Darlow south, & the highway north.

In Pishwell Hole 4 lands, Mr Morgan west, Mr Cannon east.

On the Elme Tree furlong 4 lands, Mr Morgan north & south.

Upon Blackwell Hill 4 lands, Mr Morgan north & south.

In the North Field:

Upon Frost 4 lands, Mr Cannon north, Edwd Causby south.

Upon Caudwell Head 4 lands, Mr Brookhaven north, Thos Aspitall south.

Att ye Parsonage Town's End 5 lands shooting upon the Meadow, Wm Atkins south, Mr Morgan north.

Upon Millbrook 4 lands, Dr Connant west, the Mill baulke east.

Upon Mill furlong 4 lands, Mr Brookhaven north, Mr Cannon south.

In the new Inclosure, one close about 3 acres, Mr Cannon south & Dorothy Jenaway north.

In the North Meadow:

One piece of meadow ground, John Cooper north & the Towne hook south.

One head dole in the upper Mill holme, the Brook east.

One dole in the same meadow, the Bayliffs hook south, Mr Cannon north.

One dole of meadow next the Moore hedge south & the Towne baulk
north.
One piece of Furzes in the great heath, Mr Morgan south & Thomas
Childe north.
[Signed]   Ed Reynolds, Rector; Edward Casey[?],
ye mark of Richard Hollis,
Churchwardens.

The description changed somewhat over the ensuing years, not
least because of the changed ownership of many of the contiguous
lands. By 1 July 1758 the picture remained much the same, except
that there were then eight lands (instead of four) upon Ingles furlong
in the Park Field, and an additional "inclosed piece of pasture 3½
acres within the Parsonage Yard, the Yard north, Sir John Robinson
south." The Terrier of that date ends with the following statement:

There is also a right of pounding cattle trespassing upon the Glebe or
Tythes belonging to the Rectory. Item, all Tithes within the said
Parish, excepting Tythe Hay of the Meadows, are paid to the Rector
or his Tenants in their proper kinds. In testimony of the Truth of the
above mention'd particulars, we the Minister, Church Wardens and
chief Inhabitants, have set our hands the Day and Year above writ-
ten.
[Signed]   Edward Lockwood, Rector.
Richd Stanton, Richd Wood: Churchwardens.
Henry Tibbs, Thos Green: Chief Inhabitants.

It is interesting to note that a number of the old names of the furlongs were still in use well after the inclosure of the open fields of
Kingsthorpe. But some of them became rather corrupt, for instance:
St David's Ash Furlong, mentioned above, became Sindews Ash, and
eventually Cinders Ash!

In a collection of Poor Rate Assessments for 1833 and 1834 the
names of the pieces of land occupied by farmers and others are given.
The first of these, for 14 March 1833, is an assessment at 1/3d in the
£ Quality; it names William Green and Thomas Cox as
Churchwardens, and Charles Mead and Charles Fitzhugh as Overseers
of the Poor. It then gives the names of the occupiers of lands, houses, cottages and so on; the following selection consists of the major

occupiers:

Thomas Green: Cherry Tree, Spring, Thicket, Hackett Spinney, Top, Long, Lime-Kiln, Orchard and Bush Hill Closes, Shortlands, Clayelands, Home Close, Homestead &c.

Mary Cumberpatch: First & Second Sneller, Knight's and Cotter's (Cottager's) Closes & Meadow, Homestead & Quarry, Hollow & Top Closes, Blackwell Hill, Shortlands & Sourlands.

William Hartley: Mill Holme, Meadow, House, Mill & Premises, Top, [Shuttlewell *deleted*], & Brittin's Closes, Northfield Mill Close & Buildings.

Abraham Abbott: Wall, Northfield & Cottager's Closes, [& Cordle Head *deleted*].

Charles Fitzhugh: Highway & adjoining closes, Coles Old Homestead Close, Harbro' Road, Middle Heath, Spring Barn, Great Highway, White Hill, Old John's, Mile End & Lucas Closes, House & Premises.

William Worster: Wallbank Close.

John Cumberpatch: House & Buildings, Little, two Northfield Closes, & Cordle Head.

Charles Danes: Stone Pit, Middle, Ashton's Hollow & Slade Closes, Close near Windmill, Margett's Gd. & two cottages, House, Buildings, Garden & Orchard, Home, Hayrick & two Mill Furlong Closes, & Meadow.

William Green: Mortar Pit, Bush, Little Leys, Dovehouse, Abraham & Long Closes, & Meadow, Home, Welford Road, Millbrook & Windmill Closes, and close adjoining, Harbro' Road Close, Simmerlong, House & Homestead, Millbrook.

John Brown: House & buildings, House, Barnet, First, Middle, New & West Closes, Goosebeach, Shortlands & Clayelands.

Thomas Burton: Pond, Top & Bowling Green Closes, & two closes adjoining, Wallbank, Great House & two Knight's Closes, Bowling Green, Garden, White Horse Inn & Premises, Bakers, Bridleway, Crabtree [& Kitty *deleted*] Closes.

Robert Treslar: Gleaner, Picker, Northfield, Soap & Shuttlewell Closes, Addlecroft, House, buildings & Homestead.

John Gardner: Mortar Pit, Cordle Head, Walker's Pond, Top, Bush Closes, Coal Track & House.

John Fitzhugh: Homestead, Warren, Wall, Addlecroft, Petty Furlong, two

Willow, Peach's Closes, Horseshoe Inn, Garden &c., Quaker's Close.

George Dunkley: Homestead, Warren, Wilkins, Milestone, Middle & Spring Closes, Meadow, Cock Inn, Garden &c., Elm, Mortar Pit, & Wallbank Closes.

Robert Lucas: Five Bells PH, Homestead & buildings, Garden & Corby's Close.

Stephen Manning: Close, Homestead & buildings, Garden, Quarry Close & Windmill.

John Walton (& Assignee): House & Homestead, House & Quarry Closes, Shortlands, Old Charles, Bason & Middle Closes.

Jerom Green, junior: Bottom, Conduit Furlong, Old Pits & Treslar Closes and close adjoining Field Barn.

Jerom Green, senior: Barn Close, Berry Locks & Race Ground Closes, Northfield, First & Second Town Pieces, Homestead & Leys, House and premises.

Thomas Cox: Two Thistle Holm, two Parson's End, & two Blackwell Hill Closes, Meadow, House & premises.

Harriet Boddington: Park, Great House [i.e. the Hall], Garden & premises.

Edward Perkins: Barn Close & next close, Gallows Close & next close, Spinney, Cottage, Barn &c.

Thus, despite the old furlongs having been divided up between various owners, their names remained in use for describing the situation of various pieces of inclosed land.

THE ROBINSON ESTATE

There still exists a book that contains "A Terrer [sic] and Survey of the Estate of John Robinson Esq lying in Kingsthorpe in the County of Northampton, taken in November 1727 by Thomas Crane". This survey, taken forty years prior to the inclosure of the common lands of Kingsthorpe, gives a very good indication of the way in which land was divided and used at that time. The survey is organised initially farm-by-farm, and the individual plots of land leased to each farmer are described in detail. Then, beginning on page 50, there is a summary for each farmer – Richard Billingham, John Fitzhugh and William Green – and a summary of the land in John Robinson's own possession. This is followed by lists of holdings of other persons and the lands pertaining to each of the mills (known at that time as Cradock's Mill [i.e. the North Mill], Mount's Mill, and St Andrew's Mill). Finally there is a page which summarises all the foregoing, listing each person with the amount of arable & ley ground, meadow, closes, and bush ground occupied by them.

Some of the entries refer to a map; this would have been of huge interest to us now but, alas, it seems to be no longer extant. There is, though, a small map bound into the book on page 56 which relates to a piece of land called 'Syndren Meadow', which extended to 18a.2r.38p. It was bounded on the north by part of Boughton (in which parish it was situated); on the east and north by a road or track; on the south by 'Nosters Home' (otherwise known as Woosters Holme, which was at the northern extremity of Kingsthorpe parish, next to the river); and on the west by the river 'Nin'. On a map included in a survey of the adjoining parishes of Church and Chapel Brampton, drawn in 1584 (NRO: FH 272), this same piece of land was then known as 'St Dewe's Meadow'. It had obviously once formed part of the holdings of the Hospital of the Holy Trinity, or St Dewe (St David) as it was also known. Following the dissolution, the Hospital buildings and lands came into the possession of the Morgan family and later passed by marriage to the Robinson family. So the name 'Syndren Meadow' is a corruption of 'St Dewe's Meadow'. In Letters Patent (a renewed Crown Lease) of 13 October 1747 Sir John Robinson was granted, along with other property and lands, 'one close of meadow called Sindridge at Boughton' – a further corruption of the original name. A note on the map of 1727 says: "NB. The crop of grass or hay of this meadow belongs to Mr Robinson. The Spring bit and latter crop to Boughton." This piece of grassland still exists, not having been built on at the time of writing, although it was crossed by a railway line in the 19th century.

Returning to the survey itself, this illustrates how, prior to inclosure, the arable and ley land in Kingsthorpe was divided into a number of open 'Fields'. The North Field obviously lay to the north of the village; the Park Field lay to the east; the Brook Field to the south and south-east; the Manhill Field consisted of the area we now know as

Kingsley; and the Semilong Field was the area around St Andrew's Mill or the South Mill. There were also areas known as 'Hay Broom', 'Nether Leys', and 'Haddle Croft' between Semilong and the village. Until 1767 there would also have been an area of Common land not under cultivation that would have provided pasture for sheep, cattle and horses.

The large Fields were divided into 'Furlongs', each of which was named, and these in turn were divided into 'Lands', which were cultivated by individual tenants. (In strict measure one furlong, or furrow-long, was ten chains in length.) A farmer would have one or several separate plots of land within a particular Furlong, and usually those plots would each consist of one, two, or three Lands (or Leys if the ground was not ploughed) but could sometimes consist of up to six or eight contiguous Lands. Each Land was a ploughed strip varying in width from about one third to two thirds of a chain, but probably 10 yards on average; its length varied greatly, ranging from five chains (about 100 yards) up to fifteen chains. (For information about these units, see under *Currency, Measurements & Abbreviations*.)

There were no dividing fences or hedges between any of these Fields, Furlongs or Lands; they would have been separated by strips of unploughed land, or by furrows in the case of leys. Although the land cultivated by a particular farmer was referred to as his 'farm', it looked nothing like a modern farm: it consisted of a large number of separate pieces of land in the various Fields of the parish.

There were also a number of Closes: these were pieces of land that had been inclosed at various times in the past, and they usually had individual names. The 1767 map shows a group of 14 contiguous closes known as 'Kingsthorpe Old Inclosures', but also bearing the name 'Edmunds's Farm', which belonged to the Robinson estate. It was situated to the north of the Brook Field, to the east of the North Field, and south of Moulton Park. In the 1727 survey Jeremiah Green is shown as the occupier of closes having an area of 119a.0r.26p. This corresponds well with the total for Edmunds's Farm in 1767 of something in excess of 117 acres. This farm would have looked far more familiar to us, since it consisted of separate fields ranging in size from 3½ acres to 19 acres.

To exemplify the information provided in this 1727 survey of the Robinson lands, here are some measurements from Richard Billingham's farm in the Brook Field. (The 'F' of Furlong has been capitalised when it refers to a named piece of land rather than to a unit of measurement.): In Sindews (St Dewe's) Ash Furlong he had one Land, 40 links wide on the north, 35 links on the south, and 7 chains 18 links (7.18 chains) in length. It was bounded by Mr Craddock on the west and Mr Warner on the east. The area of this Land was 1r.3p. – just over ¼ acre. In the same Furlong he had another plot, consisting of three Lands, the width being 1.36 chains on the north and 1.63 chains on the south, and the length 13.12 chains. The total area was 1a.3r.33¾p. – almost two acres; this plot had Mr Foster to the west and Thos. Atkins to the east. This illustrates the accuracy with which the surveyor was able to make his measurements. This level of detail continues to be used in the specification of every plot of land, with a total for each Furlong and for each Field; and then the process is repeated for the other farmers.

In the Brook Field, Richard Billingham held a total area of just over 27 acres made up of 26 plots of land in 15 Furlongs. In the Park Field he held a little over 14 acres in eight Furlongs; in Mannings Field about 1½ acres in two Furlongs; and in the North Field just over 9 acres in six Furlongs. He held about 2 acres of meadow ground in Woosters Home, North Meadow and South Meadow; also, his summary includes "one close in Park Field lying under Claitlands [Furlong] marked in the map 'S': 2a.2r.24p.; his house and homestead marked 'D': 1a.2r.11p.; one North Field close marked in the map: 4a.2r.32p." His total holding amounted to about 63 acres.

John Fitzhugh's farm consisted of (approximately) 27 acres in the Brook Field, 20 acres in the Park Field, 8 acres in Mannings Field, and 10 acres in the North Field. He also had nearly 4 acres of meadow ground together with some closes; one of these, described as "Dr Morgan's Close", had Bretch Lane to the east and Boughton Field to the north; it extended to just over 8 acres. A further two closes, described as "Boughton Field north, Welford Road west" together comprised nearly 9 acres; and finally there was "One close called in the map Wright's Land Close: 3a.1r.23p."

William Green had 31 acres in the Brook Field, 27½ acres in the Park Field, 12 in Mannings Field, and 12 in the North Field. He had just over 7 acres of meadow ground, one close of nearly 5 acres with Welford Road to its west, one piece of bush ground of 4½ acres with Town Piece on its south, and finally "Homesteads and fold yards marked F on the map: 3a.0r.24p."

On page 53 there is a description of the land in John Robinson's own possession:

Name	Mark	a.	r.	p.
The Capital House with the gardens & courtyard marked in ye map [This would have been the old Morgan mansion standing east of the church in Great House Close.]	B		1	30
The farm yard	a		1	04
The Turkey yard	b			24
Fir Tree Walk	c		1	14
Fir Tree Spinney	d			30
The New Orchard	e		2	11
Gooseberry Garden	f		1	14
Kitchen Garden	g		2	02
Laurel Garden	h			12
The Rookery	i	6	1	21
Elm Spinney	x			17
One piece of Bush Ground in Park Field on Blackwell Hill, Dassill Slade west, John Stephenson north, Blackwell Hill east, the Common south				32½p
One piece of Bush Ground east & butting to Mortar Pitts ye west and to Frost Furlong, Thos Dickenson north, Thos Hollis south, marked	2			38p
One piece with three sides, Northampton Road east, Mill Brook Slade north, Frost Furlong south-west, marked	3	1	0	05½
One piece bounded by Northampton Road west, Boughton Road east, Mr Ward north & south, marked	1	3	0	38
One piece, Town Piece south, Birch Closes north 4		3		12
One piece, Town Piece south,	6	1	2	24
One piece, between Harborough Roads Common east & west	8	2		28
One piece lying betwixt ye roads	10	1		13
One piece, Boughton Moor north...Long Hill south	11	2		½
One piece, Boughton Moor north	12	2		3½
The Long Hill	9	24	1	0

Next are described the holdings of a number of other individuals:

William Chapman, one piece of Bush Ground   1   3   11

Mr Thomas Richards

The Walbank Closes as described in the map		13	1	21
The Moors Close		7	0	02
The Moore Close Leys		3	1	0
Knights Close		2	1	26
A house & garden in ye tenure of **Mr Mills**				
One garden marked in the map	i		1	0
One Terrace walk	1			13
The Orchard where ye house stands			3	33
The Homestead		3	0	24
The Road Close		2	1	07

Theo: Grim; his house, homestead & fold yard

	E	3	3	38
Barnaby's Close		4	3	34
Corner Close	R	2	0	03
One piece in Haddle Croft	Q	1	2	09

Thomas Parr, his house, orchard & field

			3	22
Yard marked	G	7	2	08
The Warren...				

Cradock's Mill marked	H			
One house	H	2	0	0
One home [i.e. Holme; corrected hereafter]				
	Hx	2	1	30
One holme	Hy		1	20
One holme	Hz		3	32
		5	3	02
Mounts Mill marked	I			
One holme	Ix			24
One holme	Iy	2	0	16
One holme	Iz	1	0	36
		3	1	36
St Andrew's Mill	K			
One Mill holme	K	1	1	14
One holme	Kx		2	31
One holme	Ky	4	1	11
One holme	Kz		3	23
		7	0	39
Barnaby's Garden	N		1	24

35

St Andrew's Mill holme, of which Mr Robinson has the latter [crop?] but several people has the crop of grass or hay   5   0   01

Hollis Spinney Close   M   1   27

Mr Wallis: Elm Close   L   1   1   33

George Barwick: three lands in Northampton Field on Brith Hill Furlong, Mr Web north, Mr Peach south   1   3   03

The Survey ends with a "Total of the several particulars" as shown in the table opposite:

The Robinson Rent Rolls

Another Robinson Estate document in the collection of the County Record Office is a bound ledger containing rent rolls and certain items of expenditure relating to estates at Cranford, Tower Hill, and Kingsthorpe. The records for the latter begin with a rent roll covering the half-year from Lady Day until Michaelmas 1754, and finish with the half-year ending Lady Day 1762. The first, and largest, rent (£60 per annum) gives the tenant's name as Widow Edmunds, so this may be why the area of old inclosures recorded in 1767 is known as 'Edmunds's Farm'. The next name is Lucas Green, with an annual rent of £50; perhaps he was a descendant of the Jeremiah Green who rented the whole of this enclosed farm in 1727.

A good example of these rent rolls is that for Michaelmas 1755:

Name	½ year's rent			Sundry payments or allowances
Wid: Edmunds	30	0	0	
Lucas Green	25	0	0	17 3 6 Tax, Bush rent &c.
Thos Richards	12	0	0	
Daniel Cole	23	16	6	15 0 Carr. of thorns &c.
John Dines	17	18	4	
Thos Tallis	15	10	0	[For the South Mill]
Wm Cradock	10	10	0	[For the North Mill]
Wid: Johnson	24	0	0	2 4 0 for flood gates at her mill.
Wm Bernard	13	12	0	
(Do. for Fishery)	1	10	0	3 0 0 Pd. a year's rent
Manning	2	10	0	

LAND AND ITS OWNERSHIP

TENANTS' NAMES	ARABLE & LEY GROUND	MEADOW	CLOSES	BUSH GROUND
Jeremiah Green			119a. 0r. 26p.	
Richd Billingham	52a. 0r. 11p.	2a. 0r. 36½p.	8 3 27	
John Fitzhugh	66 1 21	3 3 4½	20 3 0	
William Green	82 1 13	7 1 1¾	7 3 31	4a. 2r. 7p.
John Robinson			9 1 19	33 1 35
Wm Chapman				1 3 11
Thos Richards			26 0 9	
Mr Mills			6 2 37	
Theo: Grim	1 2 9		10 3 35	
Syndren		18 2 38		
Thos Parr			8 1 30	
Cradock's Mill			5 3 2	
Mounts Mill			3 1 36	
St Andrew's Mill			7 0 39	
Barnaby's Garden			1 24	
St Andrew's Mill Holme		5 0 15		
Hollis Spinney Close			1 27	
Geo. Barwick	1 3 3½			
Mr Wallis			1 1 33	
	204 0 17½	37 0 15¾	237 0 15	39 3 13

37

Richd Morris	1	5	0	16	0	For nails, spikes &c.
Wid: Billingham		10	0			Forgave her rent.
Joseph Billingham	1	5	0			
Edwd Page		7	0			
Geo Barrat	1	0	0	3	0 0	Pd. 1½ yrs
Will Butlin	2	15	0			
Joseph Kenning		1	6			
Wm Dines	15	15	0			
Robert Billing		10	6			for Flaggs.
Syndrin Meadow	12	8	6			
Mrs Eliz. Hartnoll	13	10	0			
Mr Ellis	4	3	0			
Mr Campion		12	6			Pd. to Lady Day 1756.
Jos. Clerk		12	6			

For the half-year ending Lady Day 1760 Tallis was paying £19 for the South Mill; Manning was paying £23.6s.6d for the Nether Mill and £2.10s.0d for the Bakehouse; and Cradock was paying £10.10s.0d for the North Mill. 'Morris ye Blacksmith', was still paying £1.5s.0d; Bernard and Coles were renting Syndrin (which was in Boughton parish) for £15.10s.0d; and Jerom Green was renting the 'Barn at ye Great House' for £1 and Knights Spinney for 2/6d per annum. The Great House refers to the old Morgan mansion. An example of a record of expenditure occurs in October 1757:

Pd Battin ye Plumber a bill for work done at ye Great House: 19/6d.
Pd ye Vicar of All Saints for an annual sermon preached there ye 20th September last: £1.
Pd Richard Morris a bill for spikes: 1/-.
Pd Bernard ye Dinner bill for ye tennants and while I was there: £1.11.4.
Gave to Billy Robinson for his pocket: £1.11.6.
Pd for his coach hire to London: 12/-.
Pd at S Smiths: 16/4.
Pd Williams ye Millwright: £40.
Pd Mrs Remington for Mr Yeomans: £20.
Pd Johnson ye Mason: £14.7.0.
Pd Cuffley ye Carpenter: £9.6.0.
Pd Lucas Green's Disbursements: £15.12.1.

On a slip of paper between the pages of the book is an interesting example of personal expenditure that illustrates some retail prices at this period:

Pd Goodwin of Harborough ye Hatter for hats for Nanny and [Bet?]: £1.14.0.
Pd Bellamy of Kettering for 2 qrs. [i.e. 56 lbs.] of Oats: £1.14.0.
Pd ditto for Pork 19½ pounds at 3d: 4/10½d.
Pd Cheater ye Butcher for Breast of Veal at 3¾d per pound
– weight 8 pounds: 2/8d.
Spent 6d.
Pd Mr York at Farming Woods a fee for a Buck: £1.1.0.

THE INCLOSURE OF THE COMMON LANDS OF KINGSTHORPE

The purpose of this section is to show exactly what the process of inclosure involved for those who owned or leased land in the parish, and to indicate some of the effects it had upon those poor people who had only a cottage.

During the period 1760-1797 about 1500 private Inclosure Acts were approved by Parliament; since these were costly and time-consuming, legislation rendering private Acts unnecessary (in most cases) was passed in 1801: the *General Inclosure Act*. In 1766 a private Bill for Dividing and Inclosing the Open & Common Fields, Common Meadows, Common Pastures, Common Grounds, Heath & Waste Grounds, within the Manor & Lordship of Kingsthorpe in the County of Northampton was passed by Parliament .

The Patron of the Act was the Master of the Royal Hospital or Free Chapel of St Katharine, near the Tower of London, and the Brothers and Sisters of the Hospital: they were Patrons of the Rectory and Parish Church of St Peter in Northampton, with the Chapels of Upton and Kingsthorpe. This makes it clear that the Rector at the time, the Rev. Edward Lockwood, a Brother of St Katharine's Hospital, was a prime mover in this process of inclosure. The Act states that he was entitled, in right of the Rectory, to approximately 39 acres in the open and common fields, to a meadow called Parson's Meadow lying within the North Meadow, to several other pieces of meadow which were in lieu of the Tithe Hay of all the meadows, and to the sole right of cutting furze or bushes on Parson's Hill in lieu of the tithe of the Bushes or Furzes. (It was the purpose of the Glebe Terriers, examined in the chapter *The Open Field System*, to specify this entitlement in detail.) He was also entitled to all the great and small tithes arising annually on all the other fields. (The Great Tithes, consisting of grain and hay, were due to a Rector; the Small Tithes, consisting of fruits, eggs and dairy produce, depending on local custom, were due to the vicar who had been appointed to care for a parish.)

The Act, still as part of its preamble, then states that the poor persons living in Kingsthorpe "have for several years last past been Indulged and Permitted to cut furze and bushes for fuel of and from other part of the said Heath or Bush Ground." It then gives the names of the main landowners who were apparently the other prime movers in the process: Sir George Robinson, baronet; the Revd. John Conant, Clerk; Richard Hill, William West, William Wood, John Danes, and Thomas Green. It seems strange that James Fremeaux is not mentioned, since he was the next largest owner after Sir George Robinson; perhaps it was because he was not then resident in Kingsthorpe. Then the Act gives the ostensible reason for the inclosure: the fact that the lands belonging to the various owners were dispersed in small parcels in the open fields. The owners of large amounts of land felt that the land could not be improved in that situation, and desired that the whole of the open fields and common land should be inclosed and divided proportionately between all the owners. They felt that in this way the profitability of the land could be increased, much to their advantage. These were more or less standard reasons used in many similar Inclosure Acts. Among the attractions of inclosure to many landowners was the change to freehold tenure of their land and the settlement of any long running disputes about boundaries.

Then follow the directions for electing Commissioners "...for setting out, dividing, allotting and inclosing..." the common fields and meadows; also, the oath which they would be required to take was defined. The lands were to be 'Qualitied' and "such Quality shall be reduced into writing..." which any proprietor could inspect, or get a copy of any relevant portion upon payment of an appropriate fee. The Commissioners were to arrange that "a perfect Survey and Admeasurement as to Quantity and Quality" would be carried out and put into writing, with the amount of land belonging to each proprietor specified in acres, roods and perches.

The Commissioners were then to make allotments to the various landowners in amounts that were proportionate to their original holdings and common rights. They were to have due regard to the quality, situation and convenience of the allotments, and they were empowered to settle any disputes. All this was standard practice for inclosures at that period.

A number of specific provisions then follow, particularly one relating to the ten acres or thereabouts called Abington Church Lands, which were part of the open fields of Kingsthorpe. The rents and profits of this land had, from time immemorial, been taken by the Churchwardens of Abington and applied to the repair of that church and to the purchase of bread and wine for the Sacrament. Provision was made for a Trustee (John Harvey Thursby was appointed in due course) and his heirs, who would ensure that the rents &c of the allotment were applied as before.

Certain pieces of an ancient inclosure called Cottagers' or Cottiers' Close and Cottagers' or Cottiers' Meadow were to be included in the open and common fields and so allotted. One gains the impression that, because these lands were of good quality, they should, unlike a number of other old inclosures, go into the pot. Cottiers' Close or Meadow, otherwise known as Woosters Holme, was at the north end of the parish, bounded by the river on the west and by Boughton parish on the north. It was essentially an area of land where 'Cow Commons' were held: in other words, where cottagers who owned no other land could at least have pasture for grazing a cow. But such rights would disappear under inclosure, and so this land could be included and divided with the open fields.

Another special provision related to Thomas Powys Esq., of Moulton Park Farm, who was to receive land in lieu of £3.14s.5d per annum Bush Rent; alternatively, land could be set aside to produce such rent. In practice, he received just over 4 acres of land for this, together with just over 3 acres for his open field estate.

The Act then goes on to define the allotments to be made to the Rector in lieu of his Glebe of 39 acres or thereabouts, for Parson's Meadow and his Bush Rights. Then, in lieu of the Great and Small tithes, he was to be allotted a proportion (to be decided) of the open fields and common lands remaining after allotment to the poor and for the new public roads, but before the allotments were made to the other proprietors. He was also to be compensated for the tithes previously paid by several homesteads, gardens, orchards, home closes and ancient inclosures. This latter compensation was to be taken out of any allotments made to those owners; or out of the actual homesteads &c themselves; or by payment of a Rate Tithe to the Rector; or else by continuing to pay tithes as before. The Rector's allotment for Tithe was to be fenced, or otherwise enclosed, at the expense of the other proprietors – except those who had the rights of common belonging to one cottage or property of lesser value. Unless otherwise directed by the Commissioners, all such fences, ditches &c were to be on the land of the other proprietor, not on that of the Rector. The Rector was empowered to grant leases of his lands, with the consent of his Bishop.

Provision was to be made by allotting a piece of land "for the use of the Poor in lieu of such Indulgence and Permission..." for cutting furze as mentioned previously. The Rector, Churchwardens and Overseers were to hold the land "in trust for the most necessitous, industrious and honest poor inhabitants." The rents were to be disposed of either in money or in fuel, as the trustees thought proper.

Public stone and gravel pits were to be allotted for the use of the proprietors of lands and estates, for the use of their tenants, and for road repairs. Private roads were to be set out leading to four properties of Sir George Robinson: Edmunds's Farm and each of the three water mills; and one for Thomas Powys from Moulton Park Farm to the private road to Edmunds's Farm, with rights of way over that road. Turnpike roads were not to be altered or diverted. Trees and bushes growing on land could be removed as desired by the present owners, but existing boundary hedges or fences had to remain.

The Award was to be drawn up in writing. All leases would cease to have legal force upon inclosure, with the exception of those in favour of Thomas Tallis, William Manning, and William Craddock at the three mills. The guardians of minors &c could formally accept allotments on their behalf. Lands had to be inclosed with fences or similar within a period of months (to be specified) after the Award. Power was given to the Commissioners to approve exchanges of lands between proprietors, to make their holdings more convenient. The Commissioners' fees were to be settled and agreed beforehand, and the proprietors were to pay all the fees and expenses of the whole operation.

In due course, five Commissioners were appointed, who were allowed one guinea per day for their expenses. They were: Rev. Henry Jephcott of Kislingbury; William Pywell, a gentleman of Barnwell; William Smith, a gentleman of Moulton; Tresham Chapman, a gentleman of Old; and Thomas Baseley, a gentleman of Priors Marston, Warks. They made their headquarters at the "House of William Barnard called...the White Horse" (not, of course, the present building, but standing on the same site). Their first meeting was held there on 27 May 1766. Three of their number were appointed as Qualitymen: Wm Pywell, Wm Smith and Tresham Chapman.

It is interesting to note that, according to Steven Hollowell's excellent book about inclosure records (p.66), that when the Rev. Henry Jephcott, Rector of Kislingbury, died in 1776 he was a member of six inclosure commissions in Northamptonshire alone. Altogether he had apparently served on 41 such commissions in this county!

The Award refers to the proprietors or owners of certain ancient inclosures that were to be exchanged as part of the inclosure process, as provided for in the Act. These were: Sir George Robinson of Cranford, Baronet; Rev Edward Lockwood, Clerk and Rector; Deborah Atkins of Alvesley in Warwickshire, a spinster; Richard Hill and William West, both of Dallington, gentlemen; and William Wills the younger of Northampton, cordwainer, as father and guardian of Ann Wills, a minor.

The Act referred to a total of 1743 acres, though the subsequent Award refers to only 1583a.1r.37p; this included the public and private roads and ways. The Award was made on 15 April 1767 and enrolled on 15 September of the same year. The major allotments made were as follows:

	a.	r.	p.
The Rector, for Glebe	24	0	7
for Tithe	239	3	15
The Crown	49	0	38

Sir George Robinson	219	0	20
James Fremeaux	90	0	11
Mrs Atkins	84	0	22
John Ford	75	0	09
Revd. Gooday	62	0	25
Richard Wood	60	0	30
Christopher Smyth	58	2	07
Revd. Conant	58	0	06
Thomas Green	52	1	02
John Danes	50	3	01
Abington Church Lands	8	0	34
The Poor's Allotment	14	0	11
Town Land Trustees	14	2	14
Maiden Hook trustees		2	22

Allotments were also awarded to 40 other proprietors, along with four stone pits of 2 roods each. An alphabetical list of land holdings following inclosure has been extracted from the Commissioners' map and associated documents; this will be found as Appendix 1.

Public roads, all 60 feet in width, were introduced as follows: from Johnson's Lane to Stamford Lane (now known as Boughton Green Road); from the Bowling Green to Northampton Heath (now known as Kingsthorpe Grove and Kingsley Road); from the NW corner of Gallows Furlong to Moulton Lane (i.e. the Kettering Road from White Elephant Junction to the end of Park Avenue North); from the NE corner of Swabidge Head Furlong to Abington Gate (i.e. most of what is now Park Avenue North, running south from the bottom of Spinney Hill). Private roadways 30 feet in width were provided to the three water mills and to Sir George Robinson's farm, known as Edmunds's Farm and marked on the 1767 map as Kingsthorpe Old Inclosures. A 20 ft private road was provided from the Welford Road, through the southern end of the North Field Closes to Bretts (otherwise Bretch) Lane, and a 12 ft bridle road from the northern end of those Closes to the Harborough Road. This enabled traffic to pass between here and the North Mill. A 12 ft bridle road was also provided to Cradock's Windmill. A number of 4 ft wide footways were defined, and these specifications provided the starting point for settling any subsequent disputes about public footpaths. The course and uses of Pishwell Hill Spring was also directed by the Award; this was a valuable source of fresh water which had its rising to the north of what is now Boughton Green Road, ran through the lands below, and fed a well at the lower end of Johnson's Lane. (Pishwell Hill was also known as Pitchwell Hill, Pitchell Hill or Pitch Hill.)

Out of the total area of 1583 acres the Rector was awarded 240 acres for Tithes; this is 15% of the whole; but including the 24 acres awarded him for Glebe, and a further 11 acres exchanged for closes, his total holding was 17% of the whole. The Rate Tithes that were allotted to the Rector for ancient inclosures previously subject to tithes were to be paid each half year on 25 March and 29 September. Two inclosures (not defined, but presumably in the North Field Old Inclosures) had to pay 25s.3d and 29s.9d respectively each half year. Other closes, gardens or orchards paid amounts varying from a few shillings to a few pennies. For instance, Wm Craddock was to pay 1/- for his Windmill Close, and the garden belonging to the Town House paid 6d per half year.

It should be remembered that the glebe and tithes in Kingsthorpe were solely for the support of the Rector: they were not for the repair and upkeep of the church, which was paid for out of the Church Rate or, later in the 19th century, by church collections. The Award also freed the Rector from the requirement to keep a bull or a boar for the use of the inhabitants. It was also made clear that none of this was to affect his income from Surplice Fees (for baptisms, marriages and burials) or the customary Easter Offering.

The Poor's Allotment (some bush ground in what was known as Kingsthorpe Heath) was very poor land, as its later trustees had to admit, and was estimated by the Commissioners to have an annual value of only £7. In practice a distribution of two or three shillings each was made to poor people on 21 December each year; details will be found in the section entitled *Bush Close* in the chapter on *Charities for the poor.*

Sir George Robinson, according to the survey of 1727, held an estate of 281 acres of arable, ley, meadow, and bush ground, but this must be reduced by 19 acres for Syndren Meadow, which was in

Boughton parish. He also had 237 acres of closes, of which 119 acres was Edmunds's Farm and did not go into the pot. Out of his initial allotment he set aside 42a.1r.30p, together with his ancient inclosures of Town Holme (6a.1r.23p), Cradock's Little Holme (1r.22p) and a private access road to the latter (0r.3p) at Cradock's Mill; also an unspecified portion of Great Wallbeck Close, shown on the plan but not mentioned elsewhere. All of this land he exchanged with The Crown for 53 acres of arable and 3 acres of meadow, "late parcel of the possessions of the Hospital of the Savoy..." being part of the lands held under a lease from The Crown. In the Letters Patent (a renewed Crown Lease for specified rents) of 13 October 1747 Sir John Robinson was granted "the site and hospital called St Davys, otherwise Saint Trinityes...also 53 acres of arable and 3 acres of meadow in the fields of Kingsthorpe; Walbeck Close...two small parcels of inclosed land, and one close of meadow called Sindridge at Boughton." Sir George also exchanged other ancient inclosures with the Rev Lockwood for an equal area of open field: the Moor Leys; the North and South Moor Meadows, (the three together containing 10a.1r.19p); and the north part of Tallis's Holme at St Andrew's Mill (3r.12p). So, unless he had previously sold off some of the land included in the 1727 survey, his net award of 219 acres may not seem fair on the face of it; but he did have the largest holding (apart from the Rector), and his tithe payments were reduced to a negligible amount.

The total expenses of the inclosure process came to £1039.7s.8½d, but there is no record of how this was made up. There is a schedule that allocates the payment of this amount among the various proprietors, according to the size of their holdings – except that the Rector only paid expenses for his Glebe, not for his Tithe lands. He paid £32.3s.6d, which was less than 'Our Sovereign Lord the King', who paid £39.17s.6d in respect of the land which Sir George Robinson exchanged with him. Sir George himself paid £189.6s.0½d, and James Fremeaux £120.12s.11¾d. All other amounts were less than £100. Christopher Smyth, an attorney in Northampton, was to collect the payments.

As described in the chapter *The problems of the poor*, this legal process of inclosure was a very significant event in the life of the villagers of Kingsthorpe; it contributed greatly to the increase of poverty during the next 100 years, particularly among those many inhabitants who were landless.

THE FREMEAUX/THORNTON ESTATES

The various pieces of land included in this estate are detailed in a Disentailing Assurance and Abstract of Title dated April 1862; the property was originally referred to in the 1799 Marriage Settlement of T R Thornton to Susannah Fremeaux.

First is described a "messuage or tenement at the north end of Kingsthorpe, with barns, stables, outhouses &c, with three several closes, 4a.2r. by estimation," adjoining the premises and homestead. This was the property known as Court Farm, later to be known as the Court House after rebuilding, and then as Wardington Court. There were also five closes: Over Home Close, Nether Home Close, Mill Brook Pond Close, Windmill Close, and Bushy Close; this land had been allotted to Richard Wood at inclosure. Reference to the Inclosure Map shows that the land, 54a.2r.14p. in area, extended along the Welford Road from the farm, and included what is now the Recreation Ground. A note attached to the document says: "...21 November 1912: 21 acres between Harborough Road and Welford Road adjoining the Court House were sold to the Northampton Corporation for a Recreation Ground."

This document helps to make clear where a second windmill in the North Field of Kingsthorpe was actually sited, since an earlier Abstract of Title and two conveyances of 1780 and 1825 also concern this area of land. (An older Windmill is referred to in the Inclosure documentation of 1767; it was situated to the west of the Welford Road, almost opposite the 'Windmill' Inn.) In 1780 these five closes were conveyed (along with other property) to Peter John Fremeaux, but specifically excluding the windmill. Also in 1780 the "windmill in Windmill Close with a circular plot of land (diameter 22 yards)" was conveyed by Mary Wood, the widow of Richard Wood, to William Manning of Kingsthorpe, a miller, together with a "carriage and horse road or way (breadth 10 feet) from the turnpike road [to Welford] through Millbrook Pond Close and into, through and over part of Windmill Close into the circular plot of ground". In 1825 this circular plot of ground "whereon a windmill or building heretofore stood" was conveyed by Stephen Manning, yeoman of Kingsthorpe, to Revd Thomas Cooke Thornton of Brockhall.

Examination of the OS Map of 1884 shows the boundaries of these five closes; it also marks a track or bridle road, about one third of a mile north of the Court House, from the Welford Road into the northernmost close, but leading nowhere. The windmill must have stood on the brow of the slope, beyond the modern Penfold Close, near to where the school now stands. The modern housing development that reaches into this area from the Harborough Road includes 'Wallbeck Close'. This is not anywhere near to the original of this name but, oddly enough, that is mentioned next in the documents under examination.

Returning now to the original documents, another piece of land is described as being in 'Simeylong Field' and adjoining an ancient enclosure called Walbeck (or Walbank) Close, and extending to 5a.2r.16p. (Walbeck Close was exchanged by James Fremeaux with Sir Geo Robinson in 1774 for Cock Close.) This land had also been awarded to Richard Wood at enclosure. The documents actually describe the piece of land, incorrectly, as being called Walbeck Close; but they then go on to say, correctly, that the latter is one of the pieces of land which border this 5a.2r.16p.

Next recited is a tenement "with the Malting Office in Kingsthorpe formerly in tenure or occupation of Geo. Hollis, then Thos. Allen, then Thos. Percival, then Jerom Green...and land in the Nether Leys adjoining the last mentioned and measuring 1a.3r.34p..." Examination of the Inclosure Map shows that this was the property now known as 'The Old Dairy'.

Also a close of 2r.23p, with another small close of 21p. to its north, lying to the east of White's Lane (now The Leys) and to the south of the "yard, garden and premises of Thos. Abbott"; this is where 'The Old Rectory' now stands. This land was "formerly in occupation of Thos. Abbott, then John Wright, then Chas. Garner, and then bought by Susannah Fremeaux."

It then refers to "messuages, tenements, houses, outhouses, dove houses, barns, stables, yards, gardens, orchards and appurtenances, and all those closes known as Dovehouse Close, the Moor Close, Pyke Close and Nether Orchard, together containing an estimated 8 acres. Also messuages, cottages or tenements...occupied by Widow Stephenson, Samuel Bland, John Cuffley, Wm. Gibbs, - Peach, - Pippin, Ann Peach, and – Percifall."

Next is described 90a.0r.11p of land "in Heybroom and Nether Leys" extending from Mill Lane southwards to what is now Thornton Road, bounded by the river and the main road from Northampton; also the 5a.2r.8p enclosure known as the Cock Close or Barnaby's Close, once severally occupied by Wm. Barnard deceased and Samuel Dumbleton. Immediately to the west of the Cock Close stood the homestead and premises built by James Fremeaux and now known as Kingsthorpe Hall or Thornton Hall.

It was because of its proximity to the site of his house that James Fremeaux desired to obtain the Cock Close from Sir George Robinson in exchange for Walbeck Close. The documents in the Thornton Collection relating to this exchange make clear what actually occurred. First there is a Counsel's Opinion of 1774 that recites, from the 1766 Act for dividing and inclosing the open and common fields of Kingsthorpe, the portion that related to the possibility of the exchange between proprietors of pieces of land with the agreement of the Commissioners. Several such exchanges were made, and included in the Award or Deed executed in April 1767. The document then describes why James Fremeaux desired this exchange, and states that Sir Geo Robinson had agreed to it; it then suggests that, as allowed by the Inclosure Act, the exchange could be made by an instrument additional to the Award.

However, the Opinion said that the proposed exchange could not be made under any Award or Act of the Commissioners, since such exchanges were possible only between proprietors. Sir Geo Robinson held Cock Close under a lease from the Crown, so the King was the proprietor. It then said that the true way for the parties to accommodate each other would be by granting reciprocal leases of the lands in question, with appropriate covenants by each party to grant further leases or sub-leases as necessary in the future. The Opinion was signed by J Holliday of Lincolns Inn on 8 April 1774.

The legal machinery was then put into motion in order to give effect to the matter, and there is a bill from the solicitor, Christopher Smyth, covering all the work that had been necessary to bring the transaction to its eventual conclusion. In December 1773 he had taken instructions in the matter, and in January 1774 obtained a first Counsel's Opinion – which was, in fact, the same as the later (April) Opinion. From June 1774 onwards he was drawing up the various deeds, covenants, and reciprocal leases, engrossing them on parchment, paying the stamp duties and other costs, and getting them executed. The final total was £54.7s.3d, which was paid by James Fremeaux on 22 November 1777.

THE GROWTH OF KINGSTHORPE

By 1901 the population of Kingsthorpe had increased to almost nine times its 1851 level; it was fast becoming a 'dormitory village'. And there was good reason for people to purchase their homes: freehold possession of a piece of land worth 40/- per annum rateable value entitled a man to vote for an MP. The Northampton Town & County Benefit Freehold Land Society's original Prospectus of 1848 described it as "A mutual self-help Society conducted for the benefit of all within its ranks." The Rule Book of 12 December 1848 stated:

> The grand objects of the Society are – to improve the social, promote the moral and exalt the political condition of the unenfranchised millions.

In 1851, two estates in Kingsthorpe were financed by the Society: part of Semilong Road, Hester Street, Marriott Street, Primrose Hill (part); St George's Place, St George's Terrace, & Freehold Street.

Ever since the Inclosure in 1767, plots of land had been sold for the purpose of building cottages, and this process accelerated later in the 19th century with the expansion of the population of Northampton and Kingsthorpe itself. Ribbon development began first, for example along Pitch Hill (Boughton Green Road) and Harborough Road, but then actual building estates began to be laid out. On 28 September 1878 an auction took place to sell a parcel of land that was part of the Robinson Estate; its streets were already laid out, and were later given the names of American presidents.

> 7a.3r.22p of valuable Freehold Building LAND, most eligibly situate near to the Cock Inn, at Kingsthorpe, having frontages to the Northampton and Leicester road and Park-lane [i.e. Cock Lane, now Mill Lane]...If accepted, the purchaser will be allowed to get stone from the Vendor's Pit, adjoining Gipsy Lane, free of charge, subject to the supervision of the Vendor's Agent. (Northampton Mercury 14 September 1878, page 4, col 6.)

The stone pit, also on Robinson land, lay at the junction of what is now Kingsthorpe Grove and Eastern Avenue South, and is clearly marked on the 1884 OS map. It is referred to by Diana Sutherland (*Northamptonshire Stone*, p.59), and was apparently known as the 'Nursery or Shittlewell Pit'; the latter name refers back to one of the old Furlongs of the open field system. The Parish also had a stone pit at that point, awarded by the Inclosure Commissioners.

A sale catalogue of 25 May 1861 (NRO: S.C. 268) refers to an estate at Kingsthorpe consisting of a farmhouse, garden and outbuildings adjoining the Turnpike Road from Northampton to Kettering, together with about 105 acres of land and several closes in Kingsthorpe village. The farm was occupied by George Ashby. About half this land was auctioned again in 1877. The farmhouse, with its outbuildings, was situated where the *White Elephant* public house is now, and its fields became the estate bordered by Kingsley Road and Kettering Road.

The Northampton Conservative Freehold Land Society was also active in Kingsthorpe at this time, and financed property at the northern end of Semilong Rd and new roads named Currie, Burleigh, Knightley, and Cartwright, along with frontages to Kingsthorpe Road. In 1891 they purchased just over 52 acres of land to the south east of the *Cock Inn*, to be known as the Queens Park Estate. The estate and its roads were named in honour of royal persons, royal residences, or Conservative statesmen of the time.

The share prospectus for the Northampton Street Tramways Company of December 1881 says:

> A short distance beyond the terminus [then on the Kingsthorpe Road, opposite the Roman Catholic Cathedral] is the rising village of

An electric tram on the main road at Kingsthorpe in the early 20th century. (Picture courtesy of Alan J Clarke).

Kingsthorpe, with over 3,000 inhabitants, a great number of whom are engaged in business in the town of Northampton, and will doubtless avail themselves of the tramways.

The tramline was actually extended in the following year, and in October 1882 the Vestry appointed a committee to investigate details of gas lighting for the streets. In view of the tramway coming to Kingsthorpe, they saw that it was highly desirable for the village to be lit with gas. It was agreed that 40 lamps would be required at £2.1s.2d each.

There had been shops in Kingsthorpe from very early times, of course, but the development of purpose-built shops expanded rapidly in the early years of the 20th century. By the 1930s there was a parade of shops on the Harborough Road, known as Alexandra Terrace; on the other side of the road stood the Bective Boot & Shoe Works, with the Enterprise Works behind it. There were dwellings suitable for their workers in Bective Road, Newington Road and part of Yelvertoft and Norton Roads. Houses had been built on the south side of Boughton Green Road, and behind them Ruskin Road had been developed. There were two schools in this area, and another in Kingsthorpe Grove. All the area to the west of what is now Eastern Avenue (North and South) was a housing development known as St David's Estate. Much of what had been the Great Tithes and Sir

George Robinson's land in 1767 had become two golf courses, serving Kingsthorpe Golf Club and Northampton Town Golf Club; the latter became the site of a supermarket in more recent times.

The Queen's Park Estate had been developed earlier in the century, of course, and in Osborne Road in the 1930s there was a laundry and a small tennis ground. At the junction of the Welford and Harborough Roads, next to Perkins's Nursery, there were facilities for croquet and tennis as well as a bowling green. In 1912 the Council had acquired 21 acres of land on the east of the Welford Road from the Thornton estate; this became the Recreation Ground – always referred to as 'The Rec' – where there were facilities for cricket, football, tennis and bowls, together with a children's playground. Housing development had also been completed earlier in the century in Kingswell Road, Washington Street, Lincoln Street and Garfield Street; in the latter there was a factory for the production of confectionery.

The early part of the 20th century had also seen housing built along the west side of the Welford Road, and on parts of North Western Avenue, Foxgrove Avenue and Kingsway. On the Harborough Road, beyond the *Fox & Hounds* public house, Glan-y-mor Terrace had been built. Further along, opposite the Cemetery, development of the White Hills estate had commenced. In the centre of the village a small estate of bungalows had been built facing the Green – a development that was very unpopular with existing residents. There was fortunately still much land in Kingsthorpe dedicated as allotment gardens: this would be a very important means of food production during and immediately after the Second World War.

During the second half of the 20th century housing estates, and some industrial developments, were built which swallowed up almost all of the remaining portions of the land within the boundaries of the old parish. The only land remaining in its more-or-less original state is on the west of the parish: part of Dovehouse Close; a field to the west of the church; the north and south Moor Meadows; the Moor Leys; and the other Glebe Land that once formed Town's End Furlong. Continuing northwards, between the river and the disused railway line there is the land that once formed part of the Holmes of the North Mill.

53

LOCAL GOVERNMENT

THIS section outlines the history of local government in the parish, and indicates how it was affected by national legislation. There are examples of most of the areas of responsibility of the Courts Leet, the Vestry, and – towards the end of Kingsthorpe's era of independence – the Local Board and the Urban District Council.

It is clear that the driving force of local government originated in the need to solve two main problems: poverty and the disposal of sewage. The seriousness of the latter problem only became apparent and really serious in the 19th century, although polluted water had been the (largely unrecognised) cause of epidemics for centuries. In the 16th century there were provisions for keeping the drainage ditches clear. This referred to the manner in which surface water and other waste ('slops') were disposed of; the more solid forms of sewage ('night soil') were buried. But such disposal mechanisms were totally inadequate once the population began to increase three centuries later. Since it was the problem of sewage that effectively brought an end to Kingsthorpe's independence in local government matters, this is dealt with first.

The problems of the poor, and the various attempts to solve them, have given rise to huge amounts of legislation and to the spilling of much printer's ink. So the relevant chapter confines itself to examining the local records and attempting to give an indication of some of the causes of poverty in what should have been a prosperous village. The true extent of the problem in the 19th century becomes apparent from the ever-increasing expenditure by the Overseers of the Poor. Much money was paid out directly to poor and elderly persons, and large amounts were spent in maintaining the inhabitants of the dreaded workhouse. Even at the end of that century, the UDC still had the task of finding work for the unemployed labourers.

HISTORICAL OVERVIEW

Up to the end of the 18th century Kingsthorpe was effectively self-governing. It made its own local laws, appointed a bailiff and two constables, and held its own courts to ensure that these laws were given effect. A parchment roll of 1483 contains customs and ordinances, which governed such things as the time at which the sale of beer and other victuals was to cease: 9 pm from Michaelmas (29 Sept) to Easter, 10 pm for the rest of the year. If violence was offered by anyone with a weapon, a fine of twelve pence was exacted, or twenty pence if blood was drawn. Only the time-honoured paths and roads were to be used, subject to a fine of six pence. If anyone brewed ale for the benefit of the church, then no one else should brew at the same time; penalty: twelve pence. (It should be remembered in this context that, until fairly recent times, ale or 'small beer', which was quite low in alcoholic content, was much safer to drink than water.) Reaping or mowing could only begin on a date set by the bailiff and the community, and there were sensible restrictions on the numbers of sheep or cattle that could be kept per acre of meadow.

A revised set of ordinances and statutes was produced in 1547 that stated, among other things, that strangers were not to be given lodging for more than a night and a day without the bailiff's knowledge. With the same proviso, no one was to give lodging to or buy anything from any 'sturdy beggar', the penalty in each case being 3s.4d to the Town and to the bailiff. Penalties were also exacted from those who failed to ensure that the 'common gutters' or drainage ditches were kept clear and free flowing.

These documents demonstrate that Kingsthorpe was governed by a set of byelaws that ensured that the life of the community could proceed in a manner that was as safe, peaceful, and sustainable as possible. Among the documents in the Church Chest in 1883, described by the Rev. Glover in his book *Kingsthorpiana*, were the remains of Court Rolls and associated documents of various dates from 1350 through to 1606. These Rolls contained the records of the Manorial Courts, which appear to have been held every six months. One of the 1547 ordinances requires that two Courts Leet be held each year, within 14 days of Michaelmas and Easter respectively. These courts dealt with judicial matters, such as criminal offences and breaches of the laws of the Manor, as well as administrative matters such as the appointment of constables, ale-tasters, and certain other officials. These functions of the court eventually passed to the Justices of the Peace and to the parish Vestry Meeting, a process that was complete by the 19th century.

The bailiff was, in modern terms, the senior executive responsible for all secular matters. The ale-taster was responsible for checking the quality and measures of the ale sold and the bread baked in the manor. At least two constables were appointed each year, initially by the Courts Leet and later by the Vestry. Their duties were quite wide-ranging and included: the supervision of Watch & Ward as specified by the *Statute of Westminster*, 1285; the detention of criminals and the upkeep of the stocks or other means of imprisonment; the removal of itinerant beggars; the maintenance of parish arms and training any local militia. The last appointment of constables in Kingsthorpe was in 1895.

Following the dissolution of the monasteries by Henry VIII, some other provision was necessary to assist the many poor people. Two Overseers of the Poor had to be selected by the Vestry from among the parishioners, subject to the approval of the Justices of the Peace, and they served unpaid for a yearly term. One of their main duties was to levy a Poor Rate and to supervise its distribution. At Kingsthorpe, the Vestry minutes record the names of the Overseers, along with other officers, who were appointed from 1823 to 1827 and from 1833 to 1894.

As enabled by legislation, in 1833 the Vestry appointed a paid Assistant Overseer or Collector. His main task was to collect the rates levied by the Vestry for the poor. The Rating & Valuation Act of 1925 finally abolished the office of Overseer, but many of his duties had passed to the Guardians of the Poor in 1834, under the provisions of the Poor Law Amendment Act. Two Guardians are recorded as being appointed at Kingsthorpe in 1840 and on subsequent occasions, the last appointments being recorded in 1892.

In 1285 the *Statute of Winchester* made the Manors responsible for the upkeep of the highways. The constables had the duty of supervision and the work was carried out by statutory labour provided by the inhabitants. Then the *Highways Act* of 1555 gave the responsibility for upkeep to the parishes, which appointed unpaid Surveyors or Waywardens. These were selected from the parishioners at the Easter Week Parish Meeting, along with the other officers. The *Highways Act* of 1835 permitted the levying of a highway rate and the employment of a paid Surveyor. In Kingsthorpe on 7 April 1836 a levy of 2½ pence in the £ was approved; in the following years it varied between 3d and 6d in the £. The amount each householder paid was then calculated against the 'quality' of his property – later known as the rateable value.

In addition to this, the proceeds from the letting of the Town Close were to be applied at least partly to the repair of the roads. This close consisted of 14a.2r.14p of land granted to the Town Land Trustees by the Inclosure Commissioners. It was situated on the south side of what is now Boughton Green Road, next to the boundary of Moulton Park.

In Kingsthorpe there appears to have been one Surveyor of Highways in 1823, but from 1836 two Surveyors were appointed each year until 1863, when a single Waywarden was appointed annually – very often the same person each year. The collection of rates or levies was the responsibility of an Assistant Surveyor or Collector. Regardless of job title, the main function of this person was to calculate and collect the various rates that were levied for the poor, the roads, and the church.

The other Parish Officers, who had always been appointed by the church, were the Churchwardens. This was a position of great antiquity, the main duties of which can be summarised as follows:

- Managing parish property.
- Representing the views of the parishioners in parochial matters.
- Maintaining the fabric of the church building.
- Accounting for the expenditure of the church rate.
- Assisting in the compilation of the parish register.
- Collaborating with the Overseers of the Poor.
- Controlling and exterminating vermin.

In Kingsthorpe we have records of the appointment by the Easter Vestry of two Churchwardens each year from 1823 to 1827 and from 1833 onwards. One Churchwarden was appointed by the Incumbent and one by the people.

One of the duties of the Churchwardens noted above was the extermination of vermin: sparrows were so classified, and in June 1833 a payment of 3d per dozen was authorised for sparrows or sparrows' eggs; in March 1835 the payment was 2d per dozen.

The records of the Kingsthorpe Vestry available for examination run from 1808 through to 1965 but with a break from 1934 to 1946. For most of its history this was a Public Vestry, attended by ratepayers; but for a period of time from 1823 onwards there was a Select Vestry, which had a closed membership of selected persons – normally the wealthier members of the parish. There would still have been meetings of a Public Vestry to select Church Officers and deal with church matters, with other meetings of the Select Vestry to deal with matters of local government; but the minutes do not make a clear distinction between the various meetings.

A Church Levy is recorded for most years from 1833 to 1868: it was usually between 1d and 3d in the pound, unless some considerable expense arose such as serious repairs to the church or an extension to the burial ground. In February 1869 a meeting discussed the future raising of church income, since the law no longer allowed the levying of church rates; details will be found under *Churchwardens' Accounts*.

The Vestry spared no effort in order to derive income and thus keep the levies as low as possible: even the grass verges were let for grazing. In September 1833 the Herbage of Peach's Lane was let at 5/- per year and the Herbage of Pitchel Hill or Stamford Lane was let for one sovereign from October 1833 to September 1834. As late as 1876 the Waywarden had to confer with the Highways Board on the question of letting the parish herbage.

On 10 April 1834 the Vestry accepted an offer made by the Committee for Management of the Fire Engines in the town of Northampton. In the event of a fire being attended, the Vestry agreed to pay the following charges:

- Post Master's charge for horses to draw each engine.
- Four firemen per engine at 5/- per man per day or part of a day.
- For cleaning the engine and oiling the leather pipes: 10/- per engine.
- For wear & tear of each engine: 20/- plus any actual material damage.

The problem of stray cattle trespassing into enclosed fields was raised at a meeting of the Vestry in July 1818. The solution was to appoint a regular Pinner, who would be paid 1/- per week for rounding up and impounding all stray cattle, and he was entitled to charge the owners 4d per head. In August 1836 John Buckler was appointed Pinner, and Charles Fitzhugh was to present him to the Clerk of the Peace for approval.

It was suggested in September 1833 that two women might be appointed as Searchers. Their duty would have been to verify a death and, despite having no medical training, ascertain the cause of death. But there is no further mention of this proposal. Still on the subject of death, in January 1834 it was decreed that there should be no ornamentation on coffins ordered at the expense of the parish.

Questions of Settlement or Removal occasionally arose. In March 1836 Thomas Green was instructed to see whether John Webster, deceased, had obtained a Settlement in Bugbrooke parish: four days later, Widow Webster and her family were allowed their claim of Settlement in Kingsthorpe. Had their claim not been valid, they would have been removed to Bugbrooke, to avoid their becoming a charge upon the parish of Kingsthorpe. For the same reason, it was necessary to know the identity of the father of illegitimate children: "March 6th 1834: The woman living with Charles Lewis must produce her marriage certificate or else affiliate her children." When necessary, it was the task of the Vestry to commit a person to the Asylum: in 1835 a young woman was sent from Kingsthorpe to Leicester Asylum. On at least one occasion (1833) the vaccination of the children of the parish was authorised – against Smallpox, no doubt.

It is clear from the above summary that the responsibilities of the

Vestry were many and various. As the population of Kingsthorpe began to increase, particularly during the second half of the 19th century, so the task of local government became more onerous – none more so than the problem of sewage and its disposal. Eventually some of these problems were handed over to Kingsthorpe Local Board, which held its first meeting in February 1893, and then to Kingsthorpe Urban District Council, which commenced its work in January 1895. In this respect, the most relevant entry in the Vestry Minutes is dated 16 December 1895: "To consider the proposal of the Local Government Board [LGB] to the transfer of Vestry powers to the Urban District Council [UDC]." The LGB were prepared to grant the power of appointment of Overseers, with the consent of the existing Overseers, and to grant the power of appointment of Assistant Overseers (after the next vacancy) with the consent of the Vestry. Also to transfer the civil powers of the Vestry and the powers of a Parish Council with reference to the Charities. The following resolution was passed: "In the opinion of this Vestry Meeting the civil powers of the Vestry should be transferred to the UDC and the powers of a Parish Council under Section 6(1)a of the Local Government Act 1894."

With this legal statement, the involvement of the Vestry in matters pertaining to local government finally, after many centuries, came to an end. This did not mean an end to the problems of the poor, of maintaining the roads, and of dealing with water supplies and sewage disposal for an ever-increasing population. These problems remained, and got worse; but now someone else had the responsibility for them, and had to be given (eventually) the necessary resources to deal adequately with them.

THE DISPOSAL OF SEWAGE

As the population of Kingsthorpe increased during the 19th century the problems associated with the disposal of sewage gradually became more serious, and eventually led to the end of local government by the Vestry. The question was first raised in August 1868, when the Vestry was asked to consider the provisions of the Sewage Utilization Act of 1865; their uncompromising decision was "The question will not be entertained." In March 1872 it was decided that no steps would be taken at that time in the matter of appointing a Sanitary Committee. During 1873 there was discussion about the possibility of separating off the urban portion of the parish, and joining it with Hardingstone and St James to form a local Board of Health, as well as for drainage purposes. In June of that year it was agreed to request the Local Government Board to enlarge the boundaries of the Local Board of Far Cotton to include the urban portion of Kingsthorpe for all sanitary purposes; a small committee was appointed to deal with this. In October 1873, after a great deal of discussion, the original resolution was confirmed. In November the reply from the Local Government Board was considered, and the boundaries of a proposed Urban District discussed.

In 1874, Alfred Haviland, first Medical Officer of Northampton's Sanitary Authority, described Kingsthorpe's water supplies as "contaminated by the filthy oozings and drainings from slaughter-houses": wells had been converted into cess pools, drains were obstructed, and muck heaps and surface water were everywhere. But, unfortunately, it took a further twenty years, and the establishment of a Local Board for Kingsthorpe, before such matters began to be properly dealt with.

A Local Sanitary Board was set up, which included a Parochial Committee to represent the interests of Kingsthorpe. The Northampton Mercury carried a report, in its edition of 3 November 1877, of a special meeting of the Rural Sanitary Authority which was to consider a report made by Mr Haviland, Medical Officer of Health, relating to cases of enteric or typhoid fever in Kingsthorpe. The persons affected all lived in one house and the disease was traceable to a common cause: upon inspection, he had found that a well was situated within twelve feet of a series of cesspits. The whole place seemed to be sewage-soddened, and he regretted to have to say that this was not an exceptional instance in the village. A fine supply of water had been contaminated by the reckless way in which the soil had been honeycombed with cesspits, fluid wells converted into cesspits, and drains allowed to become defective. Mr Haviland reiterated the recommendations he had given in the past on this subject, which actions he felt would render Kingsthorpe what it ought to be: one of the healthiest villages in the County.

The meeting eventually decided to prevent the spread of fever by the use of disinfectants, and by closing the suspect wells at once. Further, the Inspector would make a house-to-house visitation, and a further meeting would then be called to decide what action to take. That meeting took place in February 1878, when the Inspector, Mr Killingbeck, read his report on the house-to-house investigation. The overall picture he drew of the unhygienic conditions under which people lived in Kingsthorpe at that period is horrific by our standards.

As yet there were no main sewers, only pipes in some areas for the drainage of surface water and slops from the kitchen sinks. Toilet facilities consisted of privies in the back garden, usually over a hole in the ground; some had a cesspit into which sewage was emptied. There were many cottages that had no passages through to the front for the removal of material from privies or cesspits, so it all had to be carried through the cottages; it was no wonder that the occupants dreaded this operation. Some superior types of houses, near the Cock Inn, had been built with water closets; but these emptied into cesspools. There were numerous cesspools in Vicarage Lane and Green End; throughout the village they were a continual source of trouble and annoyance through blockages or overflowing. Even some of the more modern developments in Kingsthorpe Hollow, where they had taps and water closets, still had cesspools at the rear and no other access except through the house. Some of the water closets even drained into the river.

Kingsthorpe itself had no mains water supply at that time, and water was obtained from communal or private wells, which were open to contamination from nearby cesspools. There was a piped supply that carried water from a spring on Pitch Hill (Boughton Green Road) down Lucas Lane to High Street. This pipe fed four open cisterns in the street; the water was usually of good quality and, except in very dry weather, of sufficient quantity. But the pipe was not entirely impervious, so contamination was possible. The cisterns in the street sometimes had rubbish thrown into them by mischievous children. The Kings Well provided another communal supply further down the village.

The main problem was: where was the sewage to be disposed of? Several options were mentioned, including a filtering system, osier beds, and the Goux or dry system. The latter was certainly the method recommended by Mr Haviland; but it had to be accompanied by a reliable system of collection of the dry waste, as well as a filtering system for the slop water before it emptied into the river. Mr Haviland said that the report only corroborated what he had said in 1873, that the parish was in a very bad sanitary state; nothing could be worse than some of the conditions described in the report, and he emphasised the need for urgent action. A large sewage settling tank was eventually installed, but this introduced another set of problems caused by its tendency to overflow.

In March 1888 the question of 'The Parish Wells' was raised by the Vestry, and the Rural Sanitary Authority [RSA] was urgently requested to consider the supply of water to the village. It was suggested that a reservoir might be provided at the top of the village. On 12 April, under the heading 'The Water Question', it was reported that the Trustees of the Manor Lands were trying to improve the flow from the spring in Boughton Green Road, and were considering the installation of four pumps. The matter was taken up again on 30 October 1890, when the RSA was to be requested to compel every landlord in the parish to find his tenants a proper supply of water. One wonders how landlords were supposed to do that, in the light of the Inspector's published report. The RSA was also asked to arrange for the flushing of every drain in the parish until their Drainage Scheme was made public, "which is earnestly requested."

It must have been decided that these sanitary problems were getting too large for the Vestry to cope with: on 17 September 1891 there occurred the first consideration of the formation of a Local Board, as requested by the RSA of the Northampton Union. The estimated cost of such a Board was £200. The meeting was adjourned one week, owing to the small number attending. On 24 September between 30 and 40 ratepayers were present, and a resolution was passed regarding the desirability of forming a Local Board. The

Vestry Minutes do not mention the subject again, but the Local Board for the District of Kingsthorpe held its first meeting on 8 February 1893. The Vestry thus lost the responsibility for drainage, sewage disposal and road maintenance, and two years later handed over the remaining duties of local government to the Urban District Council of Kingsthorpe.

KINGSTHORPE LOCAL BOARD

The Minutes of the Local Board, from 8 February 1893 to 28 December 1894, show how a group of people began to deal with the growing problems of local government in the area. They took over most of the responsibilities of the Vestry and, of particular significance, undertook the duties of an Urban Sanitary Authority. The records show that the disposal of sewage remained the most intractable problem during this time, and the remedies adopted were fairly primitive. The contents of the (constantly overflowing) sewage tank seem to have been spread on local farmers' fields. Cesspits also caused problems from time to time, and must have caused a stench most of the time. There were also the urgent problems of refuse disposal, the provision of clean water, the control of slaughter houses, the notification of infectious diseases and the disinfection of houses. In addition, the roads had to be maintained to a much higher standard than previously and the erection of new buildings required strict control.

The first meeting of the newly established Local Board for the District of Kingsthorpe was held at Liberty Hall (at the junction of Washington Street & Lincoln Street), Kingsthorpe, on Wednesday, 8 February 1893. All of the elected members were present:

For Semilong Ward: James Sargeant, Henry Law, Joseph Mallard.

For Kingsley Park Ward: John Perkins, Edward Rand Cooper, John Garrett.

For Kingsthorpe Ward: Fred Perkins, William Thos. Flavell, Rev. E L Tuson.

John Perkins was elected Chairman for this first meeting and for the ensuing year, and a ballot was held in order to fix the order of retirement of the members. Meetings of the Board would normally be held at 6:30 pm on the second Wednesday of each month at Liberty Hall. The following Officers were to be appointed, following advertisement in the local press: A Medical Officer at £20 per annum; a Surveyor at £50; an Inspector of Nuisances at £20; a Clerk at £60.

The whole of the members were to form the Highways, Sanitary, Building, and General Purposes Committees, whilst the Finance Committee would consist of Messrs Tuson, Cooper and Law, plus the Chairman as an *ex officio* member.

The sewage tank in the field near to the church required emptying, and it was arranged for it to be carted to Mr Garner's land since Thos Spencer had declined any more of it for his fields. Coleman the Carter was to continue in the employ of the Board.

At a meeting on 1 March a variety of formalities were completed, including the drafting of two mortgages of the Rates to secure a total of £3,194. The sewage tank was overflowing, and the Surveyor was to see if a remedy could be found. On 8 March it was reported that the tank had a probable capacity of 30 loads, and could be emptied in one day if the inflow was stopped. But on wet days it flowed in as fast as it could be emptied. The Surveyor was to estimate the cost of a Sewerage Scheme for the old part of Kingsthorpe and, as an alternative, the cost of draining into the Borough.

By 22 March there had been five tenders for the Scavenging Contract (Dust Collector) and Billing Bradshaw's tender of 40/- per week was accepted, with a penalty of £20. The sewage cart could be lent at 1/- a time to persons wishing to empty privies.

In April the water in the well in High Street was to be analysed by the County Analyst. A new sewage cart was to be purchased and the Sanitary Inspector was to examine how the tank was to be emptied. A deputation was to wait upon the Corporation to see if they would take on the whole of Kingsthorpe sewerage. In June it was reported that the sewage tank was not being thoroughly emptied; it was to be done in one night or two mornings at 4 a.m. Clarke's tender for emptying the tank – £2 per week – was accepted for 12 months. The sewage cart would be repaired and painted, and a set of bye-laws would be framed.

In July it was reported that Coleman had been dismissed for unsatisfactory emptying of the tank. Seven days' notice had been served on Bradshaw to abate a nuisance caused by overcrowding at Kingsthorpe Hollow: there were nine children and two adults in two bedrooms. Two persons were required to empty their cess-pits within seven days, and one of them to cover over his cess-pit.

From the September minutes it appears that a register of slaughter houses was to be opened; three bakers in Semilong had closets close to their larders, without proper water supply or ventilation; and Smith, in Oliver Street, kept seven pigs which caused a nuisance because of the smell.

On 10 January 1894 the Medical Officer submitted his report, which included two cases of Diphtheria, two of Scarlet Fever, and one of Erysipelas. On 15 January the Sanitary Committee adopted the plans for the new sewage scheme. The Borough Council would receive and dispose of sewage on the basis of a 4d rate, with a minimum charge of 2/6d per house. The new sewage scheme was to be implemented with all speed.

On 9 May 1894 the Board decided that all streets were to be properly named and houses numbered: Cock Lane would henceforth be known as Mill Lane, Back Lane became Manor Road, and Church End became Vicarage Lane. High Street would continue up to the Five Bells (that portion had been known as Lucas Lane, and prior to that as Johnson's Lane), and Kingswell Road was to continue to the termination of Duck End. But that last decision must have met with some opposition, since it seems never to have been implemented, and Duck End became Green End.

In September 1894 the Local Board for the District of Kingsthorpe, acting as the Urban Sanitary Authority, issued a set of bye-laws dealing with the following areas:

• Cleansing of footways and pavements.

• Nuisances arising from snow, filth, dust, ashes, and rubbish, and for the prevention of the keeping of animals on any premises so as to be injurious to health.

• Slaughter Houses: For the licensing, registering and inspection of slaughter houses, for preventing cruelty therein, for keeping the same in cleanly and proper state, for removing filth at least once in every 24 hours, and requiring such slaughter houses to be provided with a sufficient supply of water.

• New streets and buildings: This consisted of an exhaustive and detailed set of building regulations, and made provision for the closing of unfit buildings.

The Local Board met for the last time on 28 December 1894, prior to its replacement by the Urban District Council of Kingsthorpe.

THE URBAN DISTRICT COUNCIL

The minutes of the Kingsthorpe UDC give a good picture of the conditions of life at that time, with the problems of sewage still being dealt with, the nuisance of overflowing privies, the keeping of pigs in the gardens of terraced houses, and various abuses and failures of the new sewage system. Infectious diseases were also a considerable problem.

On Wednesday, 9 January, 1895 the first meeting of the Urban District Council of Kingsthorpe was held at Liberty Hall at 6:30 pm. Those present were: John Perkins, Rev E L Tuson and Messrs Sexton, Ball, Chown, Wadhams, Sargeant, Flavell, and F Perkins.

At the February meeting the Medical Officer reported a large increase in cases of Scarlet Fever in Kingsthorpe and Semilong. Instructions for householders regarding infectious diseases were to be produced, similar to those used in the Borough.

The estimates for the financial year 1895-6 were approved at a meeting in March: the amount of £2,311.1s.4d would be found from a 2/6d rate. Suitable land was to be sought for a cemetery. Progress reports were made regarding post boxes, new gas lamps, and the sewage and drainage works. Roberts's property in Vicarage Lane was to be drained into the sewer and more closet accommodation provided: there were two closets between 35 people! Various ash pits were to be emptied, and many closets were full or overfull. Nine properties in Sunnyside (the cottages built along the north side of Boughton Green Road) had no water, and their closets were full. Tenders were to be requested for scavenging and stone carting. A committee was formed to consider the proposal for an Infectious

Diseases Hospital.

On 26 March it was decided to examine Bush Close as a possible site for a cemetery, and on 10 April an approach was made to the Trustees of Bush Close and to the Charity Commissioners regarding its purchase. Two cases of Diphtheria and six of Scarlet Fever were reported in Kingsley Park, and a pig nuisance in Milton Street.

In June decisive steps were planned to secure an Infectious Diseases Hospital. The dangerous condition of a lidless well in High Street was reported. At the meeting in July expenses of £20 were allowed to Mr Morley towards the cleaning out of Mill Dam; this was necessary as a result of the overflows of sewage in the days of the sewage tank. Twenty cases of Scarlet Fever were reported, 19 of them in Kingsley Park.

In August it was decided that ten houses on Sunnyside must have a proper supply of water within seven days. Three properties in Oliver Street and one in Byron Street must discontinue keeping pigs. Scarlet Fever: 17 cases reported, and seven more in September. Mr Masom, a butcher, was to be charged for the removal of the offal &c that he had thrown into the sewer!

At the meeting on 13 November 1895 there were six new members added to the Council: Messrs Thompson, Garner, Chesters, Sturgess, Harris and Stephens. It was reported that Bush Close would be purchased for £1,200 for use as a cemetery. Two additional Police Officers were required, one each for Semilong and Kingsley Park. In December it was decided to issue handbills to warn the public of the dangers of dropping orange peel on the pavements!

In January 1896 a committee was appointed to assist in dealing with the problems of the unemployed, in particular by employing such persons where it was considered proper and necessary. In February an epidemic of Measles was reported, along with a smoke nuisance from Olivers' brickyard; the latter had not abated by March, so a summons was issued.

In May 1896 Roadmen's wages were increased from 15/- to 16/- per week. In June a Cemetery Committee was appointed: Bush Close was to be surveyed and plans drawn up. Among the building plans approved at this time was a proposal from Lady Robinson for an additional storey for St David's. The Chairman had purchased 4 acres 13 perches of land fronting the Welford Road, and known as Myfield Hollow, for £420; the Council decided to purchase it, at the same price, for the site of an Infectious Diseases (or Fever) Hospital.

In October the LGB issued an order that transferred to the Council those powers of the Vestry of Kingsthorpe that would have been transferred if the Parish had been a Rural Parish with a Parish Council (under section 6 of the Local Govt. Act of 1894). Thus, a formal line was drawn under the long history of local government by the Vestry.

In November an increase was reported in the number of Fever cases; handbills would be distributed setting out the precautions to be taken in cases of fever in a household. In December a certain Mr Letts was given a licence authorising him to sell petroleum.

At the meeting on 13 January 1897 the authority of the LGB was requested for the Council to borrow £5,500 over 50 years to cover the costs of the Cemetery Lodge, the Chapel, and the laying out of the grounds; also, a further £4,000 over 50 years for the new Infectious Diseases Hospital of 12 beds. It was reported that the Village Greens were in a bad state owing to football and people driving horses and carts across them (nothing changes!).

In June Scarlet Fever was high on the agenda: a circular was to be sent to those houses where it was present, recommending that their children should not take part in the Processions and Tea celebrating Queen Victoria's Jubilee. The Catering Committee would allow such children some compensation for their disappointment. The Medical Officer recommended closure of the National School for a further week, in view of the spread of fever cases during the past few days. In October a petroleum licence was granted to Mrs E Kelsey.

On 12 January 1898 it was reported that there were three Show Vans in a field in Gipsy Lane; there was no water supply and no sanitary arrangements; notice was given to remove them within 48 hours. On 9 March the estimates for expenditure in 1898-9 were submitted:

Item	£	s	d
400 tons of granite, and carting	200	0	0
25 tons of chippings for paths	10	0	0
Wages: 52 weeks @ £12	624	0	0
Payment to Borough for drainage	450	0	0
Gas Company for lamps	350	0	0
Interest & repayment of old loans	179	0	0
New Sewage Loan	326	4	8
Cemetery Loan	277	5	10
Hospital Loan	260	0	0
Salaries	310	0	0
Rent of Hall for meetings	15	0	0
Payments to Borough Infectious Hospital	40	0	0
Establishment charges, including Library subscription	120	0	0
Horses, Carts, &c	150	0	0
B. B., paving Kingswell Road in front of new houses			
240 yards @ 4/9d	57	0	0
Northampton Corp Water Works for flushing	80	0	0
Surface Drain, Gipsy Lane	60	0	0
Half Share Main Road improvements	226	0	0
Contingencies, inc. Election expenses	250	0	0
Floating balance for next year, for Treasurers balance	200	0	0
TOTAL	**£4184**	**10**	**6**
DEDUCTIONS:			
Half salaries – Medical Officer & Sanitary Inspector	40	0	0
Grant on establishment expenses	36	0	0
Estimated balance in Treasurer's hand			
31st March 1898	481	0	0
GRAND TOTAL	**£3627**	**10**	**6**

Rateable value £31,677. Assessable value £26,616.
Penny rate produces £110 but it is usual to allow 10% deduction for empties &c.
The Finance Committee recommend a rate of 3/- in the £, which will produce the sum of £3,600 nett.

In June 1898 another case of Typhoid Fever was reported in Stanley Street, Semilong. On 10 August the Council decided that Mr O'Connor must abate the nuisance caused by his boiling of bones! In October a proposal was made to provide a public bathing place; a sub-committee would investigate. Lifebuoys and River Drags were to be provided at each of the Mills. In November it was reported that electricity mains were to be laid in Kingsthorpe by Northampton Electric Light Co.

The use of motor cars must have been growing, since in December 1898 a petroleum licence was granted to G K Letts of Milton Street and, in January 1899, to William Lee of Kingsthorpe. By January 1899 it was still not possible for every household to be connected to the sewage system, and in these cases an earth closet – essentially a hole in the ground with a seat above it – was recommended. County Council bye-laws relating to lights on vehicles were introduced.

On 8 March 1899 the estimates for 1899-1900 were presented: expenditure totalled £4,780.7s.6d and a 3/8d rate would be required, but this was reduced to 3/6d. Three Overseers of the Poor were appointed. A case of Typhoid Fever was reported in High Street.

At the Annual Meeting on 26 April 1899 it was reported that the new Cemetery would open the following day; on 10 May it was stated that the new Hospital would open on 1 June. A telephone connection to the Hospital would cost £17.10s.0d p.a.

On 14 June it was reported that Mr O'Connor of Junction Road was again boiling bones! Two requests were made at this time regarding the railway system. First, to the Midland Railway Co: The Council suggested a new line from Guildhall Road (i.e. St John's Station) through Kingsley Park, Moulton and other villages direct to Kettering. A reply, received in September, stated that this was not possible. The second was to the London & N W Railway Co., requesting a station at the lower end of Kingsthorpe village; a reply in August said that this would not be provided.

In September the Council decided that its workmen would be allowed to cease work on Saturdays at 12 noon. Lectures on poultry keeping would be considered for the end of October. In October a *Smith Premier* typewriter was to be purchased! In November Lord Spencer offered to let the Mill and 2½ acres of grassland, at £20 p.a., for a Bathing Place. In December it was learned that Lord Spencer was prepared to sell the land, excluding provision for a road from

Kingsthorpe to Dallington, for £500. The estimated cost of providing the Bathing Place would be a further £300.

In November it was recorded in the minutes that the proposed extension of the Borough boundaries would be opposed; the Council would retain Counsel and Parliamentary Agents. At a Special Meeting on 19 January 1900 it was reported that the Borough Boundary Inquiry would be on 31 January; the Council were prepared to lose Semilong, if necessary! £300 costs were paid to Messrs Morgan & Duke. At another Special Meeting on 31 January, following the Inquiry, it was noted that St James and Far Cotton had supported the Town Council, and obtained a deferential rating for ten years; the Town Council would also pay their costs.

The UDC decided to sue for terms to the Town Council; they wanted to secure 15 years (not less than ten, anyway) deferential rates, among other things, and their legal costs to be repaid by the Town Council. They also asked for the same number of representatives for each Ward as they currently had. The next mention of this matter was in March 1900, when it was noted that the Council resolved to strenuously oppose the inclusion of Kingsthorpe into the Borough!

But it was all to no avail: by the *Borough of Northampton Extension Order 1900* part of the old parish of Kingsthorpe, then wholly in the County, was added to the Borough; of the part not added, a portion was added to the parish of Moulton Park and another portion to the parish of Boughton. Thus ended the independent government of Kingsthorpe after at least seven centuries. It was provided by the Order of 1900 that

> ...nothing therein shall affect the ecclesiastical divisions of any parish, or prejudice, vary, or affect any right, interest, or jurisdiction in or over any Charitable endowment which, at the date of the Order, was applicable for the benefit of any of the then existing parishes affected by the Order.

In 1931 the remainder of the old parish was absorbed into the Borough.

THE PROBLEMS OF THE POOR

The purpose in this chapter is to look at the problems of the poor people of Kingsthorpe, particularly during the 19th century – the period for which we have the best records. It also considers the reasons why there was such a problem of poverty in what should have been a prosperous agricultural community.

Historically, provision had been made for the poor in several ways. Initially it had been the responsibility of the Church to assist the poor. The Hospital of St David had been founded in the year 1200 for the reception of travellers and of the local poor. The Rule of the house made provision for old garments, and also the remnants of the table, to be given to the poor. The hospitality of the house was to be observed and the infirm duly attended, just as they would have been at any monastic establishment; but at St David's this was the primary purpose of the foundation.

Those who benefited from the income derived from tithes also had responsibilities towards the poor: there was an Act in 1391 (15 Rich II, c.6) which made it clear that tithes were designed among other objects for the relief of the poor. This was confirmed a decade or so later by an Act of Henry IV. Following the Reformation many of the monastic holdings, including the Great or Rectorial Tithes of about a third of the parishes of England, fell into the hands of the Crown and then into lay hands. It seems that few owners of these tithes, whether lay or clerical, were troubled by any feelings of responsibility for the poor.

Following the dissolution of the monasteries the poor had nowhere to go for assistance. Even when such establishments were serving an essential purpose in the community, they were still swept away. For instance, the King's Commissioners reported that the Abbot of St James, Northampton, was a godly man who was loved by the people, and that around 70 poor persons received relief at the abbey gates. But such considerations were ignored. The dissolution seriously affected local economies, and caused distress to local inhabitants who relied on the religious houses, not only for charity in times of need, but for trade in normal times.

It was presumably at about this time that the income of a piece of meadow ground known as Maiden Hook was set aside for the provision of food and drink for poor travellers through Kingsthorpe. But this was a poor substitute for a monastery Guest Master or the services of the Hospital. The Government had to introduce legislation in an attempt to make up the national deficiencies that quickly became apparent, and the *Poor Law Act* of 1563 made two persons in every parish responsible for the collection of charitable alms from the people of the parish. Then the *Poor Law Act* of 1598 established the office of Overseer of the Poor, which the *Poor Relief Act* of 1601 made compulsory. As mentioned earlier, one of the duties of the Overseers was to distribute doles to the poor, using funds from the Poor Levies. From time to time people would leave bequests for the poor, and the details of those relating to Kingsthorpe will be found in the section relating to *Charities*.

At Kingsthorpe the earliest records of the work of the Overseers run from 1681 to 1689. During the year ending in April 1686 £30.10s.0d was levied and £30.10s.5d paid out in allowances and other expenses. It is interesting to compare these amounts with a Poor Rate Assessment of 1786: the total on that occasion was £50.4s.0¾d, and this was only one levy among several that were taken up during the year. During that period of 100 years the population of Kingsthorpe increased from around 600 to less than 700. So what had caused this large increase in expenditure on poor relief by 1786? The most significant event in the life of the community during that century, and probably during any century, had been the inclosure of the common lands and open fields of Kingsthorpe in 1767.

Before inclosure the cottager, the ordinary inhabitant of the village, may have been a labourer on someone's farm, but he also had the use of some of the common land; after inclosure he was a landless labourer who now had no independent economic basis, since he had lost a number of valuable rights for which he received no compensation. He lost the right to cut furze or turf on the common land, and would no longer be able to graze a cow or some sheep or geese unless he had the means to rent some land. He also lost free access to welcome additions to the diet such as rabbits, wildfowl, berries and other wild fruits, nuts and fungi. Gleaning rights, following the grain harvests, were also affected in many areas, although in Kingsthorpe there is some evidence from the Overseers' records for

1810-11 that gleaning continued into the 19th century. In Kingsthorpe the right to cut furze was replaced by the provision of a piece of very poor-quality land, which produced a rental that was distributed once a year on 21 December. But whether the distribution of two or three shillings just before Christmas was an adequate compensation for free firing is rather doubtful. A man who rented his cottage received nothing in compensation for the loss of access to the common land. If a man actually owned his cottage, he received a small allotment of land – which he had to fence at his own expense as well as paying his share of the expenses of the Inclosure Commissioners. Small wonder, then, if he found he had no other option than to sell the allotment.

The loss of these rights, and the resulting increase in poverty among village labourers, was experienced across the whole of England following the process of inclosure, and Kingsthorpe was no exception. Added to this were the effects of the French Wars and the following depression in agriculture during the 19th century. The problems of the poor could undoubtedly have been much better alleviated by sensible, and sensitive, legislation. The relief of poverty would have been aided above all by the provision of allotments of land to those who had none, and the huge Poor Levies would have been much reduced thereby. It should not be forgotten that the Tolpuddle Martyrs of 1834 were actually a group of agricultural labourers who had banded together to organise a Trade Union: they were transported as a result.

During the 19th century there was a movement to obtain allotments of land for those labourers who had been deprived of resources by the inclosures. There had been an act of Elizabeth I that forbade the erection of cottages with less than four acres of land around them, "that poor people might secure for themselves maintenance, and not be obliged on the loss of a few days labour to come to the parish". But this prohibition had been repealed in1775, just at the time when inclosure was becoming popular! Some individual experiments with allotments were tried, particularly by Lord Winchilsea, but he had few imitators. His estate in Rutland included four parishes within its boundaries, and the tenants included 80 cottagers. If for some reason a labourer had to resort to the parish, he was given an allotment of land and a cow rather than a weekly cash payment or, far worse, taken to the workhouse. The effect was to give these cottagers a measure of self-reliance and self-respect, which actually resulted in a work force that was more steady and trustworthy.

William Cobbett once made a proposal to the Vestry Meeting of Bishops Waltham, suggesting that they should ask the Bishop of Winchester to grant every married labourer an acre of waste land. But apparently this proposal received only one vote in its favour, since the local farmers thought that the ownership of a bit of land would make the men too 'saucy', that they would have bigger families and want higher wages. The large farmers wanted a pool of labour that they could draw on whenever they required, and that would be maintained by the Roundsman system when they did not. (See *The Work of the Select Vestry* for details). The 1834 *Poor Law Commission* reported that they could do little or nothing to prevent poverty; the farmers insisted on it, preferring that the labourers should be slaves; they objected to their having gardens, saying, "The more they work for themselves, the less they work for us." It was often the case that the Select Vestry included these very farmers in its membership.

Under the provisions of the *Select Vestry Act* of 1819 parishes were enabled to buy or lease 20 acres of land and put the poor people to work on it, or to lease it to poor and industrious parishioners; but little use was made of these powers. In 1831 a further Act increased the amount of land to 50 acres, and some use began to be made of this facility – mainly because discontent among the poor agricultural workers had been clearly and forcefully exhibited, particularly in the southern counties, where farmers' ricks were set on fire. Kingsthorpe seems to have availed itself of this provision at around that time, since by 1833 the Poor Levy assessments included a list of labourers who were occupying allotments in Sourlands – a name that goes back to the old Furlongs of the open field system. Most of them had one rood of land, but a few had less and some two roods. And, yes, they did have to pay Poor Rates on them, averaging 3½d almost every month!

OVERSEERS RECORDS FROM THE LATE 17th CENTURY

The Overseers' Account Book for the end of the 17th century provides a number of insights into their work and into the life of the
poor people whom they served. These accounts include records of
income from levies made from 1681 to 1689, based on the 'quality'
(rateable value) of the properties owned by parishioners. So the main
landowners paid more – for example 15/- from the Rector – and those
who owned only a cottage paid perhaps 2d. The number of persons
levied was usually between 60 and 65, but this obviously does not
include all the households in the parish, some of which would have
been exempt.

Records of expenditure begin on 18 April 1685; a number of pages
have been lost prior to that date. During the year ending in April
1686 around twelve persons, mainly women, were paid an average of
1/8d every two weeks. There were also occasional payments for
coffins or shrouds, and for burials. Mary Johnson received rather
more than others at this time because she was looking after the
Mewes children, who had been orphaned; details are in an endnote
to this chapter.

In May 1686 there is recorded the expenditure involved in apprenticing one of these children, Ann Mewes; the amount was just over
£1 for clothing and £6 for an apprenticeship fee. An extra levy was
normally taken up in order to defray the expenses of such apprenticing. A few years later Elizabeth Mewes was apprenticed, and then
were recorded the expenses relating to John Mewes, for whom a levy
had been taken up which yielded £7.5s.0½d:

Hat 1/10d, Shoes and stockings 2/10d for John Mewes	4/8d
4 yds cloth 8s. buttons, thread &c 1/-	9/-
3 shirts 5/-, 3 neck cloths 1/-, Linings 1/6	7/6d
Making his clothes 2/-. Spent at his binding 6d.	2/6d
Making his indenture	2/-
January 4th 1692: Paid to John Neale for placing John Mewes to him an apprentice for 11 years	£5.

Amounts expended for the years ending in April 1690 to 1698 were:

Year	£	s	d	Remarks
1690	17	11	4	£18.0s.6d was levied
1691	14	11	1	£15.14s.2d was levied
1692	23	13	3	Including an apprenticeship.
1693	16	1	2	
1694	28	12	1	Including an apprenticeship.
1695	24	1	3	
1696	22	16	3	
1697	25	17	0	£26.3s.5¾d was levied.
1698	26	13	7	£27.18s.10½d was levied.
TOTAL	£199	17	0	Yearly average £22 approx.

The number of persons on the lists for distribution of allowances varied from six to twelve during the period covered by these accounts, with most of the payments being made to women – not all designated as widows – and only one, two or (occasionally) three to men.

Included among the many documents in the Parish records is the 1691 Will of Ann Timms. Its presence is explained by the fact that she "being sensible of the kindnesse of the Inhabitants of Kingsthorpe...in giving me a Weekly allowance and taking care of me in my illnesse" appointed four trustees for "All that my little house with ye appurtenances lyeing in Kingsthorpe...soe as the same may be disposed of by them and the Overseers of the Poor of Kingsthorpe for some poore body from tyme to tyme to inhabitt as they shall thinke fitting." She appointed the trustees and the Overseers as Executors of her will. Examination of the Account Book reveals that Widow Ann Timms received an allowance from the Overseers of 1/- on 18 May 1689 and the same amount every two weeks until19 October, when she began to receive 8d every two weeks until 19 April 1690 inclusive. On 26 April she got 4d, then from 10 May 1690 to 31 January 1691, 8d every two weeks. The fortnightly payments continued up to the end of the Account Book in April 1698, varying from time to time between 1/- and 2/-, occasionally dropping to 1/8d, 1/4d or even 10d. On 13 October 1694 appears the entry: "To George Timms his wife for tending Ann Timms in time of her sickness: 2/6d." The Parish Register shows that Ann Timms was buried on 21 October

1709.

The book includes a number of other items, such as a transcript of the 1688 will of William Gardner; a legal document relating to the control of sheep within the Parish; records of the names of Parish Officers for some of the years; and a couple of entries relating to 'Horse Lotts' or plots of land let for grazing. There is also an extract from a Land Tax assessment for 3 March 1696/7, at the rate of 3/- in the £: Francis Morgan was clearly the largest landowner, assessed at £35.19s.0d, followed by the Rector, Dr Reynolds, at £14.19s.0d, and Francis Cooke at £11.12s.6d; Henry Milward is then listed at the much lower figure of £2.5s.0d.

ENDNOTE

There is a Grant of Administration dated 31 January 1684/5 from William, Bishop of Peterborough, to Wm Atkins, tutor & guardian of Thomas, Anne, Elizabeth, and John Mewes, children of John Mewes, late of Kingsthorpe who had died intestate. This family previously had property in Kingsthorpe, since in 1646 John Mewes, yeoman, granted to his eldest son George, husbandman, a dwelling house &c in Kingsthorpe for £6.13s.4d annuity to John for life. John Mewes is mentioned as having possession of a piece of land in the North Field inclosures in 1674. Then there is a Feoffment dated 26 March 1683 from John Mewes, victualler, and Judeth his wife...to Wm Atkins of Kingsthorpe, gent. Consideration £4.10s.0d, five acres of grass in the open fields of Kingsthorpe.

THE WORK OF THE SELECT VESTRY

On 20 April 1823 the minutes record the first meeting of the Select Vestry for that year. Present were the Rev. R W Baxter (Rector), James Cumberpatch, Thomas Cox, Jerom Green, Thomas Green, Charles Fitzhugh, and John Walton. These members made decisions about the allowances to be paid to various poor persons; the legal actions to be taken against householders who had not paid their levies; and the authorisation of new levies. Similar meetings, though they undoubtedly took place quite regularly, are recorded intermittently (once with a gap of nine years) until 1835. Levies – the vast majority of them for the poor – are recorded on 12 occasions during 1833, 14 during 1834, eight during 1835, and three during most years from 1836 until 1846. Road levies occur once in most years from 1836 until 1849.

The problems of the unemployed and poor labourers required the continuous attention of the Vestry. In 1817 concern was expressed about the gross abuses connected with the sending of men out to various farmers as 'Roundsmen': it was resolved to discontinue this practice, which effectively subsidised the farmers out of the poor levies. But it continued nevertheless, for in 1819 the Overseer again expressed his concern at this abuse. An attempt was made on 31 January 1820 to regulate the situation so that these men would receive fair payment, assisted by a special levy.

It was agreed in 1826 that unemployed men should be set to work from 7am to 6pm, with 15 minutes break at 10am and an hour for lunch; on Saturdays they only worked until 5pm! If they were not present at 7am they would not be employed, and they could be discharged if they disobeyed orders.

In 1834 it was decided to pay 1/- per day to each unemployed man; also, they were to stack and burn bushes on Charles Fitzhugh's land at White Hill, for which they would be paid 5d per pole by the Vestry; Mr Fitzhugh would pay the Vestry £1 per rood (40 poles). On 26 December that year it was decided that the unemployed would dig land at a rate of 1d per pole. In January 1835 rates of 2d per pole for stacking and 1½d per pole for digging were agreed. The following winter saw no change: the Board of Guardians asked the Vestry to devise the best means of employment for labourers applying for relief, and the solution was – to dig land at 1½d per pole!

To enable people to buy coal at a reasonable price, the Vestry organised its purchase in bulk, with some of the farmers lending their carts for transport. It was then sold to parishioners at cost price during the winter. On 7 November 1834 100 tons of Wednesbury coals were ordered from Wm. Higgins at 13d per cwt., with carriage at 2/6d per ton; this was to be sold at 13½d per cwt. However, the Overseers' records make it clear that the costs were not always met, and an expense was often recorded against 'Sunk by Coals'.

On 11 February 1841 the Vestry requested the Guardians to apply to the Poor Law Commissioners for consent to sell certain properties belonging to the Parish: first, the building that had for many years been used as a Parish Workhouse, then unoccupied, and the garden adjoining it, occupied by John Fitzhugh. (Perhaps they had over-looked the fact that the building in question belonged to the Kingsthorpe Manor and Town Lands Charity.) There were also two cottages adjoining the above property on the south side, occupied by John Fitzhugh and John Craddock, and an adjoining plot where once a cottage formerly stood "containing 4 square yards approximately" (presumably 4 yards square!). There was also a cottage with hovel, shed or outhouse, and garden, occupied by Francis Causby (or Cosby), Chas. Lack and Thos. Greaves, and six more dwellings with out-offices and gardens occupied by Elizabeth Green, Thos. Haddon, Samuel Cumberpatch, Geo. Wingrove, John Love and Thos. Percival.

The 1841 census shows that these persons occupied properties on the road from Northampton, the 'Turnpike Road', adjacent to the *White Horse*. Most of the area has since been rebuilt, including the *White Horse* itself, but one remaining portion, now an electrical appliance shop, has upper windows of a shape reminiscent of ecclesiastical buildings. This may mean that it was built as a house for the poor of the parish some time after 1817 (see below), or it may have been part of the workhouse, since the 1767 Inclosure map shows a 'Poor House' next to the *White Horse*. At a Vestry Meeting in 1817 the suggestion had been made that some suitable houses should be built for the poor of the parish. The subject is not mentioned again, but some houses must have been built or acquired, since in 1834 payments of 6d or 1/- per quarter were agreed as acknowledgements from people occupying the parish houses. Occasionally a house would come into the possession or use of the Overseers of the Poor by virtue of a testamentary disposition.

Traces of the original frontage of the two cottages adjoining the south side of the old Workhouse, originally the Town House, in Kingswell Road can still be discerned in the wall, where the windows and doors have been filled in with brickwork. Each cottage had a frontage of just over 11 feet, a window about 3 feet 6 inches wide and a doorway just under 3 feet wide. The door would have opened straight into a room with a width of about 10 feet.

By 25 May 1841 permission had been granted to sell the cottages and land to assist in defraying the expenses of the Union Workhouse in Northampton. But these properties were clearly not sold, since the minutes of 1843 and 1846 are concerned with the difficulty of getting payments from the occupiers; in 1844 Charles Danes and Charles Fitzhugh were appointed to look after these houses and to agree rents with the tenants. The whole question arose again in 1850, when the properties 'near the Turnpike' (excluding one cottage) were to be sold, together with the land previously used as the parish pound for stray cattle, and two half-acre public stone pits, then exhausted.

OVERSEERS' RECORDS FROM THE EARLY 19th CENTURY

There are records still in existence of the payments made by the Overseers from 1802-1834. The first of these is the 'Club Book', which begins with the payments made by William Stanton from April to October 1802. These Club payments were made each week, with little variation in the numbers of persons paid; from 1802 to 1811 the average number of recipients was 12. The individual payments did not change during this period, remaining at 1/3d, 2/6d, or 5/- and varying only from person to person, presumably according to their needs. The number of recipients does not vary much when compared with the records for the late 17th century, though the amount paid out then, £22 average per year, was a quarter of the Club payments made in the early 19th century: £88 average. But in the 17th century these payments were normally made every two weeks, and the individual amounts were roughly half those paid weekly in the 19th century. This system is no doubt the origin of the term "On the Club" used to describe being off work owing to sickness or infirmity; this term was still in use during the 20th century.

One interesting aspect of the system in the 19th century is that one or two persons made regular contributions to the funds that were distributed to the Club members, and others made occasional payments. For instance, in the year 1802-3 Elizabeth Shaw, a widow, was contributing 9/9d most weeks; the total received in this way was

£22.17s.9d. In 1803-4 a total of £53.15s.9d was received: £23.7s.3d from Elizabeth Shaw; £26.1s.0d from Miss Fremeaux (whose own ledgers note the repayment of £25 plus interest to Kingsthorpe Club in June 1803); £2.2s.0d from Elizabeth Ward; 13/- from Sir George Robinson; and a further £1.12s.6d "from the Indigent". In the following year Thomas Freeman paid £17.10s.7d; Sir Geo Robinson 6/6d; and £1.6s.6d came from elsewhere. Thomas Freeman paid £15.9s.0d in 1805-6; he continued to be the major contributor to the Club, giving £22 and £15 in subsequent years, and then settling at £1.1s.0d each month. Miss Elizabeth Fremeaux usually subscribed £1.1s.0d each year, and Sir Geo Robinson 6/6d each half year – though this was not always received. The Overseers referred to these contributions as "Received from the Club", and to the weekly allowances as "Paid to the Club"; any balance still required was called "Sunk in the Club". In the 17th century however, these payments to poor persons, together with funeral expenses and the occasional apprenticeship, represented the whole of the expenditure of the Overseers – apart from the distribution of bread or other income from parish charities. There was no Workhouse to maintain at that time, for instance.

But this was by no means the case in the 19th century: as well as the Club payments there were many other disbursments made to the poor persons of Kingsthorpe, as the second book in the series illustrates. Between 28 April and 8 May 1802 over 30 payments were made to individuals, usually between 1/- and 5/- but occasionally more, the average being 3/-; and several payments were sometimes made to the same person during that period of ten days. There was also an item of £4.14s.0d for "the weekly poor", so those other payments must have been additional to this weekly dole.

The account continues from 8 May with similar small payments to individuals, together with larger items such as small beer, bread, cheese, meat, coals, clothing and other items for the workhouse. Then there were the payments made to the Roundsmen, those unemployed labourers who were sent round to the various farmers to work for a small wage; the Overseers paid these men sums varying between 2d and 8d for one day's work. Between April 1802 and April 1803 at least £85 was paid out in this way, which gives some indication of the number of man-days involved. The unemployed labourers must have experienced very hard times in the years following the end of the French wars, when payments to Roundsmen were as follows: 1815-16: £178; 1816-17: £230; 1817-18: £338.

The Vestry admitted in 1817, 1819 and 1820 that there were gross abuses connected with this method of employment, and some unsuccessful attempts were made to regulate the situation. What was happening, in effect, was that the farmer's payments to the labourers they employed were being subsidised by the community out of the Poor Levies. This practice, with its attendant abuses, was widespread throughout England at that time.

At the end of the half-year April to October 1802, William Stanton had paid out a net amount of £348.10s.3d, which was repaid to him out of the Poor Levies. In the next period up to Easter 1803, when the books were examined, Francis Causer paid out £431.18s.7d; he received £385.8s.3d from the levies, leaving £46.10s.4d owing.

The books were then examined and approved by Vestry members: Thos Abbott, Wm Green, Jerom Green, Chas Danes, Chas Fitzhugh, Wm Campion and Thos Wood. It is worth noting that these persons, together with the Overseers themselves, were the very farmers who benefited from the Roundsman system. The books were then verified, on the oaths of F Causer & W Stanton, by Edward Bayley, a Justice of the Peace.

Francis Causer then paid further sums to the Club after Easter, until the new Overseers took office in May. He also recorded about £70 paid to Roundsmen between mid-October 1802 and March 1803; for the most part these were payments of 6d or 10d per man per day. Other payments he made included quarterly payments to the Chief Constable in October and January of £5.12s.6d and £6.15s.0d respectively; £10.6s.8d in Constables' bills; and £1.4s.0d to Soldiers' wives. A further Levy of just over £100 still left £18 owing to him.

In round figures, then, we can see that the total expenditure on the poor of the parish in that 12-month period was £900 – forty times as large as it had been just over a century earlier. But the population of Kingsthorpe had only increased by about 50% in that time, from roughly 600 at the end of the 17th century to 909 in 1801. This gives a clear indication of the extent of poverty in the community in the early years of the 19th century. The amounts paid out each financial year are summarised in the following table, which illustrates the rate at which expenditure on the poor increased across this period.

YEAR	OVERSEERS	TOTAL EXPENDED £
1802-03	Wm Stanton; Francis Causer	900
1803-04	Thos Wood; Chas Fitzhugh	688
1804-05	Jerome Green; Richd Manning	870
1805-06	Abraham Abbott; John Fitzhugh	992
1806-07	Thos Green; Valentine Smith	960
1807-08	William Danes	933
1808-09	Thos Flavell; Wm Briggs	1275
1809-10	Thomas Green	950
1810-11	Wm Stanton; Abraham Abbott	938
1811-12	Richard Manning; Chas Fitzhugh	905
1812-13	James Cumberpatch; Abraham Abbott	1130
1813-14	Abraham Abbott	1208
1814-15	Abraham Abbott Junior	989
1815-16	John Fitzhugh; Thomas Green	1172
1816-17	Charles Fitzhugh; William Gardner	1084
1817-18	Charles Danes; William Green	1564
1818-19	Jerome Green; Abraham Abbott	1521
1819-20	Richard Earl; Thomas Burton	1532
1820-21	John Fitzhugh	1554
1821-22	Thomas Green; Charles Fitzhugh	1764
1822-23	Chas Fitzhugh; James Cumberpatch	1629
1823-24	James Cumberpatch	1063

Note: The final entry may not include all expenditure for that year.

Returning now to the details of expenditure, the next financial period ran from May 1803 to April 1804, and included items such as medical expenses and legal expenses; an example of the latter was Mr Howes's bill for attending trials and other business for the Parish: £86.10s.2d. This being the period of the French Wars, there were military expenses, including amounts paid to men who were prepared to be substitutes for those selected for militia service: "Three men of Army Reserve £76.19s.8d"; "Two Militia Men £17.16s.6d"; "Paid a

Militia Man for Smith's son £7.14s.0d". One of the members of the Parbery family must have moved to Weston Favell, and then become a soldier. His wife was paid an allowance of 2/6d per week which, under the Settlement legislation, Kingsthorpe Parish had to repay to Weston Favell Parish.

In 1804 the payments included £18 to the wives of the following soldiers: Will Kirby, John Smith, Thomas Cuffley, and John Chatham; and Parbery's wife at Weston Favell was still being paid 2/6d per week. During 1805-06 it becomes clear that they were keeping pigs at the Workhouse, since three were purchased during the period, together with potatoes and pollard "for the Hog"; there was also a payment of 1/6d "for killing the Hog". They also grew cabbages in the garden. In March 1806 14/- was paid for making 16 shirts and shifts – presumably for the inhabitants of the workhouse; Doctors' bills and Infirmary subscriptions totalled almost £30; and the Parish Mole Catcher received £3.3s.0d. During the 1807-8 period the sum of £123 was paid in respect of five Militia. These payments for Militia and to soldiers' wives show that the Poor Levies were actually subsidising the war effort!

During 1808-9 William Briggs' own bill for meat for the Workhouse during his six months tour of duty as Overseer came to £105. Dinner at the White Horse on Easter Monday cost £4.12s.6d; but in this connection it should be remembered that the Overseers received no payment for their services to the Parish. The income from eight Levies during this period is recorded as £1200; this was from about 230 families, most of whom were poor and who had to pay levies for the roads and the church as well. But at least those who lived in 'Town Houses' (small cottages owned by the parish and let at very nominal sums to poor and aged persons) did not get assessed for the Poor Rates.

In 1810-11 military expenses still appear, totalling almost £43. An unusual item, which also appears in subsequent years, is "Crying the Gleaning", for which 6d or 1/- was charged; so apparently gleaning was still allowed in the inclosed fields. In 1811 and 1821 payments were made to the census enumerators: 15/- and £2 respectively. In 1811-12 Dr Thomas received £12.12s.0d and Dr Osborne £5.5s.0d, the latter for attendance on Club members. In 1814-15 small beer was still quite cheap at £1.17s.0d for 111 gallons. Coach hire to Leeds cost £6 in February 1815, and William Gardner received £9.12s.0d for taking Thomas Calvert and family to Sherborn; these were probably journeys made in connection with removal orders.

Included between the pages of one of these record books are examples of what must be the earliest form of 'Sick Notes'. These consist simply of a scrap of paper bearing words such as "Thos. Craddock – Sick [*signed*] T Osborne, March 10th 1806" and "John Bradshaw – Lame [*signed*] T Osborne, March 17th 1806".

THE WORKHOUSE

The 1767 Inclosure map shows a 'Poor House' next to the White Horse, on the Northampton side; and then the Town House was used as a Workhouse for a period during the 19th century. The books of the Overseers of the Poor from 1802 to 1824 record expenditure in respect of the Workhouse including, in November 1802, a payment of 5/6d for "Advertisement to let the Workhouse". This shows that the property near to the White Horse was to be rented out, and that the Workhouse referred to from 1802 onwards was the old Town House. It is clear from a collection of deeds relating to contiguous property that the latter was used as the parish workhouse in 1801.

From the Overseers' records referred to above, it appears that Mr Whitsey was running the workhouse in 1802-03, and then Mr Lawrence took over. He left the workhouse in June 1804, and was replaced by Richard Taylor. His annual salary appears to have been £2.2s.0d, increasing to £3.2s.0d in 1805-06. In the financial year 1809-10 William Gardner took on the task, receiving a salary of £20. This building appears in the Vestry minutes from 1833 until 1850, though it ceased to function as a workhouse in 1836. In 1833, Benjamin Cuffley and his wife were asked to be caretakers. Later the same year, Hannah Billingham was to be given 1/6d per week for taking care of it – to be increased if she gave satisfaction. In October 1834 an advertisement was to be placed in order to find a caretaker, and in the following month we learn that Mr Sanderson with his wife were to supervise the workhouse for 6/- per week plus board, lodging and firing, "...on the same principle as the Bedford House of Industry is managed."

Thomas Treslar was to supply bread for the workhouse at 1/- for ten pounds until a tender was arranged. In March 1835 butchers and bakers were requested to tender for the supply of meat and bread for the workhouse for the next three months. Mr Treslar's tender was accepted in April: he was to supply white bread at the rate of 1/- for 11 pounds until midsummer. Later that month the Vestry authorised 9/- per week to be paid to John Fitzhugh and his wife to take charge of the workhouse, plus coals and candles at the expense of the parish; also, Mrs Fitzhugh was to be paid 25/- "...for her trouble at the workhouse prior to them residing there."

Early in the century, on 5 September 1805, Abraham Abbott, Overseer, took an inventory of the goods in the Workhouse. This gives some indication that the number of persons occupying it at any one time would have been around fifteen. There were apparently only ten beds, some of which would have been shared by families. A transcript of the inventory is included in the Appendices.

A set of Rules and Regulations governing the Poor House still exists. They specify that The Keeper was to maintain the House, Apartments and persons in a clean and wholesome state. He was to employ those poor persons, that he thought most suitable and able, to assist him in this and in the preparation of food. Refusal resulted in confinement or alteration of diet at the discretion of the Keeper. Following a second offence, a complaint would be made to the Justices of the Peace who, on conviction, would commit such person to the House of Correction for between one and two months. This was usually the County Gaol, where vagrants, beggars and unmarried mothers would be sent, and where they would be given hard labour.

The Keeper was to place in the best apartments those who had been reduced by misfortune, in preference to those who became poor "by vice and idleness". There were to be separate apartments for the "sick and distempered poor", and an Apothecary or Surgeon was to attend them when necessary at the expense of the parish.

Those who were able to work had to start at 6 a.m. between Lady-

Day (25 March) and Michaelmas (29 September) and finish at 6 p.m. During that period they were allowed a break of one hour at noon and half hour breaks at 8 a.m. and 4 p.m. From Michaelmas to Lady-Day they began work at 8 a.m. and finished at 4 p.m. with a one hour break at noon. Refusal or neglect of work, or leaving the House without permission, was punished by confinement or alteration of diet; a second offence was referred to the Overseers of the Poor. The Keeper had to maintain records of all goods, utensils and materials used, and of all items manufactured. He also had to visit each person at least once each day to ensure that there was no waste of fire, candles or provisions. Lights and fires were to be extinguished at 9 p.m. in summer and 8 p.m. in winter.

The Keeper had to remove the body of any person who died to a separate apartment: they were to be decently buried as soon as possible, the Overseers paying the costs. No one was to enter or leave the House without permission. No "spirituous liquors" were to be brought in or consumed without permission, and then only at the prescription or direction of the physician, surgeon or apothecary. The Constable, Headborough or other peace officer could be empowered by the Justice of the Peace to search the premises if necessary. Anyone illegally having spirits in the House, following conviction before a Justice of the Peace, could be sentenced to not more than three months hard labour in prison or the House of Correction.

All poor persons able to do so were to attend Divine Service each Sunday. Anyone thought to be "improper to continue longer there" was to be dismissed by the Keeper. At least once each month the Keeper had to ensure that these Rules were publicly read to all poor persons kept in the Poor-House. Refusal to work, or other misbehaviour, was punished, upon conviction, to not more than 21 days hard labour. Anyone running away and taking with them any clothes or goods provided for their use could find themselves in gaol for three months. But the Keeper himself could not administer corporal punishment to any adult under his care, nor confine anyone for more than 24 hours; nor was he allowed to use manacles, chains, etc.

Returning now to the Vestry minutes: handbills were issued in 1835 offering a reward of 5 guineas for the discovery and conviction of those who broke the workhouse window; and window shutters were to be made for the Fitzhugh apartment at the workhouse. It seems that the workhouse master was not the most popular person at that time!

In June 1836 all the former inhabitants of the workhouse had been removed to Northampton, under the new Act for the Management of the Poor. It was resolved that the former master, John Fitzhugh, and his wife were to remain in residence as caretakers until further notice, free of rent; John was to be paid 6/- per week for repairing the roads. In 1837 seven bedsteads were to be lent to the workhouse of All Saints parish for use by the Northampton Poor Law Union.

CHARITIES FOR THE POOR

Bridges quotes the following charities, which he says were taken from the Parish Register, and originally extracted from the Charity Commissioners Orders in 1683, which resulted from their Inquisition of 16 August 1682:

> Five shillings per annum, the gift of Thomas Knaps, to be distributed by the Minister and churchwardens on St Thomas's day [21 December].
>
> Six shillings & eight pence p.a., [the gift of Walter Burnell,] to be distributed by the Overseers of the Poor on Good Friday.
>
> Five shillings p.a. on the same day, the gift of Simon Rogers.
>
> Four shillings, the gift of John Smith, to be divided on St Thomas's day by the Overseers.
>
> Two shillings p.a., given by Henry Weston.
>
> The rent of Maiden Hook in Worcester's [Wooster's] Holme, to buy bread & beer for poor passengers through Kingsthorpe.
>
> Mr George Clark of London, a merchant, left the interest of £20 to be annually distributed by the Minister [and Overseers] on St George's day.

Mr Gooday left the interest of £5 annually to be given to the poor on St Thomas's day by the Minister and churchwardens. This item is not included in the 1683 Commissioners' Order.

The Order describes the situation of each property subject to a rent charge and names the present owner as the person who should be making the payment. It also recites the appointment of Francis Morgan Esq., Edward Reynolds DD, and Wm Atkins, with the Churchwardens and Overseers of the Poor, as trustees in respect of these Annuities or yearly rent charges. It also made provision for the appointment of additional persons when the original trustees had been reduced (by death) to two; such replacements were to be "discrete, honest and substantial inhabitants of Kingsthorpe."

Following the extract from the Commissioners' Order transcribed into the Parish Register, the following note occurs:

> The benefit of the Legacies left by Mr George Clark & Mr Gooday was lost to the Parish for several years, but was restored to the Poor by the generosity of Sir Geo Robinson in the year 1766, and the interest agreed to be distributed annually amongst the most necessitous industrious Poor of the Parish not receiving collection, on St George's Day.

Maiden Hook

Following the Inquisition into Charities, the report of 1683 says:

> A certain piece of meadow ground, called by the name of Maiden Hooke, lying in the parish of Kingsthorpe aforesaid, in a certain place called Worsters Holme, was heretofore given and appointed to the use following, viz., that the rent and profit thereof should yearly for ever be laid out, employed, and disposed in buying drink for...passengers through Kingsthorpe aforesaid.

The term 'hook' was usually applied to a piece of land that was used for a different type of crop from that on neighbouring land. Since a holme is a pasture of water meadow, Wooster's (or Worcester's) Holme must have been near to the river and was in fact part of the land at the north of the parish, otherwise known as Cottagers' (or Cottiers') Close and Meadow. Its name may have been derived from that of one of the millers. At the 1767 Inclosure 2r.22p of land near to Moulton Park was allotted in lieu of the original piece of meadow, but it was still known by its original name.

The Bread Fund

The following entry was made in the Account Book of the Overseers of the Poor in 1690:

> Mr George Cooke, Merchant of London, his dole of Bread to be given at the Church on the Lord's Day to the Poor of Kingsthorpe the first dole was given July 2nd 1690. The names of ye persons are Widow Waterfall, Luck, Swane, Walden, Holmes, Wright, Timms, Reviss, Smith, Thomas Billingham, Hesther Binion 2 loaves by the donor's Agreement for her life, but to be no precedent for the future.

In 1916 the Vestry Minutes noted that "...the Bread Fund would soon be insufficient to supply the weekly loaf. Perhaps it could be supplemented from the collections for the Sick & Needy."

Lady Prichard's Gift

In the Will of Dame Sarah Prichard (1637/8-1718), one of the provisions was for the payment of £5 annually for the apprenticing of poor boys who had been born in Kingsthorpe. They were to be instructed in the School for two years, so that they could read, and then apprenticed to a suitable trade. The School referred to was, of course, that which had been built and endowed by her brother Thomas Cooke (1634-1694) in 1693, and which stood in the High Street; its history is described in the *Education* section. By the middle of the 19th century apprenticeship fees had increased in many areas, and were augmented from Baxter's Charity (see below). For instance, in 1859 the sum of £5 was augmented by £7 from Baxter's and awarded to William Fitzhugh, who was apprenticed to a Shoemaker.

Bush close

The Inclosure Commissioners allotted a piece of land comprising 14a.0r.11p, known as Bush Close or the Poor's Close, to provide income for those poor people of the parish who had previously been able to collect furze from the common land. As noted elsewhere, this land was of very poor quality; this is reflected in the difficulty sometimes experienced in letting it for a reasonable rent. The records of its administration, where they exist, illustrate the informality of the process of letting the land during certain periods – a situation which the Rev Baxter, and later the Rev Glover, attempted to rectify. Greater formality and firmness of administration is noticeable as time passes and as difficulties are experienced in obtaining the rent. Eventually it had to be admitted that the land was not suitable for cultivation; most people would have known this anyway, since it had been part of Kingsthorpe Heath and consisted of poor grazing land with trees and gorse. The amounts paid out were never very generous, varying from 1/- to rarely more than 2/6d each for around 150 to 200 poor persons on 21 December each year.

With the consent of the Charity Commissioners, Bush Close was sold in 1896 to Kingsthorpe Urban District Council for £1200, for the purpose of a cemetery. Being a Parochial, not an Ecclesiastical, Charity, (along with the Bread Fund and Prichard's Charity) the UDC appointed Trustees to act with the Vicar in place of the Churchwardens and Overseers. That sum of money was invested with the Charity Commissioners, and on 21 December the following year 118 persons received 3/6d each.

Baxter's Charity, otherwise known as the Kingsthorpe Bounty

This charity was founded by the Rev R W Baxter by deed poll dated 21 December 1842, which directed that £24 per year was to be distributed equally among 12 men and 12 women. A further £7 p.a. was to be applied to the apprenticing of boys, and £5 paid to the Parish Clerk. On 14 November 1900 a deed poll executed by the Rev J H Glover augmented the annuities paid by the Kingsthorpe Bounty.

In 1897, as reported to the Easter Vestry on 18 April 1898, 24 Annuitants received 8/9d each in April and in December, a total of £21. Also, the Parish Clerk (J Hayes) was paid £5; and an Apprenticeship fee of £7 was paid to Messrs Wingrove & Stanley for Ernest Croft. Four amounts of £8.5s.0d each had been received from St Katharine's Hospital during the year, and there was a balance in hand of £7 at the beginning and at the end of the year.

The Mark Bailey Charity

At a Vestry on 5 October 1888 it was reported that Mark Bailey died at Wolvey in Warwickshire, and under his Will left £10 to Kingsthorpe Parish; it was to be invested and the income used to provide bread for the poor. Legacy Duty was £1, so £9 was handed over to the Vicar and Churchwardens, the Trustees for the Charity, and they passed it on to the Charity Commissioners for investment. The income was actually joined to that of the Cooke Charity in order to provide a Weekly Loaf for twelve poor persons.

Other Collections for the Poor

An item in the Northampton Mercury of Saturday, 7 March 1795 reported that sums collected towards the relief of the poor of the parish of Kingsthorpe, and distributed in bread, meat, fuel and clothing, amounted to £101.7s.5d. It is not clear whether this was reporting the result of a normal Poor Levy, or a special collection following some sort of economic failure.

An entry in the earliest Vestry Book records the following, dated 16 January 1812:

Names and Rent Charge & contributions collected for the Poor at St Thomas's Day [21 December] each year:

Richard Stanton, Abington Lodge	2/-
Thos Johnson	1/-
Wm Green	5/-
Chas Fitzhugh	5/-
John Boys	6/ 8d
Wm Briggs	2/-
John White	6d
Mrs Green	6d
[Total]	£1.2s.8d

Clothing and Coal Clubs

A Vestry Meeting was held in the School Room on 11 November 1853 to consider the best means of administering the Clothing and Coal Clubs belonging to the Parish. It was decided that a committee of three inhabitants were to act and assist the Minister to determine which members of the Clothing Club were entitled to receive, at the close of any year, any benefit from the common fund of the Society, in addition to their yearly subscriptions. These two societies were to be confined principally to the industrious poor and labouring classes with large young families. Tradesmen and mechanics were to be eligible for admission, but they would be excluded from any benefit arising from the common fund, unless the committee should determine otherwise. A Vestry Meeting would be held at the close of every year to choose a committee, which would carry out these objectives. Only parishioners, and persons who had resided five years in the parish, would be admitted as members. Any members convicted of any immorality of conduct would be excluded from both societies.

Nothing more appears in the Vestry Books on this subject, but an item in the Parish Magazine for October 1895 says, under the heading 'Clothing and Coal Clubs', that these Clubs closed on the last Monday of September, and re-opened the first Monday in October in each year. Members could join for the last six months, from 1 April, if they are unable to pay through the winter months. Children at school could pay into the Clothing Club, and receive a bonus of one halfpenny for each week in which they have not once been marked as late or absent! The Clothing and Coal Club members could take their cards to specified shops or suppliers in the area.

Kingsthorpe Club

The payments made by the Overseers of the Poor in connection with 'The Club' were eventually superseded by the Kingsthorpe Equitable Friendly Society, which was established in August 1835 and enrolled in February 1836. By 1886 it had 282 members and 12 honorary members. The members – who could be anyone between 15 and 50 in good health – could assure for a weekly payment in sickness until they were 65, or until death, with medical attendance and medication. At 65 they would get a weekly pension, and there was a reversionary payment upon death.

There was an associated Medical Assurance Club, which had about 900 members in 1886. Subscriptions were 3/4d annually, payable half-yearly in advance.

The Free School Charity

This charity replaced the Free School itself when it closed; free education was introduced in Voluntary and Board Schools in September 1891, so the old Free School could no longer compete. The properties belonging to the school were sold and the proceeds invested in order to provide income to support Exhibitions.

The accounts for 31 December 1897, as presented to the Easter Vestry in 1898, showed that the income included rents for land. £150 had been placed on deposit at the Union Bank.

Exhibitions:	Term: 1:	Five	£12 12 0
	2:	Five	12 12 0
	3:	Six	17 10 0

School fees: £8:8:0 in respect of four boys, first term 1898 at Northampton & County Modern & Technical School.

Charity Accounts

At the Easter Vestry on 26 April 1886 it was decided that more publicity should be given to the accounts of the various charities and to their recipients. On 7 April 1890 it was decide that the names of those receiving the Baxter and Bread Fund charities would be published in the Parish Magazine. This decision, though rather insensitive to our minds, was actually given effect. A page from the Magazine (published probably in May 1898) records the accounts of the Bush Close, Bread Fund, Prichard's, and Baxter's charities for 1897, together with the names of the annuitants under Baxter's Charity and the names of the recipients of the Weekly Loaf.

ECONOMIC HISTORY

THIS section begins by assessing the population levels of Kingsthorpe across the centuries. Then it examines some examples of the type of event that often affected population levels in the past: epidemics.

English communities have always had to be ready to contribute towards the defence of the realm. In her book Papers relating to *MUSTERS, BEACONS, SUBSIDIES &C in the County of Northampton, 1586-1623* (NRS Volume III), Joan Wake says that at the Musters of 1591 Kingsthorpe could provide two corslets (light body armour) and one caliver – a kind of light musket. The names of the men chosen in 1591 were:

Rich: Prettye	Nich: Tailor	Wm: Brookes
Wm: Causbye	Tho: the	Tho: Morrice
Jo: Wright	Millar	Edwd: Wallice
Robt: Robinson	Robt: Pikmer	
Rich: Batten	Rich: Jeffes	
Wm: the Millar	Tho: Childe	

The Northamptonshire militia was created in 1762, the men being chosen by ballot. The first lot of 160 men from the administrative district known as the Hundred of Spelhoe and four other hundreds were brought to Kingsthorpe in February 1763 for swearing in and enrollment. But most of them were actually substitutes, paid by the men originally chosen. Despite this possible shortcoming, the Militia List of 1777 has been analysed in order to compare the occupations of the men listed.

But a much more accurate analysis is provided by the information from the census return of 1851, from which can be seen the numbers of people involved in various occupations, and particularly in agriculture – a most significant element in the economy of the mid-19th century.

Bread and beer were important elements of the diet at that time, so this section provides some information about bakers and beer-houses in Kingsthorpe. The importance of the quarries in the parish is illustrated by examples of advertisements; the situation and history of the three water mills and three windmills are also described in some detail.

Charles Fitzhugh was a farmer who not only produced basic food-stuffs, but also processed them and sold the finished products in the surrounding area. His account books provide an interesting insight into these varied activities.

POPULATION STATISTICS

As far as the population prior to the first official census is concerned, estimates can only be based on surviving documents that give the numbers of people in certain categories – such as those paying Hearth Tax, for instance – and then extrapolate from such figures. One such figure for the population of Kingsthorpe can be estimated from the Domesday survey of 1086, which mentions 27 families if we include the Mills; multiplying by a factor of 4.75 we get a population of around 130. An estimate for 1548 could be based on the Survey of Chantries undertaken in that year, which says that Kingsthorpe had 400 'Houseling people.' (Houseling people were those who received the sacrament of the Eucharist, presumably counted at Easter.) But this figure sounds like an estimate in the first place! It should have included only persons of 15 years and above, and the proportion of the population under 15 is usually taken as 33%; so the original 400 (assuming it to be reliable) could be increased to 600; however, this seems much too high when compared with what we know from other sources.

A more reliable estimate of population for that period can be derived from the Subsidy Rolls of the reign of Henry VIII, held in the Public Record Office. These listed persons over 16 years of age who merited taxation, and some of the returns for Kingsthorpe can be found on microfilm copies of the Rolls at NRO. For the year 1523 there appears to be 80 persons listed, and for 1542 there is a single clear list of 87 names. Multiplying these by a factor of 4.75 gives a result of 380 and 413 respectively.

The Hearth Tax returns of 1674 list 121 dwellings; and the Compton Census of 1676 (an Ecclesiastical survey) provides population figures of 570 Conformists, 6 Non-conformists, and no Papists. Dividing that total of 576 by 121 households gives an average of 4.76 persons per household; but this assumes that children were also counted in the Compton Census. Since the average persons per household during the period 1650-1749 has been estimated by historians as 4.25, it seems that 576 is indeed a reasonable estimate of the total population at that time.

The return for the 1777 Militia List contains 108 names of men between the ages of 18 and 45. It is usually considered that a good population estimate can be obtained from these lists by using a multiplier of 6: in the present instance this gives an approximation of 648. That figure seems to be supported by Bridges, writing in the late 18th century; he speaks of 140 families which, when multiplied by 4.75, gives an estimated population of 665 persons.

There is a relationship between the numbers of children baptised and the total population of a community. It appears that the average number of baptisms over at least a ten-year period, multiplied by a factor of 30, gives a good indication of total population. Since the annual numbers of baptisms can be found from the Parish Registers, it is possible to produce estimates of population from about 1550 onwards. Checking the relationship between known populations, from the Censuses of 1801-1831, to the average number of baptisms during the previous ten years, gives a factor of around 35. Adopting this factor, and applying it to a rolling ten-year average of baptism numbers, gives a picture of likely population levels of Kingsthorpe from 1549 to 1831. The figure so obtained for 1676 is 591, which is a good approximation to that given by the Compton Census. And the figure for 1777 is 651, which compares favourably with the 665 obtained from the Militia List of that year.

Going further back, a figure of around 400 for the year 1550 is confirmed by the result obtained from the Subsidy Rolls. This makes the

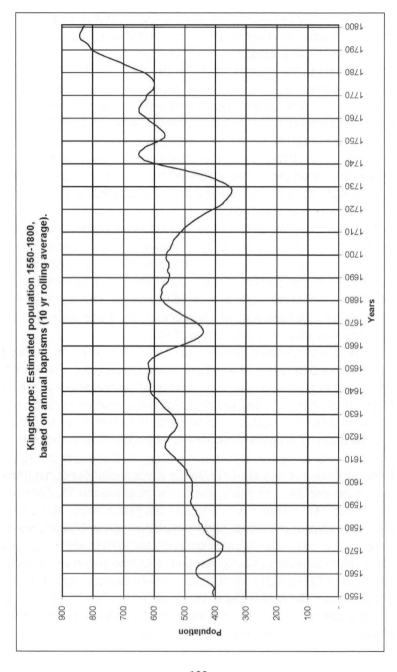

Kingsthorpe: Estimated population 1550-1800, based on annual baptisms (10 yr rolling average).

1548 figure of 400 Houseling people look like an estimate of the total population after all, rather than the number of communicants.

From 1801 onwards there were censuses every ten years, from which we have the following numbers:

Date	Total Population	Families	No. per Family
1801	909	216	4.2
1811	1,009	231	4.4
1821	1,226	279	4.4
1831	1,344	293	4.6
1841	1,467		
1851	1,586		
1861	1,906		
1871	2,409	590	4.1
1881	3,054	692	4.4
1891	7,697		
1901	14,099	2,965	4.75
1911	15,476	3,434	4.5

Up to and including 1871 the above figures are for the original Parish of 1,800 acres; but from then until 1911 they are for the Civil Parish of 1,020 acres. From 1921 onwards there are only figures for Wards, which makes comparisons with the past even more unreliable. Notice the huge increase in the twenty years from 1881 to 1901, and particularly from 1881 to 1891 when there was an increase of 152%; during that same ten years the population of Northampton itself increased by only 18%, so there was obviously an exodus to the suburbs at that time.

In his analysis of the 1851 census, Alec Brooking found that, out of a total population of 1,586, no less than 1025 (64.5%) were born in Kingsthorpe. A further 248 inhabitants (15.5%) were born outside the parish but within a radius of five miles, 84 of them in Northampton, in fact. The remaining 313 (20%) were born outside that five-mile radius, but almost half of them were born in Northamptonshire. The true strangers, he says, were therefore small in numbers; but perhaps this was little different from many another village in the mid-19th century. Railways were only just beginning to make their influence felt on the migration of populations, and economic conditions hardly made it easy for the poor to move from one district to another.

EPIDEMICS IN KINGSTHORPE

During the research for this history, a number of peaks were found in the 16th century Burial Register, indicative of a series of epidemics. These occurred in May 1547, June 1548, and particularly in July and August 1549; so the cause certainly seems to have been connected with the summer months. The pattern is well illustrated by the chart showing the burials for those three years, together with the year 1550 that shows the norm. The second chart of the eleven-year period from 1540 to 1550 illustrates the unusual nature of the peaks when compared with the previous years. Also provided (in the Appendices) is a transcript of the Burial Register from 1539 to 1555, where some of the families worst hit are indicated, and the christening dates are shown where possible. The Parish Registers at that time recorded the absolute minimum of information, so this is all that is known.

What disease might have been active in the situations illustrated? Looking further ahead in the Burial Register indicates that there was a much smaller peak of six burials in June 1594, which may not be significant. Then in 1597 there were eight in October, nine in November, and seven in December; but these seem to be related to something quite different since they occur much later in the year. A similar pattern of seven in October and six in November occurred in 1644. In 1638, returning to the summer occurrences, there were ten burials in July. This was due, in all probability, to Cholera: there had been an outbreak of that disease reported in Northampton on 1 May 1638, but at that time it had not affected Kingsthorpe. In 1676 there were nine burials in July, but no other years have anything significantly above the average, and nothing like the 1549 peak.

Considering possible causes, the diseases that come to mind are Cholera, Typhus, or Smallpox; also something called the 'Great Sweat', which apparently occurred around 1551 and affected only the richer people! Bubonic Plague (or whatever it was that was the cause

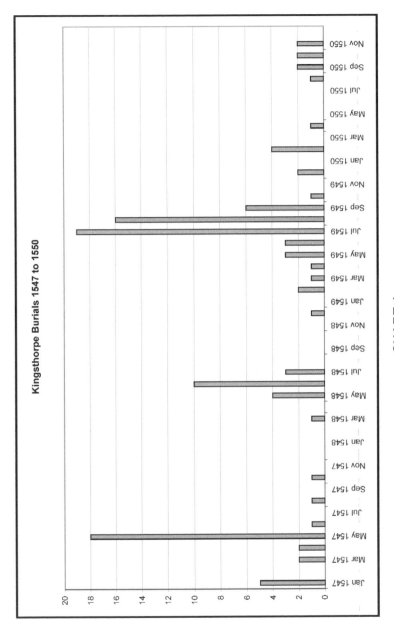

Kingsthorpe Burials 1547 to 1550

CHART 1

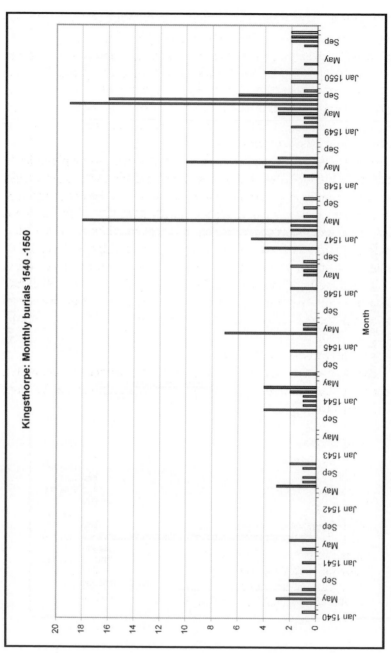

CHART 2

of the Black Death in the mid-14th century) was still active in the 16th century, but was not ravaging the population as it had in earlier times. Since so many members of particular families were affected in Kingsthorpe, it may well have been a disease spread by close human contact (as opposed to the fleas carried by black rats, as in the case of Bubonic Plague). The only other Parish Registers in the surrounding area that go back so far are those of Brixworth, and there is no corresponding pattern there.

As suggested above, the time of year at which these epidemics (if such they were) are recorded may indicate their nature. Since they occurred mainly at or around midsummer, it could be that the harvest of the previous year had been poor and that food had run out before the new harvest provided a fresh supply. This would have left the population in a weakened state and thus susceptible to infections. Also, the warmer months would have been the time when many micro-organisms were able to multiply, and the cause may have been in the drinking water; but the actual identity of the disease will no doubt always remain a mystery.

OCCUPATIONS IN 1777 AND 1851

A list of persons selected in 1777 for Militia service, in occupation order, will be found at Appendix 4. Those occupations can be summarised as follows:

Blacksmiths	3
Breeches makers	2
Carpenters	5
Farmers & Gardeners	14
Labourers:	31
Millers & Bakers	8
Servants &c.	23
Shoemakers	3
Sieve (or basket?) makers	2
Stone cutters & masons	3
Weavers, Wool-combers, and Wool-staplers:	10
Others	4

The above analysis can only give an approximate picture, since it lacks the more detailed information that began to be available from the censuses in the following century. But, when compared with the 1851 census results, there are some parallels in terms of the proportion of people employed in each trade. The number of shoemakers is extremely low in comparison with 1851, and it can only be assumed that the majority of labourers, and craftsmen of various types, were outside the age range for militia service: 18 to 45. Some of the other persons excluded were clergymen, apprentices, and poor men who had three or more legitimate children.

In his study of the history of Kingsthorpe, Alec Brooking made a careful analysis of the Census returns for 1851. The results, in terms of people's occupations at that time, are of great interest, and are largely reproduced below. Here is a generalised analysis:

Category	Number	% of total
Gentry and Clergy	10	1.7
Farmers and agricultural trades	251	43.6
Crafts and Industries	121	21.2
Distribution trades, clothing, food, etc.	102	17.7
Miscellaneous, services, etc.	91	15.8
Total	**575**	

In addition there were ten entered as Annuitants and ten who described themselves as Paupers. Detailed classification within the above groups will be found at Appendix 5. If the individual occupations are placed in rank order according to the numbers of persons, the first ten are as follows:

Agricultural Labourers	220
Shoemakers	55
Servants	35
Stone Masons &c	25
Laundresses	18
Lacemakers	17
Farmers	16
Carpenters	15
Dressmakers	10
Cordwainers	9

On the other hand if they are placed in rank order according to groups of closely allied occupations, the first ten are:

Agricultural labourers, gardeners and a shepherd	228
Shoe makers, closers, finishers, binders & leather workers	73
Building trades workers	71
Servants	35
Laundresses	18
Lacemakers	17
Farmers and a farm superintendent	17
Blacksmiths, machine workers, farriers & wheelwrights	13
Dressmakers	10
General labourers	9

From the above analysis note the prominent numbers of building trade workers, which brings their work very close to shoemaking in importance. But it would be a long time before the latter was ever anything other than a cottage industry in Kingsthorpe. The term 'boot and shoe maker' under the heading of occupation probably covers several aspects of shoe making because the separately listed terms of shoe closers, finishers and binders indicates the way in which this work was becoming increasingly fragmented and more specialised.

The fact that servants rank third highest in order of occupations should not be too surprising. In 1851 they formed about one sixth of the working population. Fifteen servants were kept by nine of the farmers, some of whom were also innkeepers and millers; but these were followed closely by just two of the gentry, who between them kept no less than twelve servants, ten of whom were at Kingsthorpe Hall. Others who kept servants were the clergy, two of the innkeepers, a machine worker, a stone sawyer, a butcher and two of the annuitants.

It should be remembered that many farmers employed bonded servants on twelve-month contracts at absolutely minimal wages. Examples will be found in the extracts from the account books of Charles Fitzhugh; see the chapter so named. The Royal Commission on Agriculture in 1895 refers to this type of worker as "...young men and women [who] were content to receive board, lodging, clothing and a little pocket money as their remuneration..."

The existence of the freestone and limestone quarries near the village accounts for the high number of stonemasons and stonecutters; no doubt some of the labourers were also employed at those places. Laundress was the occupation of 18 of the women and girls, and it is certain that this entailed no more than taking in washing; there would be no laundry in the parish for another 50 years.

It is interesting to see that lacemaking was still lingering as an occupation. The Northamptonshire villages in the south of the county, and particularly near to the border with Buckinghamshire, were well known for their pillow-lace from the 17th to the 19th centuries, when wives and children supplemented the meagre earnings of the men folk. As with so many other cottage industries, of course, it disappeared with the coming of mechanisation. The Kingsthorpe census reveals that just one man, aged 33, was a lacemaker; he was also receiving parish relief. The other sixteen were aged between nine and forty-eight years, and for the most part were daughters or wives of agricultural and general labourers; the remainder were widows.

Agriculture

Since this was the largest single employment in the economy of 1851, over 40%, it is worth separate consideration. Alec Brooking analysed the information given by individual farmers in the census, and this is set out below. Geological surveys show that the Inferior Oolite series, and principally the Northampton Sand, covers a large portion of the parish, producing a good arable soil that Baker refers to as a light, porous red earth. With good land we would expect that arable farming would predominate, and the Poor Law Commissioners' Report of 1834 confirms this as far as the adjoining, similar parish of Moulton is concerned, where 2,738 out of the parish total of 3,094 acres were arable. The report said that the farms were mostly from 100 to 200 acres in size, and one informant gave a figure of four men to every 100 acres as being sufficient for proper cultivation of the land; another suggested six men to every 100 acres. The latter approximate ratio seems to be borne out by the following analysis from the 1851 census returns for Kingsthorpe, which gives an average of 6.5 men or boys per 100 acres.

Farmer	Address	Acreage	Men employed
Thomas Cox	Welford Road	160	7
William Green	Welford Road	210	9
William Trasler	High Street.	100	4
John Gardner	High Street	55	3
Thomas Tatham	High Street	40	5
Mary Cumberpatch	High Street	70	3
Mark Cumberpatch	High Street	23	1
Charles Danes	Back Lane	140	9
William Dunkley	Dunkley's Lodge	130	16 men, 10 boys
Thomas Green	Green's Lodge	150	5
George Ashby	Ashby's Lodge	104	4 men, 2 boys
Robert Norman	Harborough Rd	30	1 man, 1 boy
John Brown	Harborough Rd	120	4
George Dunkley	Harborough Rd	88	4 men, 1 boy
Charles Fitzhugh	Welford Road	117	9
[Source: Brooking, 49]	**Totals:**	**1,537**	**98 employees**

The picture of agricultural employment illustrated by the above table changed radically during the following decades of the 19th century, and the 1895 Royal Commission on Agriculture outlines part of the reason when it refers to the depression which then rested very heavily on all those connected with the land and farming in the counties of Bedford, Huntingdon and Northampton. The problems apparently began with the cold, wet seasons between 1875 and 1880, accompanied by falling prices.

But it was not only the weather that caused this depression: the *Free Trade Act* of 1875, and the import of cheap food from abroad, almost destroyed British agriculture. (Why do we not learn from our own history? A similar situation obtains at the beginning of the 21st century!) Also relevant to this picture is the chapter entitled *The Problems of the Poor* and the data from the Overseers' records in the early 19th century, particularly the iniquitous system of 'Roundsmen.' At that time there was increased poverty owing to the alarming increase in the cost of living, caused mainly by the

Napoleonic wars of 1793 to 1815.

Wright's Directory of 1884, which lists eleven market gardeners, says that one or two of the larger farms had been made into garden allotments, and a large quantity of produce was being grown for the Northampton and other markets. Another notable industry at that time was the breeding of pigs. Gradually the number of farmers continued to decrease until eventually there were no longer any farms, or even market gardens, in Kingsthorpe.

Bakers

The 1851 census listed six persons who described themselves as Bakers: Thomas Tatham (who was also a Miller and Farmer); Stephen Tatham his son; William Birch; George Banks; Joseph Trasler (in the property which later was known as Church View); and Thomas Bates, who was listed as a visitor in the household of Richard Ellis, the Miller at Perry's Mill.

The NRO indexes for Bakehouse and Baker in Kingsthorpe, and the associated early documents, have been examined to see if the descriptions of the properties enable them to be located within the village. Only one early bakehouse can be precisely located: Kingswell Cottage. The Order issued by the Charity Commissioners in 1683, following their Inquisition of the previous year, mentions the annual payment of five shillings to be given to the poor out of the rent of this house, then called The Bakehouse. Its name indicates how the property had been used at some point in its history, if not at that time.

A certain document mentions Richard Dickenson of Kingsthorpe, a baker, and refers to a small dwelling house or tenement with barn and yard or orchard, formerly in the tenure of Elizabeth Bland, widow, and late of Mary Wood, since deceased. Another document refers to a messuage, cottage or tenement with the Bakehouse and appurtenances thereunto belonging, which was being leased to William Perrin of Moulton, a baker, for 9 years at £4 per annum. The lessors are named as Elizabeth Tresler, widow of William Tresler of Kingsthorpe, a baker; Thomas Tresler of Harlestone, also a baker; and Robert Tresler of St Giles, Northampton, another baker. This indenture is dated 7 October 1758. The Trasler family seems to have come to Kingsthorpe from Moulton, according to a Settlement document relating to William Trasler, Baker, of Moulton; this is dated 17 July 1740. As noted above, Joseph Trasler was listed as a Baker in the census of 1851.

Coming forward to 27 November 1918, there is a document setting out the particulars and conditions of sale of the extensive estate of T J Trasler, deceased. The estate consisted of 'Homehurst', 'Yew Tree Lodge', 'Church View', and 26 cottages in Kingsthorpe, so the Trasler family obviously prospered here – although Thomas Joseph Trasler was a farmer of Ravensthorpe. 'Church View', of course, had a bakehouse attached, and was at that time occupied by Mr W Cooke, a baker. It continued in use as a bakehouse by the Cooke family well into the 20th century. In the 1851 list of Farmers above, occurs another William Trasler; he was the son of Joseph and nephew to Robert, Joseph's brother. Robert left his farmhouse, closes, &c. in Kingsthorpe (estimated at 73 acres), along with two cottages, to his nephew William in 1843, the will being proved in March 1844. William had retired by August 1892, when he conveyed at least some (but eventually all) of his estate to his son Thomas Joseph. The Vestry minutes tell us that Thomas Treslar's tender to supply bread to the Workhouse was accepted in April 1835.

A document dated 1796 mentions Richard Manning of Kingsthorpe, a baker, and refers to a bakehouse in the Drapery, Northampton. We know from the records of the Overseers of the Poor that Richard Manning was supplying bread to the Workhouse in the early years of the 19th century.

INNS AND BEERHOUSES
Alec Brooking says in his useful document that Commissioner Richardson's report, on the operation of the Poor Laws in Kingsthorpe in 1834, mentioned that the beer-shops were numerous and flourishing. From the census returns it can be seen that this was still clearly so in 1851. The Northamptonshire Police returns quoted in the Northampton Mercury of 18 January 1851 give Kingsthorpe's population as 1,467; it was served by a total of five public houses and seven beerhouses; this amounts to one tavern for every 122 men,

women and children in the parish. Comparing this with Brixworth, where there was one tavern for every 240 persons, it would seem that Kingsthorpe must have had an unusually thirsty population!

Pigot's Directory of 1830 and 1841 list these public houses and their licensees:

	1830	1841
Cock:	Geo Dunkley	Robt Elliott
Five Bells:	Robert Lucas	Mary Ann Lucas
Horseshoe:	John Fitzhugh	George Dunkley
Rose & Crown:	Wm Parrott	Wm Parrott
White Horse:	Thos Burton	Thos Burton

Kelly (1847) and Whellan (1849) give the following names:

	1847	1849
Cock:	Robert Norman	Robert Dunmore
Five Bells:	Bryan Lucas	Bryan Lucas
Horseshoe:	Geo Dunkley (& farmer)	Geo Dunkley
Rose & Crown:	Wm Parrott	Wm Parrott
White Horse:	Thos Burton (& farmer)	Robert Norman
(& Bowling Green)		

Kelly (1854) and Melville (1861) list the following:

	1854	1861
Cock:	Wm Bunker	Wm Bunker
Five Bells:	Miss Rebecca Whitworth	Mrs Ann Davis
Fox & Hounds:		Geo White
Horseshoe:	George Dunkley	
Rose & Crown:	Wm.Parrott	Geo Leonard
White Horse:	No longer listed.	

The Post Office Directory (1869) and Whellan (1874):

	1869	1874
Cock:	Francis Longland	Francis Longland
Five Bells:	John Davis	William Goode
Fox & Hounds:		Geo White

Half Way house:		Thomas Plumb
Rose & Crown:	Geo Leonard	Geo Leonard

(In connection with the appearance of the *Half Way House*, under the management of Mr Plumb, reference should be made to the chapter *Entertainments at Kingsthorpe*.)

Kelly (1877) and Provincial & Metropolitan (1878-9):

	1877	**1878-9**
Cock:	Benjamin Law	Benjamin Law
Old Five Bells:	Mrs Anne Goode	Mrs Anne Goode
Half Way house:	Richard Chas Tooby	Richard Chas Tooby
(Albert Recreation Grounds, Kingsthorpe Road).		
Prince of Wales:	Robert Cross (& builder)	Robert Cross (& builder)
Rose & Crown:	Geo Leonard	Geo Leonard
White Horse:		John Dix (& builder)

In 1881 the *Five Bells* was occupied by Joseph W Fitzhugh, 28, who described himself as a Butcher and Victualler. *Windmill House* was occupied by Susan Hawkins, 82, Publican; but also resident was Richard Coleman, 51, Manager and Farmer, together with his family. Wrights (1884) and Kelly (1885):

	1884	**1885**
Cock:	Benjamin Law	Benjamin Law
Old Five Bells:	Thomas Miller, jnr.	Thomas Miller
Fox & Hounds:	Geo Brazier (& bricklayer)	Geo Brazier (& bricklayer)
King William IV:	William Parbery	William Parbery
Prince of Wales:	Wm Thos Flavell	Wm Thos Flavell
Queen Adelaide:	Thomas Love	Thomas Love
Rose & Crown:	Geo Leonard	Geo Leonard
Royal Oak:	Mrs Matilda Ruth Johnson	Mrs Matilda Ruth Johnson
White Horse:	John Dix	John Dix (& plasterer)
Windmill:	Richard Coleman	Richard Coleman

The beerhouses were not listed by name, although the licensees were given. It is noticeable, from the Directories and the census returns, that the keepers of inns and beerhouses often had other trades as well. Selling beer was a part-time occupation for them, or perhaps for their wives.

In 1847 the following beer retailers were listed:

Abraham Abbott
Mark Bryan (& chair turner)
Charles Gardner
Cornelius Love (in 1850 he was also a boot & shoe maker and a
    butcher at various times)
William Parbery (& pork butcher)
William Tarry (& tailor)

In 1854 Charles Meade was listed as a farmer and beer retailer, and George Waterfield puts in an appearance. William Flavell appeared in 1861, presumably in the house that eventually became the *Prince of Wales*, and was known in 1866 as a beer retailer & maltster. Also in 1866 appear the following:

Henry Brazier
Thomas Coleman
James Cross, mason & beer retailer, but by 1869 listed only as a mason.
Benjamin Johnson
Mrs Rebecca Parbery (William's widow)
George Waterfield (Stone Mason; he called his beerhouse the Mason's
    Arms).

In 1874 the beerhouse keepers were:

George Brazier (& bricklayer)
Robert Cross
John Dix
William Gardner
Benjamin Johnson
Cornelius Love
Mrs Rebecca Parbery
George Waterfield (In 1877 & 1878, Mrs Eliza Waterfield)

And in 1885:

George Brazier (& bricklayer)
Richard Coleman
John Dix (& plasterer). [Was this the origin of the phrase 'getting plastered'?]
Thomas Sambrooke Godfrey (& shopkeeper)
Mrs Matilda Ruth Johnson
Thomas Love (Cornelius now called himself a market gardener).
William Parbery (Rebecca's son).
George Weston (& shopkeeper & Assistant Overseer of the Poor).

ADVERTISEMENTS AND SALE PARTICULARS

The following items give an indication of the stone and lime production industry carried on in Kingsthorpe during the 18th and 19th centuries. To the east of the Harborough Road there was a quarry of white freestone having a sandy texture, with a tendency to harden on exposure to the air. Kingsthorpe Hall, the older portions of the General Hospital, the Barracks, and several country houses in the area were built of this stone. Near Moulton Park there was a quarry producing a dense oolitic limestone with very good wearing qualities. There were also a number of lime-kilns, producing material that was much in demand by farmers for improving the fertility of their land.

Advertisements in the Northampton Mercury:
21 April 1783:

STONE, COALS, LIME, &c. JOHN JOHNSON of Kingsthorpe, near Northampton, begs leave to acquaint the public, and his friends in particular, that he sells at the Quarries (lately occupied by Mr Boswell) that durable white Free-stone, so justly esteemed for Ashlar, Springers, Water-tables, Coping, Cornice, and all other ornaments in building &c. Also, flat Grave-stones, Paving, Hearth, Stock and Sink-stones; chimney-pieces &c finely interspersed with a beautiful variety of shells, being the best of that product on commonly called Moulton Park stone.

Every article at each place will be carefully executed, in such a manner as shall do honour to the chisel and the hand that directs it.

N.B. At Hillmorton Wharf he likewise sells COALS, equal in price and quantity to any other landed there; attended with one peculiar circumstance, advantageous to the consumer.
And, at Kingsthorpe, LIME, on the usual terms.
The kind encouragement of his friends, and others, will with gratitude be acknowledged and received, and every order punctually performed by their obliged humble servant, JOHN JOHNSON.

29 April 1803:
Kingsthorpe and Duston Lime Kilns: JOHN WALTON begs leave to inform his friends and the public in general that he still continues to sell LIME at 2s.6d per quarter.

29 May 1819:
To Builders and Others: T. MASTERS, having purchased the WHITE SAND STONE QUARRIES at KINGSTHORPE (lately occupied by Mr J. Lucas), begs leave to inform his friends and the public in general, that he sells the under-mentioned articles at REDUCED PRICES:

White ashlar, rubbed & squared, per foot	8d
Red ditto	7d
Chopped wall stones at, per yard,	13d

Sandstone coping, of any width, in proportion. Moulton Park Paving at reduced prices.

Common bricks, per 1,000, delivered in Northampton	37s
Ditto, at the kiln	35s

A discount of 2s. per thousand for money.
Pantiles £4.15s.0d per 1,000; £4.10s.0d for money.
(*Northamptonshire Studies Collection*).

Sale particulars:
On 18 February 1841 the Kingsthorpe Lodge Estate was to be sold: 104 acres of land in Boughton Green Road, with frontage to the

Harborough Road, then in the occupation of W Dunkley. Lime, building and paving stone quarries. This property was put up for sale again in 1848.

THE ROMANCE OF THE MILL

Kingsthorpe used to have three water mills and three windmills. The water mills go back at least as far as the Domesday survey of 1086, which says that the rent for them was £2.3s.4d per annum. They were known as the Upper or Farre Mill, the Nether Mill and St Andrew's Mill. The details that follow make use of information compiled by Geoffrey Starmer for a course, with the name of this chapter, tutored by him in 2003.

WATER MILLS
Kingsthorpe Upper Mill

It was located at map reference SP 73776400. On a leat from River Nene North Water, the site of the mill is immediately north of a bridge carrying a footpath between Kingsthorpe and Harlestone Heath. The original access road, now only a footpath, runs from the A5199 (Welford) road, immediately south-east of the site of Highfield House (now redeveloped as The Old School House). The earliest specific reference to this mill is in a document of 1439. Milling continued here until around 1953. The top storey collapsed about ten years later and the mill was demolished. In 1992 some sections of wall were still standing, and the curved brickwork at the bottom of the wheel race and the framework of the wheel were still in position. Three millstones were lying around the wheel chamber. In the late 1990s the wheel-race was opened up as part of flood prevention work and the rubble and millstones cleared away.

In 1844 the mill had two pairs of stones, driven by great spur wheel gearing. Before the mid-20th century, there was a breast-shot waterwheel driving three pairs of stones by a layshaft, with all the gearing of iron except for the bevel gears on the layshaft, which were of iron with wooden cogs. In addition to the millstones, there were a smutter, a winnowing machine, an oat crusher, a wire dressing machine and a jumper, all driven from the waterwheel.

Millers:

1521 John Hopkin

1777 Abraham Abbot *(Militia List)*

1840 Charles Fitzhugh, miller (Assignee in affairs of Thomas Coleman, baker)

1841 At Kingsthorpe Upper Mill: Stephen Spokes, 40, journeyman miller, with wife Mary, 45, and Sarah Townsend, 70. In Welford Road: Charles Fitzhugh, 30, farmer and miller, with wife, 2 daughters, 2 sons and 2 female servants (15 & 20 years)

1851 At Fitzhugh's Mill: Henry B Smith, 30, miller, with wife, Mary, 29; 6yr. daughter and 4 yr. son (both born at Oxendon). In Welford Road: Charles Fitzhugh, miller & farmer 117 acres employing 9 labourers, with wife, 3 daughters and 3 sons.

1861 At Fitzhugh's Mill: Jabez Springer, 43, miller, with wife, nephew (agricultural labourer) and niece.

1864 C. Fitzhugh, miller *(Kelly's directory)*

1871 At 'First Mill': John C. Barratt, 27, miller employing 2 men & 1 boy, with 55 yr. female servant.

1881 At 'Watermill Welford Road': Jeffery Sarrington, 49, Higgler & miller, with 3 nieces and 2 male boarders, both agricultural labourers.

1904-1951 John Walker.

Kingsthorpe Mill (The Nether Mill)

This was located at map reference SP 74526263, on the River Nene North Water on the north side of Mill Lane, which headed west from the Cock Inn towards Dallington. The realigned modern road from Kingsthorpe to Kings Heath crosses over the site on an embankment. The last recorded miller here was in 1898. In 1900 the millpond and part of the river were converted into a bathing place. By the 1930s only some of the outer walls of the mill buildings were standing.

Millers: 1777-90 William Manning *(Militia List & Admons.)*

1814 Richard Manning, miller & baker *(Insurance policy)*.

1823 Thomas Hands of Kingsthorpe, miller & baker. (In 1798 Thomas Hands listed under Northampton corn millers and flour dealers, with an address in Drury Lane; in 1830 he was at Horse Market, Northampton, and in 1841 at Gold Street.)

1841 At Kingsthorpe Mill: William Kilborn, 35, journeyman miller with wife and son, together with Thomas Tatham, 80, miller. In High

Kingsthorpe Nether Mill from the south, towards the end of the 19th century. (Picture from the late Alec Brooking's collection).

Street: Thomas Tatham, 30, miller & baker, with wife and 4 sons. *(Census)*.

1851 At Tathams Mill: John Chamberlain, 43, miller, with wife, 2 sons & 2 daughters. In High Street: Thomas Tatham, 43, miller, baker & farmer 40 acres, employing 5 men, with wife, 6 sons, 2 daughters and 2 female housemaids (15 & 17 yrs).

1866 Thomas Tatham, farmer, corn-miller & baker *(Royal Directory)*.

1871 At 'Second Water Mill': Thomas Moss, 52, miller, with wife, 2 daughters & 2 sons. In Hopes Place: George Tatham, 36, miller & baker, with wife, son, daughter and 13 yr. old nursemaid.

1874 Thomas Moss, miller *(Whellan's Directory)*.

1881 In Cock Lane: Thomas Moss, 64, miller, with wife Mary, 62, and son William, 22, miller. In High Street: Thomas Moss, 29, miller, and wife Elizabeth, 30.

1885-94 Thomas Moss, Miller *(Kelly's directory)*.

1896 Mrs. Moss, miller, Kingsthorpe *(White's Directory)*.

1898 Mrs. Eliza Moss, Mill Lane, Kingsthorpe *(Kelly's Directory)*.

Kingsthorpe south (St. Andrew's mill)

This mill was located at map reference SP 74876133, on a leat from the River Nene North Water. The site is west of St. Andrew's Road, immediately behind the old service station. It is about 70 metres north of where Mill Lane (near Hampton Street) comes from the east to its junction with St. Andrew's Road. In 1411 St. Andrew's Priory, to whom the mill was let on lease, was involved in a dispute with the men of Kingsthorpe over fishing rights. In 1457 there were four watermills here under one roof, two for grinding corn and two for fulling cloth. In 1831 and 1839 it had two pairs of stones. By 1934 the mill had a straight float undershot waterwheel, and ground wheat and barley at about 2 cwt per hour or 1 ton per day. A gas engine was used at a later date. In 1941 it was still milling provender, but was then burnt out. About five years later the machinery was dismantled and the mill sold and subsequently demolished.

Millers: 1457 William Braunfield, lessee of the mill.

1608 Francis Morgan held a lease on the mill, but he was not the miller.

1777 Thos. Tallis, miller *(Militia List)*.

1831 Jabez Adkins & John Perry (also at Town Mills and Nunn Mills), millers, corn and coal merchants. *(Insurance Policy)*.

1839-47 John Perry (also at Town Mills) *(Insurance Policy)*.

1841 At St. Andrew's Mill: William Green, 45, Journeyman Miller, with wife, 3 sons and 1 daughter.

1851 At Perry's Mill: Richard Ellis, 52, miller, with wife, son and daughter (both boot closers) and grandson.

1861 At St. Andrew's Mill: George Bason, 35, journeyman miller, with wife, five sons and two daughters. (For Northampton Progressionists Cooperative Society?)

1871 George Haines, 53, miller, with son, Thomas, 15, miller, and daughter, 20, housekeeper.

1874 Geo. Haynes, St. Andrew's Mill, St. Georges Street *(Whellan's Directory)*.

1877-96 George Rushforth Swallow, 30 Market Square and St. Andrew's Mill.

1881 At 'Swallow's Mill': Henry Williams, 31, carter to miller, and wife. At 12 Semilong Place: David Bell, 59, miller, and wife. *(Census)*

1897 John Barford, on retirement of G R Swallow (who continued to own the mill).

1898 John Barford, St. Andrew's Road *(Kelly's Directory)*.

1906-28 John Robinson, St. Andrew's Road *(Kelly's Directory)*.
c.1934 Gerald Westley, corn & feed merchant (formerly of Town Mills) rented St. Andrew's Mill from Cyril Yard (seedsman).
1940 Gerald Westley, St. Andrew's Road *(Kelly's Directory)*.

WINDMILL SITES
Kingsthorpe – North

This windmill was located at map reference SP 749640, about ½ mile from the A5199 (Welford Road) at the end of a track heading east-north-east from a point on this road mid-way between the present Windmill Inn and its junction with the A508 (Harborough Road). The track is still shown on the 1884 OS map, but leading nowhere. In 1780 the 'windmill in Windmill Close with a circular plot of land (diameter 22 yards)' was conveyed to William Manning of Kingsthorpe, a miller, together with a 'carriage and horse road or way (breadth 10 feet) from the turnpike road to Welford.' The 1813 survey plan for OS marks it with a symbol and *Mill*. In 1825 the circular plot of ground 'whereon a windmill or building heretofore stood' was conveyed by Stephen Manning, yeoman of Kingsthorpe, to Revd Thomas Cooke Thornton of Brockhall. Nothing more is known about this windmill.

Kingsthorpe – North East

The converted remains of this windmill are located at map reference SP 756639, on the south-east of Boughton Green Road, by Windmill Terrace. It last appeared in a trade directory in 1894. In 1905 it was purchased by Thomas Wilson and converted to a dwelling, to which further extensions were made later.

Machinery: The three-storey stone tower mill had a domed cap, surmounted by a ball finial and fitted with a petticoat. A cradle higher than the finial carried an eight-bladed fan. There were four clockwise sails, two being common, the others being spring sails.

Millers: 1841 In High Street: William Stanton, 45, miller, with wife and son (Journeyman Shoemaker).
1851 In High Street: William Stanton, 54, miller, with wife.
1861 On Harborough Road: John Spencer, 55, farmer and miller,

The Windmill that stood at the top of Boughton Green Road. (Picture from the late Alec Brooking's collection).

with wife, son Thomas, 22 (no occupation given), and 16 yr. female servant. At another address on Harborough Road, James Hamilton, 30, miller, with wife, son and daughter.

1870 John Spencer and son, Kingsthorpe, involved in dispute re 3 sacks of barley flour.

1871 In High Street: William Stanton, 75, miller, with wife and a boarder. In Back Lane: Alfred Coley, 26, miller, with wife and son. On Pitch Hill, leading to limeworks: Charles Tite, 36, miller with wife and son.

1881 On Pitch Hill: Charles Tite, 46, miller, with wife and son, 22, shoe finisher. (Pitch Hill, Pitchwell Hill or Pishwell Hill all refer to what is now known as Boughton Green Road.)

1885-94 Thomas Spencer, Kingsthorpe, miller using wind. *(Kelly's Directory).*

Kingsthorpe – North West

This mill was located at map reference SP 741641, on the west side of the A5199 (Welford Road), about half way between that road's junction with the A508 (Harborough Road) and the old railway level crossing, and almost opposite the site of the present day *Windmill Inn*. The 1767 Kingsthorpe Inclosure Map shows a circular Close for Cradock's Windmill, with bridle road access. Eyre & Jeffery's 1791 map marks it with a symbol, un-named; Bryant's 1827 map does not show the mill but marks 'Windmill Ho.' at the site of Windmill Inn. Nothing further is known about this windmill. In the will of Robert Cooke of Kingsthorpe, dated 4 August 1574, he bequeathed to "Simon my son my windmill to him and his heirs for ever" along with "my [leys?] of the North Mill and the leys of the holme and the interest of my said Mill for my years" - which may be a reference to this windmill.

THE ACCOUNT BOOKS OF CHARLES FITZHUGH

Charles Fitzhugh described himself as a Farmer and a Miller in the trade directories from 1841 onwards. In the 1851 census he appears as a 45 year old Miller & Farmer occupying 117 acres and employing nine labourers. In Whellan's Directory of 1874 he appears under Farmers with 'and Butcher and Maltster' added. The chapter *The*

Romance of the Mill makes it clear that he leased the North Mill. Slater's Directory of 1850, along with later ones, mentions two Millers: Charles Fitzhugh and Thomas Tatham; but neither of these actually lived at the mills with which their names were associated. They obviously employed millers to do the actual work, and Charles Fitzhugh's accounts do include payments to millers.

The Account Books in the collection of the County Record Office begin in late 1840. The first book is written in an exceptionally fine, neat hand and commences with a number of notes on the flyleaves. The first entry records that he "had of Clark Hillyard Esq 6 pigs at 40 shillings" which he paid for with a cheque for £12 on 8 May 1841. On 8 June he "sold Mr Smith, Northton [short for Northampton] the six pigs which I bought of Mr Hillyard at 10/3d per score to have them in two months if fat enough."

The second flyleaf contains a record of payments he made to various persons in respect of Poor Levies, Taxes, Highway Rates, Church Rates, and Fee Farm Rents. The Tax must have included Window Tax, since in 1842 it increased from £2.8s.6d per half-year to £3.7s.2d on account of two extra windows. This record continues up to May 1843 on the fifth page. On page 3 there are some interesting records of people that he took into service: On 21 October 1841 Eliza Pell entered his service until Michaelmas 1842; she received £6.10s.0d for a year's work – most of it not paid until 15 October 1842! Nevertheless, on that date she entered into a further year's 'servitude' (a good word for it!) until Michaelmas 1843 at the same rate of pay. At the same time he hired Ann Day for a year at 9d per week. Fitzhugh also hired William Buswell into service from Michaelmas 1841 until 1842 at £5 for the year. He also recorded payment to Esther Stevenson, on 3 May 1842, of twelve weeks pay at 9d per week, and a further 1/- on 24 June. All these entries were on the flyleaves; they clearly do not represent a complete record, though obviously begun with good intentions.

Then come the accounts proper, which begin with an alphabetical index of names with page numbers. The first use of the book, from 1841 to 1843, was mainly concerned with the sale of bread, flour and some 'baking' to 122 customers. Most of these were in Kingsthorpe, but others were in the nearby villages of Boughton, Pitsford, Holcot, Overstone, Sywell, and in the town of Northampton. The second use of the book relates to the years 1864 to 1874, and relates to 'Buchering', with around 90 customers. This index is followed by 520 pages of accounts for each of the people with whom he did business; some people took up a number of pages, some only one or part of one page. The account of Mrs Lucas of Kingsthorpe, for instance, records a balance of £2.0s.6d "brought out of the old book" followed by an entry, repeated every few days, recording 6d worth of bread. This is interspersed with another entry, occurring roughly once each month, recording "I had 2½ gallons of yeast at 1/6" or similar. At the end of the year he totals up the bread to £2.11s.6d and subtracts "The Yeast £1.13s.9d", followed by "12 Jan 1841: Paid the Bill 17/9". So he received payment for a year's supply of bread to this customer at the end of the year. He also bought yeast from Mr Sears of Pitsford during 1840 and 1841, which varied in price from 6d to 3/6d per gallon; perhaps the price reflected the thickness of the liquid and thus the strength of the yeast. A similar variation in price occurs in the account of Mr Parbery at Boughton, from whom he had 2½ gallons of yeast at 9d on 14 May 1841, and 1 gallon at 3/- on 25 June; Mr Parbery kept *The Griffin* at Boughton. Charles Fitzhugh bought yeast from a number of other customers who were beer retailers; specific strains of yeast more suitable for bread making had not then been developed.

As well as bread he supplied customers with such other items as flour, pollard (a fine bran, or flour containing fine bran), and biscuit. This book was clearly his 'sales ledger' in which he transcribed his notes of the sales (and some purchases) that he made as he (or one of his family) journeyed around Kingsthorpe and the nearby villages. Most of the accounts seem to be settled on a quarterly basis, with some very small ones being left to the end of the year.

When used for the butchery trade the book changes in character, being written in a different quite rough hand. The dates are from 1864 onwards, and involve sales of meat – mainly mutton, but occasionally beef and pork – as well as flour. Various cuts of meat are mentioned as well as heads and offal. In 1867 an account for Mr

Bassett is opened: he seems to be a dealer in pelts and skins. In 1872 the trade includes items such as beans, linseed, turnips, and bushels of rye and vetches.

On page 396 an account is started which records purchases of animals – mainly sheep, but some pigs and occasionally calves and beef – on the left hand page, and a 'Money Account' (meaning money received for sales) on the right hand page. There are several examples of this type of record, but only one set is totalled: that for 1871, page 471, and this shows a total outlay of £690.5s.6d; 'Money' £764.16s. 8½d; and a profit figure of £74.11s.2½d.

The accounts for Miss Boddington (at the Hall) on pages 406, 463, 495 & 508 (the latter for 1873, the year of her death), show entries every week or so with the names of several persons, each having 2 or 2½ lbs of mutton, costing 1/4d or thereabouts. The account is settled every three months or so. Perhaps this was meat purchased for some poor persons in the village.

Another account book covers a period from 1845 to 1874, where the writing becomes shakier. Some notes on the flyleaf record amounts of corn, barley and beans, together with the note: "Rent 25, Miller 20, Horses 70". This book also includes an index of customers. Trade included flour, bran, straw, rye, pollard, barley, malt, beans, sharps (the hard pieces resulting from milling), wheat, oats and fleeces of wool. From Mobbs, Snow & Wood (seed merchants) he purchased Red & White Clover, Trefine seed, Rye grass, Talian (Italian Rye?) grass, and Kales. Towards the end of this book are some pages relating to 'Spratton Land', 'Old Grass Keep' and 'Old Land', where he kept for a time some records of his purchases of animals, rents for pasture, and sales of fleeces and animals. It is not always clear whether certain entries relate to purchases or sales, but the following examples of purchases provide interesting comparisons with the present time:

Date	Description	£	s	d
1869				
April 26	2 Cows	30	0	0
	3 Calves	20	0	0

	50 Tegs	100	0	0
May 3	17 Ewes & 20 Lambs	41	8	0
May 29	6 Welsh Runts	48	0	0
June 3	1 Cow	7	17	6
	Sheep washing and shearing[?]		8	0
June 7	Shearing Sheep		10	6
June 17	Mr Blythe, 37 Ewes & 58 Lambs	107	10	0
	Expenses fetching them		7	6
July 21	Paid Mr Peirce for the Keep	58	15	0
	Mr Stephenson, 1 Cow	8	10	0
Aug 2	11 Lambs	13	4	0
	6 Sheep	10	4	0
1870				
April 28	17 Ewes, 25 Lambs	47	0	0
	3 Hereford Sterks[Steers?]	24	0	0
	3 Steers	20	0	0
	30 Tegs	67	10	0
	6 Ewes, 12 Lambs	21	0	0
	6 Ewes, 6 Lambs	17	14	0
	9 Tegs, Mr Lowick's sale	14	17	0
	20 Cows	27	0	0
	1 Heifer from Brixworth	12	0	0

He actually spelled heifer 'Heefor', which is probably how he pro-
nounced it – just like its Old English original: Heahfore. A Teg is a
sheep in its second year.

And here is an associated list of sales:

Date	Description	£	s	d
1869				
June 5	67 Fleeces of Wool	33	10	0
June 18	50 Sheep	92	10	0
	2 Ewes, my own	36	0	0
June 25	1 Lamb	1	10	0
	37 Fleeces of Wool	14	16	0
June 29	1 Lamb	1	10	0

Aug 26	Mr Cox bought grass	5	0	0
	87 Lambs	112	8	0

3 Calves	24	0	0
6 [Welsh?] Runts	59	0	0
[Perhaps the ones he bought for £48 on May 29]			
6 Sheep	10	16	0
--------			
35 Ewes	98	1	0
1 Dead Sheep		1	0
68 Fleeces of Wool	28	4	0

Another record of sales of foodstuffs covers the years 1857-1869. There is what we would call a Cash Book for the years 1856 to 1874, with the name Henry Fitzhugh on the cover, that records receipts and payments for various goods and services. Its varied entries show that he used much hay and straw and threshed a lot of barley. On 20 February 1863 he makes the following note:

> 3 sows piged. 27 live pigs &7 dead on the 20th day of February the same day that the Prince of Wales came to Brampton Station to visit Althorpe house Fryday and meete the hounds at Welton on Sunday Monday and Brighton, to church on Sunday, through Northampton on Monday at 1½ past one.

Other example entries are:

1870

Jan 15	Wm Fitzhugh on Eggcutting [i.e. hedge cutting]	4/-
Jan 22	Wm Fitzhugh on Eggcutting	10/-
	Mr Buswell had the Bull from Brixworth.	
Jan 29	Paid Wm Fitzhugh Egg cutting	4/-
April 12	Samuel Parbery Ploughing	15/-

1871

Jany 24	Sold the old nag from Brixworth	£25.15.0

1873

Jan 4	Lost Mr W Turners check in the Corne Exchange. Mr W Reeve [...] it same & is Man denied finding it on the Monday Week following Cashed Birmingham Bank on 10 Jan 1873 & paid me 18 Jan £25.18.0	
Aug 11	2 men in the Home Close	4/-

	Crab tree	7/6
	3 men Top Home Baggars	2/-
	4 men in Home Close	5/-
Dec 14	Lent Mr Danes at the Bull	£1.0.0

Yet another ledger with the word 'Bread' on the cover runs from 1866 to about 1872, and deals with a somewhat extended range of goods, including flour, bran, pollard, barm, yeast, dough, bread, cake, baking, buns, rolls, butter, bacon, lard, ham, eggs, peas, mutton, beef and pork.

KINGSTHORPE COAL MINE

How many people know that there was once a coal mine in Kingsthorpe – or at least, a mineshaft, sunk at the top of what is now Boughton Green Road, to the east of the old windmill, in the hope of finding coal? The Northamptonshire Great Central Coal Mining Company, with a capital of £21,500 in £1 shares, was formed in the first half of the 19th century. Shares were bought by many Northampton folk who thought thereby to make themselves rich.

In the Northampton Mercury for 11 June 1836 there appeared an advertisement inviting tenders for supplying 200,000 bricks before the 1st day of July, "on which day sinking the shaft will be com-menced". In this same issue, subscription of capital in 6,000 shares of £3 each was invited. On 6 August there was a report of the First General Meeting and on 10 October another meeting to report progress, the shaft then having gone to a depth of 215ft. The work was not without danger, for on 10 December it was reported that a charge of gunpowder had gone off by accident, burning the face and arms of a Staffordshire man working in the shaft.

Doubts about the presence of coal were expressed at lectures by the Rev J C Meeke in the Mechanics Institute in Northampton towards the end of 1836; but the engineer in charge of the project apparently offered him a wager of £100 that a good seam of coal would be found. Doubts were also expressed by Mr Murchison (later Sir Roderick), a local geologist. Then one day it was announced that good quality coal had been found in the shaft. Shareholders were exultant, and hurried to the site to hear of the discovery first-hand from the Engineer. But he had disappeared, leaving a note to say that the only coal found in the pit was some that he had taken down there himself.

The shaft was allowed to fill with water; this was analysed and a proposal made that it could be the means of making Kingsthorpe into a health spa. But nothing came of that suggestion, and the shaft was eventually filled in.

EDUCATION

K INGSTHORPE apparently had a school during at least some part of the 17th century, but no record remains of its activities. The Free School began work in 1693, and continued to provide education for almost 200 years. It must have been here that Charles Fitzhugh learned to read and write; the great neatness and clarity of his entries in his account books demonstrate how well the school did its work. Although the National School was founded in 1840, its services were not free until near the end of the century. An Infant School was run privately from at least 1840 until 1873, when its patron died, and must have served the children well during that time. There is no indication that it required the payment of any fees. The parish then had to provide an Infant School, the accommodation for which was provided by the Manor & Town Lands Charity and by the Thornton family.

THE FREE SCHOOL

Thomas Cooke (1634-1694) provided the earliest recorded school for the free education of Kingsthorpe children, and the following inscription used to be over the door of the school building of 1870 in the High Street (on the corner of The Rise, and now converted into a private residence):

> This School, anciently set up for the free education of boys and girls belonging to the Parish of Kingsthorpe, was endowed by Thomas Cooke, Esq., of Hackney in the County of Middlesex, Merchant, who rebuilt the first school house in 1693 at his own charges. Mistress Elizabeth Cooke, relict of his son Thomas Cooke, Esq., of Stoke Newington, appointed the first Trustees in 1753. The second school house having fallen into decay, this building was erected by the Trustees in the year of our Lord 1870.

The Free School building in High Street, prior to its conversion into a dwelling. Following its closure in 1890 it had been used as a 'Babies School', an Infant School, a Youth Fellowship, and a warehouse. (Picture from the late Alec Brooking's collection).

This was the centre for education in the village for the next 150 years. Note that this inscription refers to a *rebuilding* of the *first* schoolhouse in 1693, and also says that the second schoolhouse had fallen into decay by 1870, when it was again rebuilt. It seems, therefore, that there had been an earlier school building, perhaps on the same site. But any such school would not have been a charity school, or the Charity Commissioners would have mentioned it in 1683, following their inquisition. Bridges says that Thomas Cooke "...bought ground, and built a school-house upon it; gave to it a neighbouring close, and settled a salary of £14 per annum upon the schoolmaster." This is not entirely accurate and does not give the full picture, as will become apparent from what follows.

The new Charity School House of 1693 consisted of a School Room, a Fire Room and a Buttery on the ground floor, with stairs going up to three bedrooms above. (Buttery was the name usually given to the room where small beer was brewed.) It was built of stone, with wood framed windows and a thatched roof. The walls were lime washed at a later date. It was financially supported by the rents of 14 acres of land in Kingston, Surrey, which in 1753 produced £20 per annum. The Schoolmaster, who had to be a man who could write and cypher well, careful and diligent in his duty and of sober life and conversation, received £12; the balance of £8 was used for the maintenance of the building.

Thomas Cooke's daughter-in-law Elizabeth (née Gould) was friendly with Philip Doddridge: she was among the donors of books to Doddridge's Northampton Academy, and Doddridge visited and dined at her house in Newington at various times between 1731 and 1749, according to his letters. Since she was a trustee of the school, she was able to introduce Non-conformist elements into the curriculum. Whellan's Directory of 1874 says that the Free School was "under the management of three trustees, who must belong to some sect of Protestant dissenters". A hand-written note in *Genealogical Memoranda* (1873) in the Northamptonshire Studies Collection confirms that the trust deed stated that the Trustees should be of this religious persuasion.

The rules drawn up in 1753 stated that the schoolmaster was to "carefully and diligently teach and instruct fifteen boys and fifteen girls of the town of Kingsthorpe to read English well, and to say by heart, exactly and distinctly, the church catechism, and the Assembly's catechism." If the Schoolmaster wished, he could also teach up to ten more scholars in addition to those admitted.

All the children should be orphans, or such children whose parents

were so poor (or so careless) that they could not pay for their school-
ing. None of the scholars were to continue at school longer than
three years, except those who learned to write: at least ten of each
sex; they were to continue six months longer. No child was to be
admitted under the age of seven years.

The school hours were from 7am to 11am and from 1pm to 5pm
when there was sufficient daylight; otherwise the school day did not
start until 8am and finished at twilight. Teaching was clearly oral,
with the children using chalk on slates. The first record of the purchase of stationery or books was in April 1830; that was also the year
in which coal was first purchased for the School Room. By 1837 exercise books were being purchased, and the schoolmaster was paid
£4.7s.6d per quarter.

George Hicks was master in 1845 and, although the National
School had opened its doors in 1840, the pupils at the latter had to
pay fees of 1d per week, so the Free School was able to maintain its
full complement. In 1852 the Rev. Joseph Litchfield, who had been
appointed as Minister at Kingsthorpe Baptist Church in 1848, became
the master. His initial annual salary was £20, but by 1866 this had
risen to £40 plus £10 gratuities.

Since the old building was deteriorating rapidly a new school was
built in 1869-70, probably behind the old one because this continued
to function during the construction period. Copybooks etc. were regularly purchased at that time, indicating that the curriculum had
developed beyond simple catechism learning. Owing to poor health
the Rev. Litchfield had to retire in 1888, and the Rev. Needham
became master in 1889. His salary of £40 per annum was less than
half the salary of a Board School Master of the time. He resigned in
1890 because his position was becoming untenable: free education in
Voluntary and Board Schools was due to be introduced in September
1891, so the old Free School would no longer be able to compete. The
building was sold to the Thornton family, and in 1901 was used as a
'Babies Department' for the National School, and later as an Infant
School until 1922.

The Charity Commissioners' Report dated 23 August 1895, resulting from an application made in January of the previous year, men-

tions that the Free School had been founded by a deed of 2 February 1753; this, of course, was when it had been placed on a formal legal footing by the Cooke family. The property consisted of the school-house, the garden attached, and a close on the east side of the Harborough Road of 14a.2r.32p. This property would be sold, and the proceeds invested. The income was to be applied to the maintenance of Exhibitions, each of an annual value not exceeding £10, tenable at any institution of education higher than elementary, or of Technical, Professional or Industrial instruction. This was intended to cover the tuition fees of the child, or otherwise to be spent for his or her main-tenance or benefit. Parents had to be *bona fide* residents of Kingsthorpe and members of the Church of England or Protestant Nonconformists. For half of the awards, other things being equal, preference would be given to children whose parents were the latter.

THE NATIONAL SCHOOL OF 1840

In October 1811 there was formed 'The National Society for Promoting the Education of the Poor in the Principles of the Established Church throughout England and Wales'. In 1818 the Society circularised all clergy in an attempt to assess the national sit-uation, but many clergy ignored the survey. However, by 1823 almost 2,000 'National' schools had been founded. Then, following the 1833 Education Bill, parliament approved the expenditure of £20,000 to aid the Voluntary societies to build "School houses for the education of the children of the poor classes in Great Britain." A Select Committee was set up in 1837 to consider the best way to provide education, and they were shocked to discover "that children were worked to death in factories and fields." As Bispham pertinently observes: "The worker was exploited, underpaid, underprivileged and of course une-ducated." But despite efforts to provide education, many families relied upon their children to earn money to help support the family. It was against this background that the National Mixed School was brought into existence in Kingsthorpe.

In 1839 Sir George Stamp Robinson donated the land for the build-ing of a school. He was the son of Sir George Robinson, who had been Liberal MP for Northampton in 1774. A letter of 5 June 1840 from Rev.

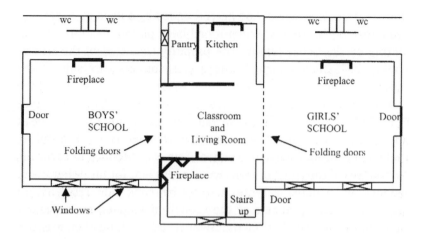

Kingsthorpe National School, 1840, ground floor layout. This sketch plan is not to scale or in proportion. It is based on the original architect's plan in NRO (SBD 33).

R W Baxter to the National Society acknowledged the proposal of the society to donate £80 towards the building of the school. On 29 July 1840 the foundation stone of the new school was laid by the Rector's wife, Mrs Baxter, and Miss Frances Boddington, who resided at the Hall.

The new school was really a master's house with two extra rooms extending on either side. In 1841 there were 100 pupils, each paying 1d per week, and the National Society donated £30 towards the master's salary. Kelly's Directory of 1847 tells us that the Master at that time was Samuel Berridge; by 1849 he had been replaced by George John Blackstone. Their wives' names were quoted as schoolmistresses, so running the school had to be a family commitment. The 1851 Census says that John Brown was the Master (and his wife the schoolmistress); he stayed until 1862, when John Robinson took over. By this time the school had just over 100 pupils, and the Free School still taught 30. There was also an Infant School run by the Misses Boddington, details of which will be found in a separate section.

According to a Log Book entry in January 1865, John Lewis became Master, with John Robinson, the previous Master, as an Assistant

Teacher. That document tells of the difficulty experienced in getting the penny-per-week school fees paid; it also records the irregular attendance during periods when there was much field work to be done on the local farms. On 7 November 1865 there were 159 children in school.

The Kingsthorpe Manor & Town Lands Charity accounts show that they contributed £12 p.a. to the school from at least 1864 to 1868, and £20 p.a. from 1869 until at least 1870. In October 1866 the Charity paid £50 towards the building of a new National School House for the Master. This was to take the form of an extension to the school on the side facing High Street, and would replace the accommodation that had originally been included within the school building. Bispham (p.67) says that this plan was rejected, and certainly a new Master's House was eventually built at the end of the school site, on the corner of Back Lane (now Manor Road) and Knight's Lane. (That house was sold for £260 in 1968.)

Attendance at the school was very poor, according to the Inspectors' reports, owing in the main to the inability of the poor

The old National School at the junction of High Street and Knights Lane. (Photo by the author).

families to find 1d per week. Attendance was also much affected by special events in the area, especially the annual Boughton Green Fair in June. On 13 January 1871 the Rev Thornton visited the school and gave a magic lantern show; he continued to take a great interest in the school until his death. By 1874 there were 250 pupils and, as Bispham says "The staff of only three were desperately overworked and the children were sitting shoulder to shoulder."

School fees were increased in the 1880s, and parents then had to pay 3d for the first child and a further 1d for each subsequent child. In January 1891 the Free School was closed, so additional scholars began to arrive; even more came with the abolition of fees in September of that year. In 1892 an extra room was built on to the school in order to provide total accommodation for 250 pupils. The Master's salary was then £120 per annum. By 1894 there were 304 pupils, and classes in cookery took place in Liberty Hall. In 1898 the cookery classes were held in the old Free School; but this became a reception class, known as the Babies' School, in 1899; and it continued to function as the Infant School, following closure of the one on The Bank, until the early 1920s.

THE INFANT SCHOOLS

The Free School did not take pupils below the age of seven, so there had always been a need for a school for infants. Prior to the opening of the National School in 1840, and for many years afterwards, this need had been met to some extent by an Infant School run by the Misses Boddington, who resided at Kingsthorpe Hall from 1832 until 1873.

Pigot's Directory of 1841 lists "Miss Boddington's Infant School," with Mary Hollowell as the mistress (presumably in 1840). Kelly's Directory of 1847 notes Bethia Treslar as mistress of an Infant School, as does also Slater's Directory of 1850, but the latter describes it as "Infant School (The Misses Boddingtons') Kingsthorpe: Bethia Treslar, mistress." The Misses Boddington resided at the Hall, but the school would have been in the village. It seems fairly certain that it was 'Rose Cottage' in Manor Road; there was a village tradition that this had been a 'Dame School.' Alec Brooking (p.39) found confirmation of this in some deeds for a group of properties including 'Rose Cottage', which had a reference to a property "formerly the school house." In the 1851 census there was "one house uninhabited" at that point, with the White family next door; Elizabeth White, aged 16, is described as a Teacher! Perhaps she was an assistant teacher. Bethia Treslar (Trasler in the census) aged 59, was the wife of Thomas, a blacksmith, living on the Harborough Road; so she evidently did not live on the school premises.

Melville's Directory of 1861 says "There are National and Infant Schools", and the Post Office Directory of 1869 says the same and gives Miss Sarah Ann King as mistress of the Infant School. Whellan's Directory of 1874, which obviously used information gathered in the previous year, knows nothing of an Infant School: the explanation for this is that Miss Frances Boddington, the last of the sisters of that name living at the Hall, died in March1873.

Perhaps partly as a result of the demise of Miss Boddington, Vestry Meetings were held on 24 & 31 July 1873 to consider how to provide a school for 90 infant children, as ordered by the Education Department of the Privy Council. Was the money to be raised by a voluntary arrangement or by appointing a School Board? A committee was appointed to gather information about the functioning of School Boards in nearby parishes. The committee reported back on 14 August, when Mr Cumberpatch suggested that the Town House belonging to the Trustees of the Manor Lands might be made available for the school. A committee was asked to investigate whether the property could be suitably adapted, and to ascertain the costs. The necessary work was obviously carried out, despite lack of mention in the Vestry Book, since on 3 September 1874 a meeting was held to appoint managers for the "new Infant School lately made." Bispham (page 72) says that the 'Town House' had been restored in the 1830s and again in 1857, and rented out; and he states that the alterations of 1874 cost £44.14s.0d.

Kelly's Post Office Directory of 1877 mentions three schools: National (mixed), Infant, and Free. It says that Miss Sarah Ann King was mistress of the Infant School; she had been mistress of the previous Infant School in 1869, as recorded above. Wright's Directory of

1884 still lists her as the mistress, and so does Kelly's of 1885, when the average attendance was 74. In 1898 Kelly says that the Infant School, built 1873, had been enlarged in 1885 to take 122 pupils; Sarah King was still the mistress.

The next mention is in the Kingsthorpe School Managers' Minute Book, which, in December 1903, stated that the Infant School on the Bank would have any absolutely necessary work carried out, but this school would not be kept on when the new school in Kingsthorpe Grove was built. As far as the Babies' School in the High Street was concerned, necessary repairs would be carried out, and enlargement was being considered. (This was the old Free School building, owned at the time in question by the Thornton family.)

In November 1906 it was the intention to close the Infant School in Kingswell Road on 31 January 1907. In June 1907 the Infants' Department in High Street was closed for three weeks by order of the Sanitary Authority. In the following January, during alterations to that Department (where 74 pupils were on the books!) the old School Room in Kingswell Road was to be used for two weeks. The alterations were actually completed in April 1908 and the official accommodation was set at 60. In July 1922 notice was given to terminate the use of the Infant School in High Street, and in October thanks were recorded to Mr F H Thornton for its use; it had been let to the Managers at a nominal rent.

PRIVATE EDUCATION
Alec Brooking (pp.38-9) quotes an advertisement from the local press:

At Kingsthorpe, one mile from Northampton.
The Rev. R.B.Woodward, M.A., of St. John's College Cambridge and twenty two years Curate of Kingsthorpe, is desirous of receiving into his house after the present Christmas Vacation, a limited number of Young Gentlemen, who will in every respect be treated and watched over as members of his own family and be carefully instructed in those preparatory branches of education which will qualify them for admission into the principal public schools, for the learned professions, or for agricultural and commercial pursuits.

The terms, including those items for which extra charges are usually made, will be moderate and may be known on application, either personally or by letter. (Kingsthorpe. December 1850.)

The 1851 census shows that in the April of that year Mr Woodward watched over and instructed his own two sons plus five other boys with ages ranging from eight to fourteen. This type of arrangement was not uncommon at the time, and must have provided a useful supplement to a Curate's stipend. Among Nonconformists, Philip Doddridge's Academy of a century earlier would have begun in this manner; and when John Collett Ryland came to College Lane Baptist Church in Northampton in 1759, he brought his boarding school with him.

There are one or two mentions in documents of a private academy for young ladies in Kingsthorpe, but details have not been found.

FAMILY MATTERS

ALTHOUGH this section contains details of the families of Kingsthorpe's landed gentry, they were not the only people who influenced the history of the community. But, owing to the fact that they owned estates, and in some cases held high office, their history is well documented. There were other people in the village who owned smaller amounts of land, or who were tenant farmers leasing land from the large estate owners. They also made their influence felt in the community, since they were normally chosen to be Parish Officers and (in the 19th century) members of the Select Vestry. Their names crop up frequently in documents that record the problems and decisions relating to the administration of the church and of the parish. And there is no doubt that there were many others who helped to keep the community running smoothly, but whose names are not recorded in the surviving documents.

So, alongside the Morgans and the Cookes there were names such as those in the selection that follows (and if your own family name is not included, it is hoped that no offence will be taken!):

Abbott	Causby /Cosby
Adams	Chown
Allibone	Cooch
Ashby	Cox
Atkins	Cuffley
Barber	Cumberpatch
Billingham	Danes
Briggs	Darlow
Brownknave	Dickenson
Brookes	Dunkley
Burton	Edmunds

Fitzhugh	Sheppard
Gardner	Stanton
Green	Smyth/Smith
Hawkes	Tatham
Hollis	Treslar/Trasler
Hollowell	Waterfall/Waterfield
Johnson	Wells
Lack	West
Parbery/Parbury	Wood
Pell	
Perkins	
Pickmer	
Ridge	
Sargeant	

THE BARNARDS AND THE LANES

The Barnard Family

George Baker (iv, 40) says that Francis Barnard, who lived in Kingsthorpe, was a son of Francis Barnard (or Bernard) of Abington. Francis's eldest son Robert, who was born in 1600, was a barrister, and was made a baronet in 1662.

The Lane Family

Sir Richard Lane was the son of Richard Lane of Courteenhall, and he came to live in Kingsthorpe in the mansion that was at the back of the Cock Inn in Wilkinson's Close; it was still shown on the 1767 Inclosure map. He was Deputy Recorder for Northampton in 1615, and later became Lord Keeper of the Great Seal for Charles I and again for Charles II. He followed the latter into exile in 1650 and died that year. It was his daughter Bridget who married Francis Cooke in December 1655. Lady Margaret his widow survived him and lived in the Kingsthorpe mansion until she died in 1669; she was buried at Kingsthorpe. (Further details can be found in Baker, iv 41, and VCH, 83.)

143

LANE OF COURTEENHALL, NORTHAMPTON & KINGSTHORPE
Based on Sarjeantson (1904) pp 180-1.

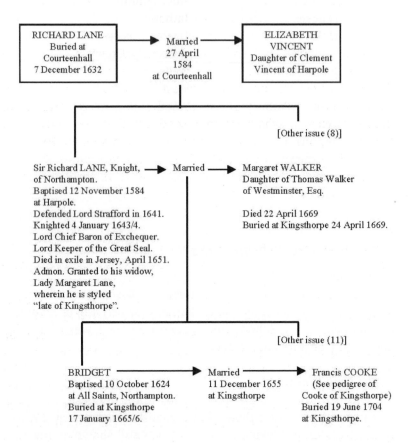

RICHARD LANE
Buried at
Courteenhall
7 December 1632

Married
27 April
1584
at Courteenhall

ELIZABETH
VINCENT
Daughter of Clement
Vincent of Harpole

[Other issue (8)]

Sir Richard LANE, Knight,
of Northampton.
Baptised 12 November 1584
at Harpole.
Defended Lord Strafford in 1641.
Knighted 4 January 1643/4.
Lord Chief Baron of Exchequer.
Lord Keeper of the Great Seal.
Died in exile in Jersey, April 1651.
Admon. Granted to his widow,
Lady Margaret Lane,
wherein he is styled
"late of Kingsthorpe".

Married

Margaret WALKER
Daughter of Thomas Walker
of Westminster, Esq.

Died 22 April 1669
Buried at Kingsthorpe 24 April 1669.

[Other issue (11)]

BRIDGET
Baptised 10 October 1624
at All Saints, Northampton.
Buried at Kingsthorpe
17 January 1665/6.

Married
11 December 1655
at Kingsthorpe

Francis COOKE
(See pedigree of
Cooke of Kingsthorpe)
Buried 19 June 1704
at Kingsthorpe.

144

THE COOKE FAMILY

Serjeantson (1904) pp 210-214 begins his history of this family with Robert Cooke, but the following pedigree chart goes back to the previous generation with Robert's father Symon. We do not know Symon's dates, only that his will is dated January 1520/1, that his wife Hawes died in 1549, and that his brother Thomas was buried in March 1539/40. The Cooke family, as one of the main landowners in the area, played an important part in Kingsthorpe's history across three centuries. Robert Cooke was the bailiff in 1547, and was one of the commissioners who went up to London in that year to represent the township in the dispute with the keepers of Moulton Park over the rabbit problem. (Details of this can be found under *Rights of Warren* in the chapter *Problems with the Neighbours* in the section on *The Manor*.) Robert was Churchwarden in 1534 and in 1565; in the latter year he provided receipts relating to repairs to the church steeple. He died in 1574 and was buried at Kingsthorpe on 28 September. His grandson, also named Robert, married Elizabeth Morgan, whose family were very large landowners in the parish; they lived in the mansion that stood in Great House Close, east of the church.

Robert and Elizabeth had one son, Francis, a lawyer, who lived at Stoke Newington as well as maintaining his interests in Kingsthorpe. In 1656 Francis Cooke, Thomas Morgan and others met with the mayor and aldermen of Northampton to discuss the subject of a water supply for Northampton. As described in the Records of the Borough of Northampton (Fox ii, 255), it was proposed that water from a spring known as Swarbutts Head in Kingsthorpe parish should be diverted for use of the people of Northampton. A rent was to be agreed in recompense for disturbance of the ground and the use of the water. Two years later Francis Cooke died, and was buried in the nave of Kingsthorpe Church.

Three of Francis's children were benefactors to the parish of Kingsthorpe. In 1690 George Cooke gave £100 to the parish, the interest of which was to be used to buy bread for distribution each week to twelve poor people. Another son, Thomas, built and endowed the Free school for the education of Kingsthorpe children. Francis's youngest daughter, Sarah, married Sir William Prichard, who was

PEDIGREE OF COOKE OF KINGSTHORPE 1521-1801
Page 1

Sources: [See Bibliographical References].Genealogical Memoranda...; Serjeantson, 1904; Glover J H; Bridges; Baker; VCH; Rev H I Longden's indexes and pedigree notes at NRO; Kingsthorpe PRs & BTs at NRO; Archdeaconry of Northampton Wills at NRO.

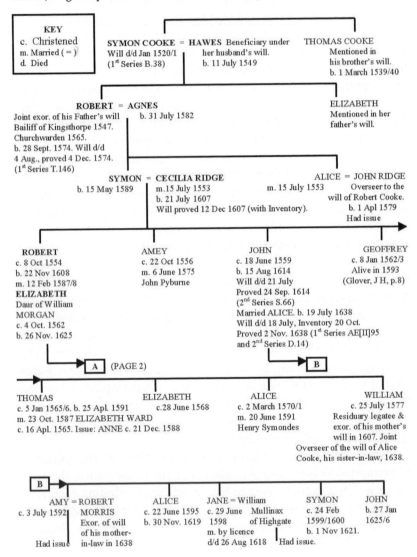

KEY
c. Christened
m. Married (=)
d. Died

SYMON COOKE = HAWES Beneficiary under
Will d/d Jan 1520/1   her husband's will.
(1ˢᵗ Series B.38)   b. 11 July 1549

THOMAS COOKE
Mentioned in
his brother's will.
b. 1 March 1539/40

ROBERT = AGNES
Joint exor. of his Father's will   b. 31 July 1582
Bailiff of Kingsthorpe 1547.
Churchwarden 1565.
b. 28 Sept. 1574. Will d/d
4 Aug., proved 4 Dec. 1574.
(1ˢᵗ Series T.146)

ELIZABETH
Mentioned in her
father's will.

SYMON = CECILIA RIDGE
b. 15 May 1589   m.15 July 1553
                  b. 21 July 1607
                  Will proved 12 Dec 1607 (with Inventory).

ALICE = JOHN RIDGE
m. 15 July 1553   Overseer to the
                  will of Robert Cooke.
                  b. 1 Apl 1579
                  Had issue

ROBERT
c. 8 Oct 1554
b. 22 Nov 1608
m. 12 Feb 1587/8
ELIZABETH
Daur of William
MORGAN
c. 4 Oct. 1562
b. 26 Nov. 1625

AMEY
c. 22 Oct 1556
m. 6 June 1575
John Pyburne

JOHN
c. 18 June 1559
b. 15 Aug 1614
Will d/d 21 July
Proved 24 Sep. 1614
(2ⁿᵈ Series S.66)
Married ALICE. b. 19 July 1638
Will d/d 18 July, Inventory 20 Oct.
Proved 2 Nov. 1638 (1ˢᵗ Series AE[II]95
and 2ⁿᵈ Series D.14)

GEOFFREY
c. 8 Jan 1562/3
Alive in 1593
(Glover, J H, p.8)

A (PAGE 2)   B

THOMAS
c. 5 Jan 1565/6. b. 25 Apl. 1591
m. 23 Oct. 1587 ELIZABETH WARD
c. 16 Apl. 1565. Issue: ANNE c. 21 Dec. 1588

ELIZABETH
c.28 June 1568

ALICE
c. 2 March 1570/1
m. 20 June 1591
Henry Symondes

WILLIAM
c. 25 July 1577
Residuary legatee &
exor. of his mother's
will in 1607. Joint
Overseer of the will of Alice
Cooke, his sister-in-law, 1638.

B

AMY = ROBERT
c. 3 July 1592   MORRIS
                 Exor. of will
                 of his mother-
Had issue   in-law in 1638

ALICE
c. 22 June 1595
b. 30 Nov. 1619

JANE = William
c. 29 June Mullinax
1598   of Highgate
m. by licence
d/d 26 Aug 1618 Had issue.

SYMON
c. 24 Feb
1599/1600
b. 1 Nov 1621.

JOHN
b. 27 Jan
1625/6

PEDIGREE OF COOKE OF KINGSTHORPE 1521-1801
Page 2

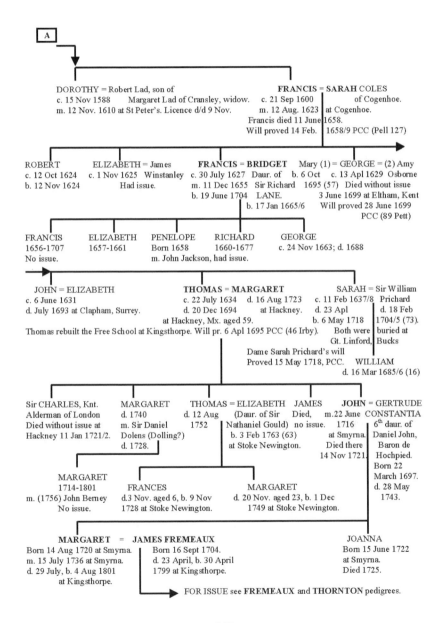

A

DOROTHY = Robert Lad, son of
c. 15 Nov 1588   Margaret Lad of Cransley, widow.
m. 12 Nov. 1610 at St Peter's. Licence d/d 9 Nov.

FRANCIS = SARAH COLES
c. 21 Sep 1600   of Cogenhoe.
m. 12 Aug. 1623 | at Cogenhoe.
Francis died 11 June 1658.
Will proved 14 Feb. | 1658/9 PCC (Pell 127)

ROBERT
c. 12 Oct 1624
b. 12 Nov 1624

ELIZABETH = James
c. 1 Nov 1625 Winstanley
Had issue.

FRANCIS = BRIDGET
c. 30 July 1627 Daur. of
m. 11 Dec 1655 Sir Richard
b. 19 June 1704 LANE.
b. 17 Jan 1665/6

Mary (1) = GEORGE = (2) Amy
b. 6 Oct   c. 13 Apl 1629 Osborne
1695 (57) Died without issue
3 June 1699 at Eltham, Kent
Will proved 28 June 1699
PCC (89 Pett)

FRANCIS
1656-1707
No issue.

ELIZABETH
1657-1661

PENELOPE
Born 1658
m. John Jackson, had issue.

RICHARD
1660-1677

GEORGE
c. 24 Nov 1663; d. 1688

JOHN = ELIZABETH
c. 6 June 1631
d. July 1693 at Clapham, Surrey.

THOMAS = MARGARET
c. 22 July 1634   d. 16 Aug 1723
d. 20 Dec 1694   at Hackney.
at Hackney, Mx. aged 59.
Thomas rebuilt the Free School at Kingsthorpe. Will pr. 6 Apl 1695 PCC (46 Irby).

SARAH = Sir William
c. 11 Feb 1637/8 Prichard
b. 6 May 1718   d. 18 Feb
Both were | 1704/5 (73).
buried at
Dame Sarah Prichard's will   Gt. Linford, Bucks
Proved 15 May 1718, PCC.   WILLIAM
d. 16 Mar 1685/6 (16)

Sir CHARLES, Knt.
Alderman of London
Died without issue at
Hackney 11 Jan 1721/2.

MARGARET
d. 1740
m. Sir Daniel
Dolens (Dolling?)
d. 1728.

THOMAS = ELIZABETH
d. 12 Aug   (Daur. of Sir
1752   Nathaniel Gould)
b. 3 Feb 1763 (63)
at Stoke Newington.

JAMES
Died,
no issue.

JOHN = GERTRUDE
m.22 June CONSTANTIA
1716   6th daur. of
at Smyrna. Daniel John,
Died there Baron de
14 Nov 1721. Hochpied.
Born 22
March 1697.
d. 28 May
1743.

MARGARET
1714-1801
m. (1756) John Berney
No issue.

FRANCES
d.3 Nov. aged 6, b. 9 Nov
1728 at Stoke Newington.

MARGARET
d. 20 Nov. aged 23, b. 1 Dec
1749 at Stoke Newington.

MARGARET = JAMES FREMEAUX
Born 14 Aug 1720 at Smyrna. Born 16 Sept 1704.
m. 15 July 1736 at Smyrna. d. 23 April, b. 30 April
d. 29 July, b. 4 Aug 1801 1799 at Kingsthorpe.
at Kingsthorpe.

JOANNA
Born 15 June 1722
at Smyrna.
Died 1725.

→ FOR ISSUE see FREMEAUX and THORNTON pedigrees.

Lord Mayor of London in 1682-3. She provided oak pews for the church and paid for the renewal of the roof and leadwork. She also built a Town House for the freeholders to meet in. When she died in 1718 she left £5 per annum for the education and apprenticing of poor boys of Kingsthorpe.

The Kingsthorpe estates, along with property in Earls Barton and Pattishall, eventually passed to Thomas Cooke of Stoke Newington in Middlesex, a son of the Thomas who endowed the Freeschool. He was High Sheriff for Northamptonshire in 1733 and Governor of the Bank of England 1737-9. His wife Elizabeth and daughter Margaret also took an interest in the school. Following his death in 1752 the estates passed to his niece Margaret, daughter of his brother John who had been British consul at Smyrna and had died in 1721. (John had married the daughter of Daniel John, Baron de Hochpied, the Dutch Consul at Smyrna.) It was at Smyrna in 1736 that Margaret had married James Fremeaux. They had five daughters and an only son, Peter John Fremeaux, who died in 1784 before his parents; he drowned whilst swimming in the river. Peter left an only child Susannah, who married Thomas Reeve Thornton, thus conveying the Kingsthorpe estates to the Thorntons of Brockhall.

FREMEAUX BUSINESS INTERESTS

James Fremeaux's business interests are well represented by a number of ledgers, now in the Thornton of Brockhall collection at NRO, under reference Th 2055-2059. The first of these, covering the years 1790-1800, contains an index or list of contents, and under item number 16: 'Building House &c.' James Fremeaux made the following note:

> 1791: The building of my house, out-houses, garden walls, orchard planting &c cost me full four thousand five hundred pounds. The enclosing of Kingsthorpe, [Earls] Barton and Petichel [Pattishall] about seventeen hundred pounds. All this, with the cost of my furniture, plate, books, horses and carriages &c were passed in profit & loss, thus nothing of it appearing in these books. I thought proper to make here this note by way of memorandum.

In 1768 he valued the following items: *(see p 153)*

FREMEAUX OF KINGSTHORPE

Based on Serjeantson, 1904, p.212.

KEY	JAMES FREMEAUX = MARGARET COOKE
c. Christened	Born 16 Sept 1704 at Smyrna — Born 14 Aug 1720
m. Married (=)	Parents: Peter & Adriana. — m. 15 July 1736 at Smyrna.
d. Died	Naturalised 1751/2. — d. 29 July b. 4 Aug 1801
b. Buried	d. 23 April b. 30 Apl 1799 at — at Kingsthorpe.
	Kingsthorpe. *(Tablet)*

ADRIANA CONSTANTIA	ELIZABETH	PETER JOHN = SUSANNAH BERNEY
Born 18 Nov 1738 at Smyrna.	Born 29 Sept 1741	Born 2 Nov 1742 — younger daur. of
d. 7 Jan 1812, b. at Kingsthorpe.	at Smyrna	at Smyrna. — John Berney of
(See tablet)	d. 7 March 1826	m. at Bath 20 Dec 1774. — Bracon Ash, Norfolk.
	b. at Kingsthorpe.	d. 28 Mar 1784, b.at — d. 25 Oct 1797 (51)
	(See tablet)	Kingsthorpe. *(Tablet)* — b. at Kingsthorpe

THOMAS REEVE THORNTON = SUSANNAH
Of Brockhall, Northants.
1775-1862

Born 1 Aug, c. 20 Aug 1776
at Kingsthorpe; m. there
31 Jan 1799. d. 2 May
b. 8 May 1846 at Brockhall.

FOR ISSUE SEE THORNTON PEDIGREE.

MARIA CATHARINA	GERTRUDE JOHANNA	MARGARET
Born 25 Dec 1744 at Smyrna.	Born 6 Jan 1750/1 at Amsterdam	Born Nov 1761
m. 16 March 1764 at St John's church,	m. 14 Dec 1790 at Kingsthorpe to	d. 8 March 1802.
Hackney, to Thomas, 5th son of	Rev Henry PORTINGTON, Rector	b. at Kingsthorpe.
Benjamin BODDINGTON.	of Wappenham. She died 28 Mar 1803,	
d. 15 Jan 1814, b. at Enfield, Mddx.	b. at Kingsthorpe. *(See tablet).*	
Thomas d. 28 June 1821, aged 85.	He died 7 Dec 1832, aged 77,	
(See tablet) Had issue.	b. at Wappenham.	

KINGSTHORPE: A ROYAL MANOR EXPLORED

PEDIGREE OF THE THORNTON FAMILY

Based on Serjeantson, 1904, page 212, and VCH Northamptonshire Families,
(Oswald Barron, 1906).

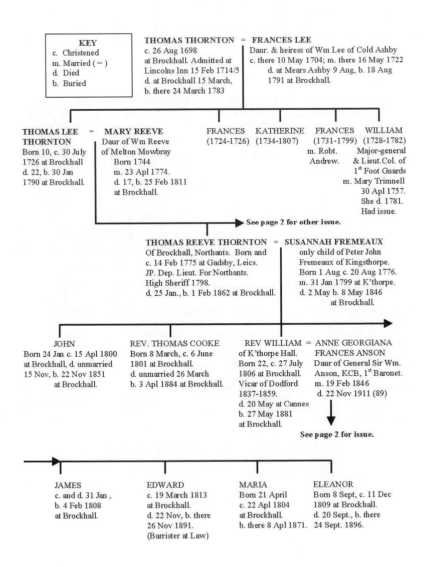

KEY
c. Christened
m. Married (=)
d. Died
b. Buried

THOMAS THORNTON = FRANCES LEE
c. 26 Aug 1698
at Brockhall. Admitted at
Lincolns Inn 15 Feb 1714/5
d. at Brockhall 15 March,
b. there 24 March 1783

Daur. & heiress of Wm Lee of Cold Ashby
c. there 10 May 1704; m. there 16 May 1722
d. at Mears Ashby 9 Aug, b. 18 Aug
1791 at Brockhall.

THOMAS LEE = MARY REEVE
THORNTON   Daur of Wm Reeve
Born 10, c. 30 July   of Melton Mowbray
1726 at Brockhall   Born 1744
d. 22, b. 30 Jan   m. 23 Apl 1774.
1790 at Brockhall.   d. 17, b. 25 Feb 1811
                     at Brockhall.

FRANCES   KATHERINE   FRANCES   WILLIAM
(1724-1726) (1734-1807)   (1731-1799) (1728-1782)
                            m. Robt.   Major-general
                            Andrew.   & Lieut.Col. of
                                         1st Foot Guards
                                         m. Mary Trimnell
                                         30 Apl 1757.
                                         She d. 1781.
                                         Had issue.

► See page 2 for other issue.

THOMAS REEVE THORNTON = SUSANNAH FREMEAUX
Of Brockhall, Northants. Born and
c. 14 Feb 1775 at Gadsby, Leics.
JP. Dep. Lieut. For Northants.
High Sheriff 1798.
d. 25 Jan., b. 1 Feb 1862 at Brockhall.

only child of Peter John
Fremeaux of Kingsthorpe.
Born 1 Aug c. 20 Aug 1776.
m. 31 Jan 1799 at K'thorpe.
d. 2 May b. 8 May 1846
at Brockhall.

JOHN
Born 24 Jan c. 15 Apl 1800
at Brockhall, d. unmarried
15 Nov, b. 22 Nov 1851
at Brockhall.

REV. THOMAS COOKE
Born 8 March, c. 6 June
1801 at Brockhall.
d. unmarried 26 March
b. 3 Apl 1884 at Brockhall.

REV WILLIAM = ANNE GEORGIANA
of K'thorpe Hall.   FRANCES ANSON
Born 22, c. 27 July   Daur of General Sir Wm.
1806 at Brockhall.   Anson, KCB, 1st Baronet.
Vicar of Dodford   m. 19 Feb 1846
1837-1859.   d. 22 Nov 1911 (89)
d. 20 May at Cannes
b. 27 May 1881
at Brockhall.

See page 2 for issue.

JAMES
c. and d. 31 Jan ,
b. 4 Feb 1808
at Brockhall.

EDWARD
c. 19 March 1813
at Brockhall.
d. 22 Nov, b. there
26 Nov 1891.
(Barrister at Law)

MARIA
Born 21 April
c. 22 Apl 1804
at Brockhall.
b. there 8 Apl 1871.

ELEANOR
Born 8 Sept, c. 11 Dec
1809 at Brockhall.
d. 20 Sept., b. there
24 Sept. 1896.

150

FAMILY MATTERS

PEDIGREE OF THE THORNTON FAMILY: PAGE 2
Other issue of THOMAS LEE THORNTON & MARY REEVE

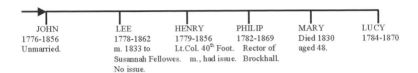

JOHN	LEE	HENRY	PHILIP	MARY	LUCY
1776-1856	1778-1862	1779-1856	1782-1869	Died 1830	1784-1870
Unmarried.	m. 1833 to	Lt.Col. 40th Foot.	Rector of	aged 48.	
	Susannah Fellowes.	m., had issue.	Brockhall.		
	No issue.				

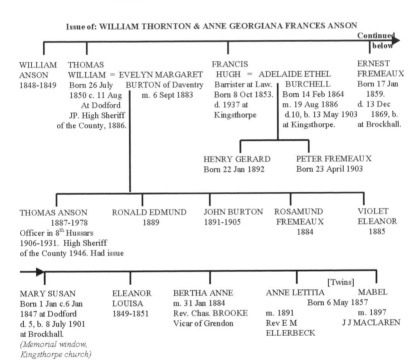

Issue of: WILLIAM THORNTON & ANNE GEORGIANA FRANCES ANSON

Continued below

WILLIAM ANSON 1848-1849

THOMAS WILLIAM = EVELYN MARGARET BURTON of Daventry
Born 26 July 1850 c. 11 Aug   m. 6 Sept 1883
At Dodford
JP. High Sheriff
of the County, 1886.

FRANCIS HUGH = ADELAIDE ETHEL BURCHELL
Barrister at Law.   Born 14 Feb 1864
Born 8 Oct 1853.   m. 19 Aug 1886
d. 1937 at   d.10, b. 13 May 1903
Kingsthorpe   at Kingsthorpe.

ERNEST FREMEAUX
Born 17 Jan 1859.
d. 13 Dec 1869, b.
at Brockhall.

HENRY GERARD
Born 22 Jan 1892

PETER FREMEAUX
Born 23 April 1903

THOMAS ANSON
1887-1978
Officer in 8th Hussars
1906-1931. High Sheriff
of the County 1946. Had issue

RONALD EDMUND
1889

JOHN BURTON
1891-1905

ROSAMUND FREMEAUX
1884

VIOLET ELEANOR
1885

[Twins]

MARY SUSAN
Born 1 Jan c.6 Jan
1847 at Dodford
d. 5, b. 8 July 1901
at Brockhall.
(Memorial window, Kingsthorpe church)

ELEANOR LOUISA
1849-1851

BERTHA ANNE
m. 31 Jan 1884
Rev. Chas. BROOKE
Vicar of Grendon

ANNE LETITIA
Born 6 May 1857
m. 1891
Rev E M
ELLERBECK

MABEL
m. 1897
J J MACLAREN

151

PEDIGREE: MORGAN OF KINGSTHORPE

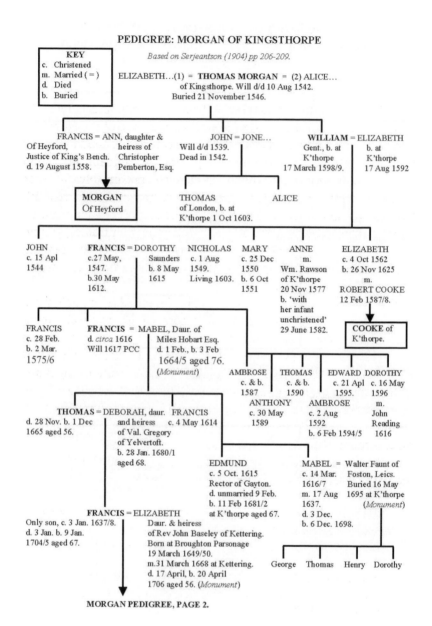

KEY
c. Christened
m. Married (=)
d. Died
b. Buried

Based on Serjeantson (1904) pp 206-209.

ELIZABETH...(1) = **THOMAS MORGAN** = (2) ALICE...
of Kingsthorpe. Will d/d 10 Aug 1542.
Buried 21 November 1546.

FRANCIS = ANN, daughter &
Of Heyford,   heiress of
Justice of King's Bench.   Christopher
d. 19 August 1558.   Pemberton, Esq.

JOHN = JONE...
Will d/d 1539.
Dead in 1542.

WILLIAM = ELIZABETH
Gent., b. at   b. at
K'thorpe   K'thorpe
17 March 1598/9. 17 Aug 1592

MORGAN
Of Heyford

THOMAS
of London, b. at
K'thorpe 1 Oct 1603.

ALICE

JOHN
c. 15 Apl
1544

FRANCIS = DOROTHY
c.27 May,   Saunders
1547.   b. 8 May
b.30 May   1615
1612.

NICHOLAS
c. 1 Aug
1549.
Living 1603.

MARY
c. 25 Dec
1550
b. 6 Oct
1551

ANNE
m.
Wm. Rawson
of K'thorpe
20 Nov 1577
b. 'with
her infant
unchristened'
29 June 1582.

ELIZABETH
c. 4 Oct 1562
b. 26 Nov 1625
m.
ROBERT COOKE
12 Feb 1587/8.

FRANCIS
c. 28 Feb.
b. 2 Mar.
1575/6

FRANCIS = MABEL, Daur. of
d. *circa* 1616   Miles Hobart Esq.
Will 1617 PCC   d. 1 Feb., b. 3 Feb
                 1664/5 aged 76.
                 (*Monument*)

COOKE of
K'thorpe.

AMBROSE
c. & b.
1587
ANTHONY
c. 30 May
1589

THOMAS
c. & b.
1590
AMBROSE
c. 2 Aug
1592
b. 6 Feb 1594/5

EDWARD
c. 21 Apl
1595.

DOROTHY
c. 16 May
1596
m.
John
Reading
1616

THOMAS = DEBORAH, daur.
d. 28 Nov. b. 1 Dec   and heiress
1665 aged 56.   of Val. Gregory
                 of Yelvertoft.
                 b. 28 Jan. 1680/1
                 aged 68.

FRANCIS
c. 4 May 1614

EDMUND
c. 5 Oct. 1615
Rector of Gayton.
d. unmarried 9 Feb.
b. 11 Feb 1681/2
at K'thorpe aged 67.

MABEL = Walter Faunt of
c. 14 Mar.   Foston, Leics.
1616/7   Buried 16 May
m. 17 Aug   1695 at K'thorpe
1637.   (*Monument*)
d. 3 Dec.
b. 6 Dec. 1698.

FRANCIS = ELIZABETH
Only son, c. 3 Jan. 1637/8.   Daur. & heiress
d. 3 Jan. b. 9 Jan.   of Rev John Baseley of Kettering.
1704/5 aged 67.   Born at Broughton Parsonage
                  19 March 1649/50.
                  m.31 March 1668 at Kettering.
                  d. 17 April, b. 20 April
                  1706 aged 56. (*Monument*)

George   Thomas   Henry   Dorothy

MORGAN PEDIGREE, PAGE 2.

Books in my Library	117	18	6
Jewels and Gold	994	11	7
Plate	401	8	7
Furniture	713	8	8

Th 2058 is a leather bound ledger bearing the title BALANCE BOEK and containing a fascinating record of the business of the Fremeaux family, Isaac, Nicolas, Daniel and James. It consists of annual balance sheets of Debtors and Creditors, beginning 'Amsterdam, July Anno 1751', and is written in Dutch or Flemish, presumably by Isaac Fremeaux, until 13 July 1755, when it is written in English in a different hand, and under the heading of Hackney. The name 'Smirna' appears frequently, since it was one of their bases for trading around the Mediterranean. There are also many mentions of Amsterdam, Aleppo, Leghorn, and Marseilles among other places. Later entries mention Dublin, India and China.

The goods in which they traded included carpets, mohair yarn, cotton yarn, needles, cloth, goats wool, corn, &c. There are also mentions of Quicksilver, Tin, Arsenicum and 'Couchinille'. They were also arms traders, as the following example indicates: "Arms under J & D Fremeaux: ½ in 300 pair Pistols £114.10s.0d." Other interesting items include "Sundry goods to Aleppo under John & Nathaniel Free: My ½ in 16 barrels Ginger £66... Jewels from Leghorn under J de B Caravaglio: ½ in a Ruby £104... Voyage to China: ½ in a box of corrals...Lottery: £40."

There are also details of the financial shares held in various trading voyages, for example:

Share 1/5 in the Constance, Captain: Honoré Pourquier under direction of Isaac Fremeaux. £231.17s.10d.

Share 1/5 in the Hermes, Capn. M Schryver under J Fremeaux. £187.11s.6d.

Share 1/5 in the Constantia, Capn. Kerkdorp. £301.4s.10d.

Share ¼ in the Sea Nymph, Captain A Hall under direction of Isaac Fremeaux. £621.9s.2d.

From the records of the Overseers of the Poor at Kingsthorpe for the early years of the 19th century it is clear that the Fremeaux family made payments into the Kingsthorpe Club, from which doles were paid to widows, sick persons and so on. From the Fremeaux ledgers it appears that the Overseers must have invested £25 (perhaps from a legacy to the poor) in the Fremeaux business. James himself notes in June 1790 that, rather than make a separate entry for 'this trifle' he regularly pays the 25/- yearly interest out of House Expenses. (The latter averaged around £1,200 per annum at this time!) In June 1803, following the death of James in 1799, his widow in 1801, and their daughter Margaret in 1802, this amount of £25 was brought forward in the ledger and then repaid to the Parish Officers. A note says: "The interest on the same was paid up to the 21st of June 1803 so that this business is now finally settled." Also relevant are entries from Edward Van Harthall's Account in respect of subscriptions to the Kingsthorpe Club of £1.11s.6d per annum, together with donations of £2.2s.0d and £1.8s.8d in 1800 "paid to the poor at Kingsthorpe [at] Mr H's desire."

Th 2059 is a Letter Book from 21 July 1794 to 6 January 1796, containing transcriptions of James Fremeaux's letters in French and English. Many concern events in Smyrna concerning the family, and would no doubt make an interesting story if properly translated and edited.

THE MORGAN FAMILY

The Rev R M Serjeantson's pedigree of this family, as set out in his 1904 book, begins with Thomas Morgan of Kingsthorpe, who was buried there on 21 November 1546. He had three sons, Francis, John and William. The oldest of these, Francis, founded the estate of the Morgans of Heyford.

Thomas's great-great-grandson, also named Thomas, is mentioned in 1656 as one of the committee that conferred with the Burgesses of Northampton regarding the bringing of water from the lands of Kingsthorpe to Northampton. He died in November 1665 aged 56 and was buried at Kingsthorpe. In 1681 Thomas's son Francis was a Bencher of Middle Temple; according to the Rev Fox (1898; ii, p.248) he was also one of the commissioners appointed to superin-

PEDIGREE: MORGAN OF KINGSTHORPE

PAGE 2

FRANCIS = ELIZABETH (Page 1)

FRANCIS	EDMUND	THOMAS	WILLIAM	ELIZABETH
c. 20 Apl. 1669	c. 24 July 1672	c. 13 Oct 1677	c. 31 July 1689	c. 26 Oct 1686
b. 21 Feb 1693/4	b. 30 Dec 1735	WILLIAM	WILLIAM	CHARLES
		Born 1 Feb	c. 23 Jan 1679/80	c 17 Mar 1692/3
		c. 4 Mar 1673/4	b. 10 Aug 1682	b. 23 Jan 1693/4
		b. 8 June 1674		

JOHN = TRYPHENA
c. 15 April 1671   Daur & heiress of Hon. Robert Sheffield
b. 31 Dec 1721   b. 14 March 1723/4

MARY (1)   =   SIR JOHN ROBINSON =   (2) ELIZABETH
Daughter and heiress   of Cranford, 4th Baronet   daur of – Perkins Esq.
d. 12 Feb, b. 18 Feb   d. 31 Aug 1765   of Marston, co. Warwick
1733/4, aged 24
(*Monument*)   Had issue.

SIR GEORGE ROBINSON = DOROTHEA CHESTER   ANNE ROBINSON
of Cranford & Kingsthorpe,   Daur. of John Chester, Esq.   c. 23 Feb 1727/8
5th Baronet.   At Kingsthorpe.
MP for Northampton 1774
c. at Kingsthorpe 27 May 1730
d. 10 October 1815.

ROBINSON
of Cranford

KEY
c. Christened
m. Married (=)
d. Died
b. Buried

tend the rebuilding of Northampton following the fire of 1675. His son John, 1671-1721, succeeded to the estate, and Serjeantson (1904, pp.207-8) tells a story concerning a quarrel with the parish clergy regarding fishing rights in the river. Apparently the curate, Mr Johnston, challenged John Morgan to a duel with swords! Fortunately the matter was settled without bloodshed following the intervention of the Bishop of Peterborough. The Rector, Richard Reynolds, expressed his opinion that Mr Morgan was a troublesome man, like his father before him and all his family. He indicated that the Morgans had always been a thorn in the flesh to the parsons of the parish, and they had encouraged rebelliousness in the parish too.

John married Tryphena, the daughter and heiress of Hon. Robert Sheffield, and produced a daughter Mary. She was the heiress to the Morgan estate, and she married Sir John Robinson of Cranford, 4th baronet. Thus the Morgan estates at Kingsthorpe came into the possession of the Robinsons. Mary died on 12 February 1733/4 aged 24, and was buried at Kingsthorpe; but she had borne a son George, who was baptised at Kingsthorpe on 27 May 1730, and a daughter, Anne, baptised 23 February 1727/8. George became Sir George Robinson of Cranford and Kingsthorpe, 5th baronet, and was MP for Northampton in 1774. He died on 10 October 1815.

THE ROBINSON FAMILY

The following notes originate from an examination of the NRO catalogue of the records in the Robinson of Cranford collection:

8 Feb 1650/1	John Robinson of London, Merchant.
25 March 1659	John Robinson, Alderman of City of London.
30 Oct 1660	Letters Patent of Chas. II to Sir John Robinson, Kt & Bt, Lewtenant [sic] of the Tower of London.
1 May 1675	Letters Patent of Chas. II to Sir John Robinson, Kt & Bt, as office of Master Forrester &c. &c.
14 Nov 1679	Will and Inventory of John Robinson of London, Alderman, Kt & Bt, late Lieut. of the Tower...manor of Newnham Courtney...manor of Grafton...Farmingwoods
1688	Copy out of survey book of Grafton Underwood –

land in Wharton, Cranford, & Wood Fields.
The Morgan Estate in Kingsthorpe: General
deeds, 1668-1722; mortgaged property 1719-
1732; Terrier 1727 [this is the doc-ument, NRO:
ML 77, examined in the chapter *The Robinson
Estate.]*

A note accompanying the catalogue suggests that the majority of
the documents did not originally belong to the Cranford branch of
the Robinson family but to the descendants of Anne Robinson, who
became Earls of Upper Ossory and lived at Farming Woods. The
author of the note does not give the reasons for that conclusion.
However, the inventory accompanying the will of Sir John Robinson
of London, 1679, includes leases of property in Tower Hill, and the
bound ledger containing 18th century Robinson Estate Rent Rolls and
expenditurPepyse (NRO: ML 62) relate to properties in Cranford,
Kingsthorpe, and Tower Hill. This appears to establish a connection
between Sir John of 1679 and the Cranford Robinsons.

PEDIGREE OF ROBINSON OF CRANFORD
Based on VCH Part II, Northants Families (Oswald Barron, 1906) page 277.

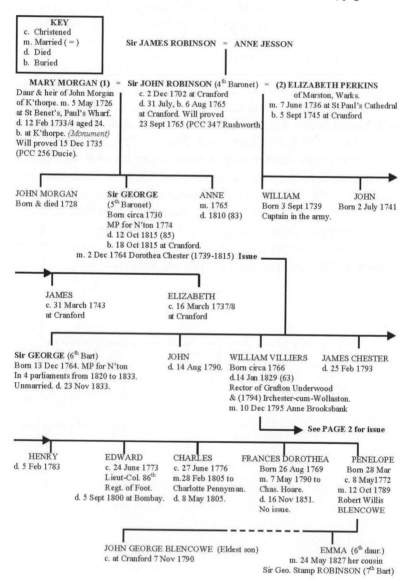

KEY
c. Christened
m. Married (=)
d. Died
b. Buried

Sir JAMES ROBINSON = ANNE JESSON

MARY MORGAN (1) = Sir JOHN ROBINSON (4ᵗʰ Baronet) = (2) ELIZABETH PERKINS
Daur & heir of John Morgan   c. 2 Dec 1702 at Cranford   of Marston, Warks.
of K'thorpe. m. 5 May 1726   d. 31 July, b. 6 Aug 1765   m. 7 June 1736 at St Paul's Cathedral
at St Benet's, Paul's Wharf.   at Cranford. Will proved   b. 5 Sept 1745 at Cranford
d. 12 Feb 1733/4 aged 24.   23 Sept 1765 (PCC 347 Rushworth)
b. at K'thorpe. (Monument)
Will proved 15 Dec 1735
(PCC 256 Ducie).

JOHN MORGAN   Sir GEORGE   ANNE   WILLIAM   JOHN
Born & died 1728   (5ᵗʰ Baronet)   m. 1765   Born 3 Sept 1739   Born 2 July 1741
                   Born circa 1730   d. 1810 (83) Captain in the army.
                   MP for N'ton 1774
                   d. 12 Oct 1815 (85)
                   b. 18 Oct 1815 at Cranford.
          m. 2 Dec 1764 Dorothea Chester (1739-1815) Issue

JAMES   ELIZABETH
c. 31 March 1743   c. 16 March 1737/8
at Cranford   at Cranford

Sir GEORGE (6ᵗʰ Bart)   JOHN   WILLIAM VILLIERS   JAMES CHESTER
Born 13 Dec 1764. MP for N'ton d. 14 Aug 1790. Born circa 1766   d. 25 Feb 1793
In 4 parliaments from 1820 to 1833.   d.14 Jan 1829 (63)
Unmarried. d. 23 Nov 1833.   Rector of Grafton Underwood
                                                 & (1794) Irchester-cum-Wollaston.
                                                 m. 10 Dec 1795 Anne Brooksbank

                                                      See PAGE 2 for issue

HENRY   EDWARD   CHARLES   FRANCES DOROTHEA   PENELOPE
d. 5 Feb 1783   c. 24 June 1773   c. 27 June 1776 Born 26 Aug 1769   Born 28 Mar
                Lieut-Col. 86ᵗʰ   m.28 Feb 1805 to m. 7 May 1790 to   c. 8 May1772
                Regt. of Foot.   Charlotte Pennyman. Chas. Hoare.   m. 12 Oct 1789
                d. 5 Sept 1800 at Bombay. d. 8 May 1805. d. 16 Nov 1851. Robert Willis
                                                         No issue.   BLENCOWE

JOHN GEORGE BLENCOWE (Eldest son)   EMMA (6ᵗʰ daur.)
c. at Cranford 7 Nov 1790   m. 24 May 1827 her cousin
                                                     Sir Geo. Stamp ROBINSON (7ᵗʰ Bart)

158

FAMILY MATTERS

PEDIGREE OF ROBINSON OF CRANFORD (PAGE 2)

Issue of WILLIAM VILLIERS ROBINSON & ANNE BROOKSBANK

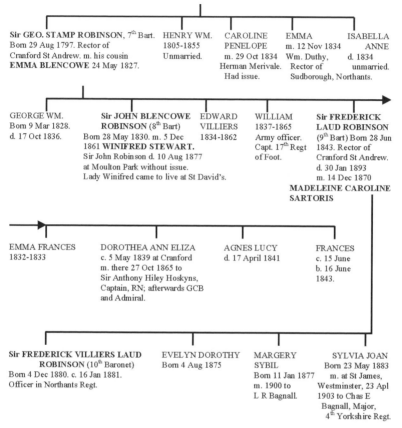

Sir GEO. STAMP ROBINSON, 7th Bart.
Born 29 Aug 1797. Rector of
Cranford St Andrew. m. his cousin
EMMA BLENCOWE 24 May 1827.

HENRY WM.
1805-1855
Unmarried.

CAROLINE
PENELOPE
m. 29 Oct 1834
Herman Merivale.
Had issue.

EMMA
m. 12 Nov 1834
Wm. Duthy,
Rector of
Sudborough, Northants.

ISABELLA
ANNE
d. 1834
unmarried.

GEORGE WM.
Born 9 Mar 1828.
d. 17 Oct 1836.

Sir JOHN BLENCOWE
ROBINSON (8th Bart)
Born 28 May 1830. m. 5 Dec
1861 **WINIFRED STEWART.**
Sir John Robinson d. 10 Aug 1877
at Moulton Park without issue.
Lady Winifred came to live at St David's.

EDWARD
VILLIERS
1834-1862

WILLIAM
1837-1865
Army officer.
Capt. 17th Regt
of Foot.

Sir FREDERICK
LAUD ROBINSON
(9th Bart) Born 28 Jun
1843. Rector of
Cranford St Andrew.
d. 30 Jan 1893
m. 14 Dec 1870
MADELEINE CAROLINE
SARTORIS

EMMA FRANCES
1832-1833

DOROTHEA ANN ELIZA
c. 5 May 1839 at Cranford
m. there 27 Oct 1865 to
Sir Anthony Hiley Hoskyns,
Captain, RN; afterwards GCB
and Admiral.

AGNES LUCY
d. 17 April 1841

FRANCES
c. 15 June
b. 16 June
1843.

Sir FREDERICK VILLIERS LAUD
ROBINSON (10th Baronet)
Born 4 Dec 1880. c. 16 Jan 1881.
Officer in Northants Regt.

EVELYN DOROTHY
Born 4 Aug 1875

MARGERY
SYBIL
Born 11 Jan 1877
m. 1900 to
L R Bagnall.

SYLVIA JOAN
Born 23 May 1883
m. at St James,
Westminster, 23 Apl
1903 to Chas E
Bagnall, Major,
4th Yorkshire Regt.

THE HOSPITAL OF ST DAVID OR THE HOLY TRINITY

THIS hospital was founded in 1200 by the prior and convent of St Andrew, Northampton. St Andrew's priory had been founded some time prior to 1076; its land bordered on the river and extended as far as the northwest boundary of the Castle. A clear description of the founding of St David's, together with plans and elevations of its remains at the end of the 19th century, is contained in an 1898 paper by Christopher Markham. He says that towards the end of the 12th century the prior and convent of St Andrew, Northampton, possessed a house in Kingsthorpe. In 1200, on the petition first of Peter the son of Adam of Northampton, and then of Henry, son of the said Peter, rector of St Peter's (and thus of Kingsthorpe), Walter the prior of the convent of St Andrew settled this house, with the chapels of the Holy Trinity and St David, for the reception of travellers and the local poor.

Robert Grosseteste, who was Lord Bishop of Lincoln from 1235 until his death in 1254, drew up statutes for the regulation of this hospital. (His diocese in those days extended so far south as to include parts of Hertfordshire). They provided for a staff of nine persons: the Procurator or Master, who could be a layman, two Chaplains, and six lay brothers to wait upon the poor. The details of these statutes are given in a MS (circa 1280) in the Cambridge University Library, for which Markham gives a transcription and translation. These statutes state that the Master was expected to eat and sleep with the brethren and attend at the canonical hours (i.e. the fixed times of prayer during the day); that there were sisters as well as brethren of the hospital, who fed apart; that the sisters and brethren owned nothing of their own; that the lay brethren in place of Matins said twenty Our Fathers and twenty Hail Marys, and at the other hours seven of each; that old garments, and also the remnants of the table, were to be given to the poor. There was to be silence in

160

chapel, refectory, cloisters, and dormitory, and also reading at meals. The hospitality of the house was to be observed, and the infirm duly attended. There was to be a weekly chapter, and the seal of the house should be kept under three keys.

Here, as so often was the case, we can see that it was the poor who suffered as a result of the dissolution of such houses in the reign of Henry VIII. The chapter *The Problems of the Poor* discusses this subject in more detail.

There were three rows of beds for the use of the poor, the sick, and the stranger; there were two chapels adjoining: one dedicated to the Holy Trinity & the Blessed Virgin Mary, and one to St David; and there was a burial ground. It was more often known as the hospital of the Holy Trinity, but the other title of St David's or St Dewe's (or Dewy's) was also used. An examination of the Public Record Office (PRO) catalogue resulted in 27 documents whose primary description was Hospital of the Holy Trinity, four more referred to it as St David's, and one other as St Dewe's; a number of them also mentioned one or more of the aliases. The question arises, how does the Welsh form Dewe or Dewy, for the name David, come to be used in this locality? It might be tempting to think that there was some connection here with the Morgan family, whose name perhaps indicates Welsh origins. But they did not come into possession of the lands of the Hospital until after the dissolution, and the use of the name Dewy goes back to at least 1398, as shown by PRO document C 146/134.

Its income was derived from the rents and benefits of various pieces of land in the surrounding area. A map of 1584, contained in the NRO document FH 272, gives the name St Dewe's Meadow to a piece of land north of the parish of Kingsthorpe that bordered the parishes of Boughton and Brampton. The VCH says that the large collection of deeds and documents at the PRO pertaining to this hospital relates mainly to lands at Boughton, Bletsoe, East Haddon, and Wollaston, and mills at Abington.

By the survey taken in 1535 in preparation for the dissolution, this hospital, with the profits arising from the various lands, houses and mills belonging to it, had a yearly value of £46.12s.10d. (More details can be found in Bridges, p.416.) In 1557 the Hospital, with its land

and appurtenances, was granted to Hugh Zully, the last master of the Hospital and master of the Savoy. The Savoy was a similar hospital in London; the well-known hotel now stands on its site.

A little later the Crown granted a lease of the premises to the Morgan family of Kingsthorpe. The ruins of the hospital and one of the chapels still remained in Bridges's time, and it then formed part of the large estate of John Morgan. Upon his death it passed by marriage to Sir John Robinson of Cranford, the 4th baronet.

At some point in time part of the Hospital buildings were converted into a blacksmith's shop, and the chapel of the Holy Trinity appears to have been destroyed. When Mr G J de Wilde wrote, in 1863, he speaks of this blacksmith's shop as being "worth looking at." Around 1870 this building was modified to make it into a private house. In 1882, when Winifred, Lady Robinson, widow of the 8th baronet, Sir John Blencowe Robinson, came to reside at the house, the cottages adjoining the building on the north side were removed, in order to extend the accommodation. Various other improvements were made in subsequent years.

The chapel of St David was at some stage converted into two small cottages, a floor being inserted about half way up the walls, and doors and windows inserted. Two fireplaces were made, one of the chimneys being carried up through the centre of the old east window of the chapel. Markham believed that this chapel stood on a site that is now between the main road and Kingsthorpe Grove. An article in The Northampton County Magazine (Vol. 3, 1930, page 180) agrees with this by clearly stating that the road from Kingsthorpe to Abington separated the two chapels, with St David's chapel standing between that roadway and the main Northampton road.

Mr Richard Barratt, who was joint managing director of a local shoe-manufacturing firm, purchased St David's House early in the 20th century. He rebuilt the house further inside the grounds, and changed its orientation towards the south. During the demolition and rebuilding, which took from 1927 until 1931, a number of skeletons were found; they were undoubtedly from the old hospital burial ground. Mr A E Davies, founder of a firm of organ specialists, installed a 3-manual organ (now in Christchurch, Northampton) in the Music Room of the new house. Their foreman on the site, David Hutchinson, described as "a serious minded Scot," maintained that he several times saw figures appear in the Music Room 2 or 3 feet above floor level – which is where the floor of the previous building would have been! A letter in the possession of Mr Leo Bell, the first Headmaster of St David's Middle School, contains the following information: Mr W A Cousner, at the time a 17-year-old Apprentice Plumber, recalled fixing lead on the Music Room roof while the men were digging out the foundations of the power room for the organ. They came across a stone slab and, on lifting it, exposed a coffin in which was a perfect skeleton. Many more skulls were found in the grounds, and stored in the garages on shelves. Another labourer was excavating when a bag of gold coins fell to the bottom of the trench.

In 1960 St David's was converted into the Notre Dame Preparatory School, which was closed in 1974 following the closure of the Convent School in Abington Street. The Good Shepherd Roman Catholic Lower School, which had been built in the grounds, was opened in June 1975. In September 1976 the house itself became St David's Roman Catholic Middle School. Mr Leo Bell says that, at the time of the building of the sports hall in 1987, a medieval skeleton was unearthed near the rear wall of the hall (the old Music Room). Following the discovery, the school was visited by an archaeologist; but it was decided not to investigate further, since the site had been dug over and built on so many times. So the remains were left *in situ*.

The conclusion of this most recent part of its history is that, as part of the reorganisation of education in Northampton, St David's Middle School was closed in July 2004 and the house put up for sale.

THREE WALKS AROUND OLD KINGSTHORPE

THESE three walks confine themselves to the examination of the older buildings that still remain in the village. Buildings associated with the history of the community, such as the Church of St John the Baptist, the old Town House, and Kingsthorpe Hall, are examined in detail. The old Rectory, which used to stand at the end of Vicarage Lane, had an interesting history; this has been reconstructed from old photographs and, together with details of some of the Rectors, forms the subject of a separate chapter following the second of these walks.

The first walk follows a route that begins at the Kings Well and proceeds up Kingswell Road to Mill Lane; there it turns left and goes as far as the Cock Hotel. It then returns by way of Thornton Park and Kingsthorpe Hall, crosses Mill Lane, goes down The Leys, and returns to its starting point.

Walk number two begins at the bottom of The Leys and examines the properties in Green End; then it turns northwards towards the church and enters Vicarage Lane by way of Hopes Place and Church Passage. A number of interesting properties are examined along Vicarage Lane, and the walk ends at the converted buildings of the old Glebe Farm.

The third walk begins at the triangular Green to the east of the Kings Well, proceeds up High Street to the Harborough Road, and ventures up Boughton Green Road before going northwards along Harborough Road as far as Glan-y-mor Terrace. It returns across the Recreation Ground to Wardington Court, and then examines the properties in Manor Road, ending (appropriately enough) at the *Queen Adelaide*.

WALK NUMBER ONE

B eginning at the Kings Well which, according to Baker, "has never been known either to fail or to freeze," this walk begins by going up what used to be known as The Bank, or Cattle Bank, towards Kingswell Road. On the right there is a high stone wall of considerable age. Where modern development has taken place this wall has been pierced or lowered, but most of it remains intact. It originally enclosed the land attached to the mansion and farm buildings that belonged to the Cooke family until the 18th century. Somewhere close to the Kings Well would have been a gateway giving access to the Green from this enclosure. G J de Wilde, writing in 1863, mentions an avenue of elms leading down to the Green from the Cooke premises.

The old Town House
Across the triangular green on the left stands the building that was once the Town House; it was built by Dame Sarah Prichard (1637/8-1718), born Sarah Cooke of Kingsthorpe; it consisted of one long room, built of stone, for the Freeholders or Trustees of the Manor to meet in. But what was the date of the erection of this building, and was it of the same ashlar facing that we see today? Since the plinth is of squared coursed rubble, the ashlar work may be a later addition. Serjeantson (1904; p.213) says that this building was used as a workhouse, and was pulled down in the middle of the 19th century. By "pulled down" he must have been referring to its conversion to an Infant School, but the extent of this conversion is not known. Was it radical enough to involve rebuilding the walls and roof? The cost, recorded by Bispham on page 72 of his thesis, was £44.14s.0d.

The Town House was used as a workhouse for a period during the 19th century, but this function ceased in 1836. Certainly it was so used in 1801, when it was mentioned in Robert Kinning's will; in describing his property, which included what is now No.1 The Green, he states that it lay immediately to the east of the parish workhouse. Perhaps it was converted from a single room, and given a first floor, when it became the workhouse. During the 1860s it was producing

The Kings Well in 2004; this spring, a source of water for local villagers over many centuries, was culverted in the 19th century. (Photo by the author).

The Old Town House. Initially provided for meetings of the Trustees of the Manor, it later became the parish workhouse, then the Infant School, and finally a Sunday School. (Photo by the author).

£10 p.a. rental for the Manor and Town Lands Charity, and then in 1874, as mentioned above, was altered to become an Infant School. In 1898 it was apparently let to the Managers of the National School for £12 p.a. It was in use as an Infant School in the early years of the 20th century, until the old Free School building was so used; also during the time when the latter underwent modification. It was purchased by Mrs Anne Thornton (who lived at Kingsthorpe Hall until her death in 1911), and eventually given to the parish for use as a Sunday School. The "Manor House" was sold in 1952 and converted into two dwellings. It is a Grade II Listed Building, having been first listed in 1952 as "Sunday School, Kingswell Road". It is a sandstone building with a plinth, quoins, a cornice and a hipped and tiled roof. It has two storeys, although originally one room only; three casement windows under lintels and keystones; and a central doorway, now altered because of the conversion into two dwellings. The official listing does not give a date for the building. It is now listed as "The Green (East Side), Kingsthorpe, *Greenbanks* and *Wayside*". These two dwellings have a delightful outlook across the Green towards the church.

Traces of the original frontage of two cottages adjacent to the old Town House on the south side can still be discerned in the wall next to the footpath. The 1884 25-inch OS Map shows a terrace of six cottages extending up the slope and then a group of others, some set further back.

The Old Church Institute

Higher up the slope, still on the left and just before reaching Garfield Street, is a house named *The Old Church Institute*. This Institute was first mentioned in the Vestry minutes in 1919, but was apparently purchased in 1911. It was in use by the church until at least 1933, but then there is a break in the records. The church again seems to have used it from 1947 to 1963. Kelly's Directory of 1898 mentions a *Liberal & Radical Working Men's Club and Institute* at 1 & 3 Garfield Street, at the rear of which this property actually stands; but the 1903 Directory places the Institute in Kingswell Road, thus confirming its origin. No doubt Lady Robinson, who was a great sup-

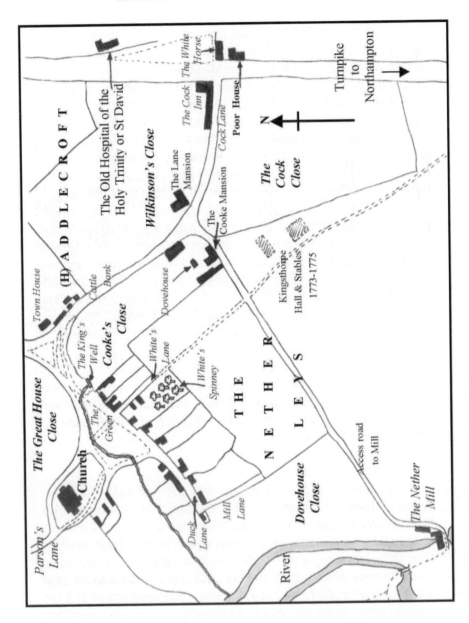

Sketch map of part of Kingsthorpe in the late 18th century

The Old Church Institute. Built in the late 19th century as Working Mens' Club and Institute, it was acquired by the church in 1911. (Photo by the author).

porter of Liberalism, financed its construction. Its Secretary was George Ogden, who was also Secretary of Liberty Hall in Washington Street; this was erected in 1887 by Lady Robinson, and used for concerts, entertainments etc.

Home Farm

Approaching the junction of Kingswell Road with Mill Lane, on the right is a very capacious stone building that was once a barn. The angle of the roof indicates that it was originally thatched. It now consists of two dwellings, the southern half having been converted into *Home Farm* in the late 19th or early 20th century; the northern half (at one time used as the dairy of *Home Farm*) was converted and extended, in a very careful and attractive manner, at the beginning of the 21st century.

As with many barns of this type, slit windows originally pierced the walls. In the east wall of the building, facing Kingswell Road, two of these have been filled with stonework, but can still be clearly traced; another has been incorporated into a modern window opening. At about the mid-point of the wall, and about ten feet up, a piece of local dark brown ironstone has been carved into the likeness of two faces. The area around the front door of *Home Farm* is of great interest, because this was originally an impressive entrance for horses and carriages to the barn and to the mansion. The carved stone architraves of a large gateway can be clearly seen, the left hand side of which remains intact within the wall to the left of the new doorway; the other side is about five feet to the right of the doorway. Higher up on this north side it has been incorporated into the side of a window opening, and cut back as necessary to receive the new sill and lintel of the window. The original gateway was about 10 feet wide and 11 feet high. A larger window opening has been formed to the left of the doorway, and the filled-in remains of one of the old slit windows can be seen at the upper left of this new window.

The Dovecote
Continuing towards Mill Lane, the old Dovecote can be seen standing within the garden of *Home Farm*. Phyllis Collins visited it in September 1971 whilst compiling the material for a thesis on dovecotes. She described it as rectangular in plan, 24 feet in length and 15 feet wide. Its gable ends are finished with stone finials, and high up in its east gable is a small square window with a weather-worn plaque below it. The building may have been erected in the early 17th century, and is built of the local ferruginous limestone. In its south wall is the original wooden door, with a curved wooden lintel and a rough stone arch above that; the door can be seen clearly from the entrance to *Home Farm* garden. Phyllis Collins measured the height of the dovecote to the eaves as 15 feet, and estimated the height of the ridge as 29 feet. The walls are about three feet thick and the stonework very irregular. There were still nesting boxes inside in 1971; these were constructed of stone on the south side and of brick on the north side, the latter presumably being of later date. The dovecote originally had a lantern in the roof to provide access for the

170

The old dovecote, which stands at the rear of Home Farm at the junction of Kingswell Road and Mill Lane. (Photo by the author).

birds, but this was removed some time ago when the building was re-roofed in slate. Since the modern usage of the dovecote is for storage, it has had additional doors and windows added, together with a brick buttress to the south wall.

There may have been another cote further down what is now Mill Lane, just above the river; there was an ancient enclosure here, known as Dovehouse Close, which belonged to the Cooke family. In Robert Cooke's will of 1574 he refers to "my orchard joining to my dovehouse", but this probably refers to the existing cote, or its predecessor, which would have stood within a yard surrounded by the house, the outbuildings, and no doubt an orchard. This was a good situation for a dovehouse, according to Phyllis Collins's research into medieval treatises on the subject. A further interesting note concerning these structures is found on page 490 of John Morton's *'The*

Home Farm: The doorway was converted out of an original high status entrance for a coach. (Photo by the author).

The old barn on Kingswell Road that once formed part of the range of buildings associated with the Cooke mansion. The far (south) end was converted into Home Farm in the late 19th century, and the near (north) end converted into a dwelling at the beginning of the 21st century. (Photo by the author).

Natural History of Northamptonshire...' (London, 1712), where he says that the construction of a dovecote above a stable has good results. As an example he gives Mr Morgan's dove-house in Kingsthorpe, which apparently had more pigeons than all the four other dove-houses in the village. Mr Morgan's dove-house would have formed part of his mansion in Great House Close, east of the church. Morton's quotation also tells us that, early in the 18th century, there were five dove-houses in Kingsthorpe. Their owners were not, of course, pigeon fanciers; the birds provided a convenient source of fresh meat and no doubt a few eggs in season, and the droppings would have provided fertiliser for at least the vegetable garden.

The Cooke mansion, still marked on the 1767 Inclosure map, had a frontage to the Kingswell Road/Mill Lane corner. It was demolished in 1774 by James Fremeaux, who built Kingsthorpe Hall on the other side of Mill Lane in 1773-5. But he left some of the outbuildings intact, including two large barns and the dovecote. The other range of outbuildings, to the west of the cote, was converted into dwellings in the late 20th century, and their doors and almost all their windows face east. The west wall of these dwellings was originally the wall of another large barn, and was pierced by slit windows and a large gateway. The slit windows can still be traced, since they are filled with stones on edge. The large gateway here has a timber lintel and rougher stone edges rather than carved architraves, since it provided working access to the land known as the Nether Leys. The stonework filling of this gateway has been pierced just below the lintel to form a modern window.

Home Farm, the Dovecote and the converted Barns are Grade II Listed Buildings "of the 17th century with group value." To the east, across the road in 'Wilkinson's Close', once stood the mansion of the Lane family; the building was still shown on the 1767 Inclosure map. Some details of the Lanes are included in the section *Family matters*.

Main Road
Continuing up Mill Lane, once known as Cock Lane, at the junction with the main road to Northampton is the rebuilt version of the *Cock Inn*, the earlier form of which was so delightfully described by George

The Cock Inn, before it was rebuilt in 1893. (Picture courtesy of Northampton Borough Council, Planning Dept.)

James de Wilde in his *Rambles Roundabout*. The present building dates from 1893 and is a Grade II Listed Building "carefully designed in squared rubble with ashlar dressings." Across the main road can be seen the rebuilt *White Horse* where, in a previous incarnation as an inn, the Inclosure Commissioners had their meetings in 1766 and 1767. It was also the venue for the meetings of the gentlemen's dining club, known as Kingsthorpe Bowling Green Club, from 1771 to 1852; see the chapter so named in the section *Entertainments at Kingsthorpe*. To the south of this once stood the Poor House, and some other cottages for the poor people of the parish. Looking further eastwards, across the triangular Upper Green, and a little to the north, can be seen the house built by a local footwear manufacturer on the site of the old Hospital of St David or The Holy Trinity. On the Upper Green itself stands a memorial to the men of Kingsthorpe and Holy Trinity parishes who fell in the Great War of 1914-18; see *Endnote 1* for details of the unveiling ceremony in 1921. A little further to the north is the stone drinking fountain erected in 1897 to commemorate the Diamond Jubilee of Queen Victoria.

View across the main road in front of the Cock Hotel at the beginning of the 20th century. The building in the picture stood a little south of St David's, the residence of Lady Winifred Robinson. (Picture courtesy of Alan J Clarke).

Kingsthorpe Hall

Returning down Mill Lane towards *Home Farm*, to the left is Thornton Park; it was once an ancient inclosure known as The Cock Close or Barnaby's Close, which belonged to the Morgan family and then to the Robinson estate. It later passed from Sir George Robinson to James Fremeaux in exchange for Walbeck Close in Kingsthorpe Hollow. Thornton Park can be entered, either here or further down Mill Lane just past *Home Farm*, in order to see the house erected by James Fremeaux. Since, like the Cooke family before him, he left no male heirs, his estates passed by marriage to the Thornton family of Brockhall. The house is therefore sometimes called Thornton Hall, but more usually referred to as Kingsthorpe Hall.

James Fremeaux had been born into a Dutch or Flemish Huguenot family who were merchant traders, and he later became a naturalized British citizen. In 1752 his wife Margaret (née Cooke), inherited the estates of the Cooke family in Kingsthorpe (and elsewhere). James

Kingsthorpe Hall in Thornton Park. Built by James Fremeaux in 1773-1775, it was designed by John Johnson of Leicester (1732-1814). (Picture courtesy of Northampton Borough Council, Planning Dept.)

and his family moved to Kingsthorpe in 1769 or 1770, but they did not live in the old Cooke mansion. James rented the Parsonage House, or Rectory, where he and his family lived until the building of the Hall was completed. The Hall was designed for James Fremeaux by John Johnson of Leicester (1732-1814), an accomplished architect and builder of London town houses and country houses in various parts of England and Wales, including Pitsford Hall a few miles north of Northampton. Kingsthorpe Hall, along with its Stables, is a Grade II Listed Building. Its ashlar facing is the white Kingsthorpe freestone, once quarried locally in the Park Field near Moulton Park. According to Baker it was also used in building the general infirmary and the barracks in Northampton, as well as in several other local mansions. The Hall has a low-pitched slate roof behind low parapets. Its plan is square, with the entrance facing west; it has three floors and is five windows wide. The windows are sashes, those on the ground floor being in arched panels. The main door has an architrave surround under a cornice, the glazed wooden porch being more recent. The

interior has carved marble chimneypieces, and there is a spiral staircase with a wrought iron balustrade lit by a lantern dome; but the
latter suffered much damage from a recent fire. The Stables are also
of ashlar construction, with a stone slated roof; they are two storeys
high, with a projecting pediment in the centre. Work on the Hall
began in 1773 and was complete by early 1775.

James's only son, Peter John Fremeaux, died in 1784 and his daughter Susannah became the heiress when her grandfather died on 23
April 1799. Just three months earlier she had married Thomas Reeve
Thornton of Brockhall, Northants, into which family the estate now
passed. Susannah and Thomas lived at Brockhall so, presumably after
James's widow Margaret had died in 1801, Kingsthorpe Hall was let
for some years to people such as Lady Sarah Cave, who gave up her
tenancy in 1810 to avoid involvement in a footpath dispute; and from
1821 to Fortunatus Dwarris, a barrister-at-law, who still lived there in
1831, according to the writer in Hone's Year Book of 1832.

*Kingsthorpe Hall, front elevation. (Picture courtesy of Northampton
Borough Council).*

Kingsthorpe Hall, entrance hall. (© Crown copyright. National Monuments Record, English Heritage. Ref: BB82/9369. Reproduced with permission.)

Kingsthorpe Hall, balustrade detail. (© Crown copyright. National Monuments Record, English Heritage. Ref: BB82/9367. Reproduced with permission.)

In 1832 the Hall, together with 14 acres of land and a 2½-acre farmyard, was leased to the Misses Boddington: five maiden ladies named Harriott, Susannah, Maria, Frances and Emma. They were grandchildren of James Fremeaux, through his daughter Maria Catharina, who had married Thomas Boddington of Clapton. The contents of the Hall were auctioned on 21 and 22 April 1873, following the death on 7 March of that year of Frances, the last of the Boddington sisters. Following her demise, the Rev William Thornton, who had inherited the Hall from his mother Susannah, lived there with his family; his widow, Anne, continued to

Kingsthorpe Hall, staircase. (© Crown copyright. National Monuments Record, English Heritage. Ref: BB82/9368. Reproduced with permission.)

live there with her family after her husband's death in 1881.

The Rev William and Mrs Thornton were known as a great benefactors to other local churches beside Kingsthorpe: St James, St Paul's, St Matthew's and Holy Trinity. Mrs Thornton purchased the old Free School building in the High Street for use as an Infant School; she also purchased the old Manor House, used for some years previously as an Infant School, and gave it to the parish for use as a Sunday School. When she died in 1911 her son, Francis Hugh Thornton, who had lived at the Hall with his mother for the past decade, continued to live there and to manage the estate until his own death in 1937. He was particularly noted for the herd of pure-

Kingsthorpe Hall, the stables - modified for use by the Council in the 20th century. (Picture courtesy of Northampton Borough Council).

bred shorthorn dairy cattle that he managed for his mother. According to L W Dickens, a local journalist, he was a county alderman, Justice of the Peace, and a director of the Northamptonshire Union Bank in the Drapery, Northampton (which later merged with the National Provincial).

In 1937 the Borough Council purchased the hall, and the park was later made available for public use. During the 2nd World War the Hall was used as a Civil Defence control centre. From 1950 onwards it became a much-used Community Centre, which hosted 14 organisations at various times. The stables were somewhat modified and, together with the old farm buildings, used as a Council Depot for the district. At the end of the 20th century the Hall was still in regular use by at least seven organisations, besides occasional functions and meetings. The Town Council then agreed to sell it for conversion to luxury flats. It suffered much from graffiti and vandalism externally and was then broken into and set on fire. This caused much damage to the roof, and doubtless much water damage elsewhere. That damage has now been repaired, but at the time of writing there is still some local opposition to the plans for development into flats.

The Leys

Leave Thornton Park by the gateway to the north of the Hall, in order to re-enter Mill Lane. The mill buildings at the bottom of the lane have long since disappeared; the last mention of a miller there was in 1898, and in 1899 arrangements were being made for a bathing place next to the mill. Crossing Mill Lane, this walk continues down the path known as The Leys. On the Inclosure map of 1767 it is called White's Lane, and the land it crossed was the Nether Leys. The stone walls on either side of the path would have been built following the Inclosure. This pathway originally ran from the village across the fields until it met the Turnpike coming from Northampton – as, indeed, it does today.

At the point where the path widens, it enters the 'Old Inclosures' of the original village. In 1767 the piece of land to the left, beginning from just before the widening of the path right down to the Green, and extending westward to the property now known as *The Old Dairy*, belonged to Sir George Robinson. There was a spinney, known as White's Spinney, which, according to the Robinson estate Rent

The river at Kingsthorpe Nether Mill, around 1910; the old mill buildings are visible to the right of the picture. (Picture courtesy of Alan J Clarke).

Roll, was let to T Hollis for two years from Lady Day 1762 for 10/- per annum. Then there was, and is, a cottage with a sundial on its south wall with a date stone above it that bears the date 1696. It has been extended on more than one occasion since then, but it originally consisted of two rooms on the ground floor, one of which had a boxed-in cupboard staircase leading to a bedroom; a second bedroom was accessed through the first. In the 1930s, when the present writer was familiar with it, it still had an outside toilet and no bathroom; but a brick extension provided additional accommodation in the shape of a small kitchen and a dining room, with a bedroom above which was accessed by means of a vertical ladder through a trap-door. The next stone cottage down the slope towards the Green is a conversion from what was originally a barn or outbuilding.

Reaching the bottom of The Leys, one can look across the Green and admire the superb view of the church from this point. There must

Kingsthorpe Parish Church, dedicated to St John the Baptist. (Photo by the author).

be something about the proportions of the building with its tower and spire, sitting securely on top of the green mound of the church-yard, which makes it so attractive. It is surely one of the most pho-tographed, drawn and painted churches in the county.

The Old Rectory

To the east of The Leys is the attractive brick and tile-hung house known as *The Old Rectory*. It had in fact been the Vicarage, and later the Rectory, from 1950 to 1979, when a more modest Rectory was provided in Green End. The latter was a recently built dwelling, which was enlarged to provide suitable accommodation for the Rector, the Rev Wolstenhulme. The original Rectory or Parsonage House (officially a Vicarage from 1850 onwards) had been at Parson's End, the furthest point of Parson's Lane, later renamed Vicarage Lane.

In 1871, according to a notebook relating to the Thornton Estate, the site of *The Old Rectory* consisted of a court of eight cottages, occu-pied by four widows and four families. These dwellings can be seen on the large scale OS map of 1884. Mary Thornton of Kingsthorpe Hall, in her diary for 1886, records that on 14 August the workmen had begun to demolish these tumbledown old cottages. Then on 11 June 1888 she says that she went into "the new Villa on the Green" and explored it thoroughly; the views from the windows she described as charming. Early in the 20th century it was apparently known as *Anson Villa*, a name that links it to Mary Thornton's mother.

Kingswell Cottage

Next to this house, between it and the Kings Well, stands the steeply roofed (and once thatched) *Kingswell Cottage*. This is a Grade II listed building, and is officially described as a "17th-century house of squared coursed rubble with stone verges and kneelers to gables of steeply pitched Welsh slated roof...three casement windows, one to centre of 1st floor retaining two lights with moulded stone jambs and mullion..." The ground floor window lintels retain evidence that all the windows originally had stone mullions. It has modern dormer windows at the rear; there is a window at attic level in the east gable, and one very small fixed window above eaves level in the west gable.

Kingswell Cottage, which stands next to the Kings Well. It was built in the early 17th century, or possibly in the late 16th. (Photo by the author).

There are some deeds and other documentation that provide further information about the history of this house; see *Endnote 2* for details.

The above mentioned notebook of 1871 shows that this cottage was owned by the Thornton estate at that time, and was let to George Waterfield. Some repairs were necessary, and the notebook lists these and includes a plan of the cottage and outbuildings. The latter were (and still are) quite extensive; apart from a pigsty and storage for wood, coals, etc., there was a thatched 'Potato House' measuring about 12 ft. by 16 ft., and an adjoining tiled barn of similar size. This cottage and its outbuildings are also clearly shown on the OS map of 1884.

The 1851 census shows George Waterfield, then aged 27, living at this property with his wife and two young children. He described himself as a Stonemason and Beer Seller, and he is described in Kelly's Directory of 1854 as a Beer Retailer; the house was sometimes known as *The Mason's Arms*. It seems that the outbuildings were used at this time as a brew house. George Waterfield continued to describe himself as a beer retailer in trade directories until at least 1874, and Mrs Eliza Waterfield was so described until 1881. In her diary entry for 1 April 1882, Mary Thornton records calling on the family of one of the servants of the Hall, who had recently moved into the re-roofed and renamed Kingswell Cottage. She says that Mrs Waterfield had left at Michaelmas 1881, and until then it had been known as *The Mason's Arms*.

The Kings Well

This walk ends where it began, at the Kings Well. The Northampton Borough Council affixed a plaque to the wall in 1995; it says that the water that springs out of the hillside at the Kings Well, sometimes known as the Long Well, was also accessed by a deep well inside Thornton Hall. The same spring probably feeds the lake in the grounds of St David's. According to Suzanne Wright (p.58) there is an old tradition in the village that one can only claim to be a true Kingsthorpian if one has fallen into the Long Well; the present writer can make that claim! The spring was culverted in the 19th century, and at the western end of the Green further provision was made for water to be obtained from it. This was known as the Jubilee Well, which continued in use until the first World War. From here it runs as a brook behind the King William IV and the other properties in Green End, until it joins the river. The plaque at the Kings Well says of this spring that "It was the proud boast of the villagers that it was of greater purity than the town's piped water supply." It clearly provided a very convenient source of water for the brewing, baking and other domestic activities of the residents of the nearby properties across many centuries.

ENDNOTES:
(1) KINGSTHORPE WAR MEMORIAL
(From NORTHAMPTON INDEPENDENT, Volume XVI, 14 May 1921 p.12.)

Graceful cenotaph Unveiled by the Mayor

One of the most artistic memorials in the county was unveiled at Kingsthorpe on Sunday afternoon by the Mayor (Councillor Harvey Reeves OBE) to the memory of the 142 men from the parishes of Kingsthorpe and Holy Trinity who fell in the war.

Standing on the Green and thrown into bold relief by the dark foliaged background the memorial, which is fashioned on the cenotaph principle, is of Portland Stone standing on three plinths and surmounted by a bronze figure of St George, whose sword, held at arms length, forms a cross, on which is a miniature crucifix. On the front of the memorial are carved the words "Lest we forget. These men were faithful unto death." The memorial is from the design of Mr Alfred Turner, B.Sc., who has designed the Mobbs Memorial, and was erected by public subscriptions, Mr F H Thornton, C.A., being Chairman of the Committee, Councillor A J Chown, Treasurer, and Mr J V Rowntree, Secretary.

Over 1,000 people were present at the unveiling ceremony, which was in the charge of the Rev J P de Putron (Vicar of Kingsthorpe), the Rev J F Winter (Vicar of Holy Trinity) conducting the prayers, and the Rev S S Black (Kingsthorpe Baptist) read the lessons. The singing was led by the combined Church and Non-comformist choirs, accompanied by the Volunteer Band. The Rev J P de Putron dedicated the memorial "to the brothers who laid down their lives for their country."

The "Last Post", Chopin's "Funeral March", and the National Anthem marked the close of an impressive ceremony, after which the relatives slowly filed past and placed floral tributes on the memorial. There were over 50 tributes.

(2) In a Conveyance of 7 January 1794 this property, described as a "messuage, cottage or tenement with garden, orchard etc., together with a small tenement, formerly a barn or workshop...and also that close of 1r.14p. in a place called the Nether Leys...lying on the south side of and adjoining to the said cottage", was sold for £406 to Joseph Hall of Northampton, who con-

veyed it to William Green of Kingsthorpe for £406 on 11 March 1794. The conveyance shows that the property was charged with the yearly sum of five shillings, "payable to or for the use and benefit of the poor of the parish of Kingsthorpe". (NRO: NPL 2427 & 2428) The premises and close were originally conveyed to Joseph Hall by the devisees of George Hollis, who had bought the cottage from Elizabeth Cooke; she was the widow of Thomas Cooke, and had died in 1763. The map drawn up for the Inclosure Commissioners shows this plot of land with George Hollis's name on it, together with the adjoining close of 1r.14p. in the Nether Leys awarded to him.

The story can now be taken back to 1683 and the Order issued by the Charity Commissioners, following their Inquisition of the previous year. That Order mentions the annual payment of five shillings to be given to the poor out of the rent of a house in Kingsthorpe called The Bakehouse, which was then owned by Francis Cooke and occupied by Mary Morris, a poor widow. Its name indicates how the property had been used at some point in its history. The same document states that the rent charge of 5/- p.a. originated from a legacy made by Thomas Knapps, whose will was proved 20 May 1613. A recently cleaned datestone reveals that this house was built in 1600.

WALK NUMBER TWO

This walk around the village begins at the bottom of The Leys and examines the terrace of six cottages which run in a westerly direction from there, facing across the Green towards the church. Their mixed appearance is very attractive, and they obviously vary in their dates of construction. The two most modern, at the corner of The Leys, appear to pre-date the 1884 OS map, and the others are considerably older, particularly the three-storeyed stone cottage. The land on which these properties stand would trace its title back to Sir George Robinson at the time of the Inclosure, and before that it would have been part of the estate of either the Morgan family or the Lane family. These houses are numbered 1, 3, 5 etc. from the bottom of The Leys to the bottom of the Lower Leys, but interrupted by the properties forming Fremeaux Terrace. This area is known as Green End, and was previously known as Duck Lane or Duck End.

The substantial stone dwelling now known as *The Old Dairy* (No. 13) was originally thatched; in 1767 it belonged to Thomas Hollis, who was awarded a further 1a.3r.34p. of land in the Nether Leys. This is a Grade II Listed Building, which is included for group value with numbers 15 & 17, also Grade II. It is defined as "a 17th-century house built of coursed rubble...with kneelers to side elevation gables". The property was certainly in use as a dairy in the first half of the 20th century, when a certain Miss White used to deliver milk from a pedal-cycle with sidecar attached. Then there is the L-shaped *Victoria Cottage*, which has a gable end facing the road, and the adjoining three-storeyed house (No. 17) with its central doorway flanked by two bay windows. In 1767 the land on which these two properties stand was owned by Catherine Walding, who received an award of a further 1r.21p. at the rear. *Victoria Cottage* (No. 15) is listed as an 18th-century building, "restored and altered", of coursed rubble with large flush quoins. No.17 is listed as early 19th-century "of red brick, some yellow headers, Welsh slated roof with brick cornice. Three storeys...Two ground floor bay windows with rounded angles. Six flush panel door and oblong fanlight in surround of fluted pilasters, frieze, cornice." This group of three properties is certainly most

Victoria Cottage in Green End. The underground garage is, of course, a 20th century modification. (Photo by the author).

attractive.

In the remaining part of Green End the original dwellings have either been demolished altogether or converted into modern dwellings. The early 20th century saw the erection on the south side of five gable-fronted houses known as Fremeaux Terrace, separately numbered from 1 to 5; number 5, also known as *Moorlands*, has a side entrance to the west. The name of this terrace indicates that it was almost certainly built by the Thornton family, which had Fremeaux connections. The next two semi-detached houses, numbered 19 and 21, built of stone with tiled roofs, are relatively modern and of high-class construction. They have mullioned windows, with a shared dormer in the roof. The land upon which they and Fremeaux Terrace stand appears to have belonged to John Archbold in the late 18th century. The remaining land on this side belonged in 1767 to James Bowker of London, who was awarded a further 1a.3r.19p. at the rear in the Nether Leys. Here stand four more dwellings: three of these, numbers 23, 23a and 25a (the two latter standing back from the

17 Green End, with its attractive bay windows. (Photo by the author).

road), are of late 20th-century date.

Green End Cottage

Then there are two semi-detached cottages, built of stone and brick with tiled roofs, that now form one dwelling, *Green End Cottage* (No. 25). The original two cottages that form this property were clearly built, or altered, at about the same time: there are clear similarities in their construction, but there is a definite dividing line. Their northern elevations to the road are very similar, but include what must have been individual preferences in the position of windows; the eastern one also has a dormer window at the ridge, and they both have a window to an attic floor in the gable ends. To the north ele-

Green End Cottage: the evidence that it was converted from two semi-detached cottages can be clearly seen. (Photo by the author).

vation they both have a simple cornice between the ground and first floors; above the cornice they are faced with brick, though their main construction is of stone.

The eastern cottage also has two courses of brick under the ground floor windows, with stones laid in a herringbone pattern below them, and another two courses of brick below that. This herringbone pattern is very attractive, and can be seen in several other buildings in the area. Both cottages originally had their entrances at the rear, as the present dwelling does, although at some point a modern, but matching, porch extension was built on to the east with a front door; but this has since been converted into a window. Further information about the history of this property will be found in *Endnote 1*.

Fremeaux House

A lane runs off to the south, once known as Mill Lane but now called The Lower Leys; it narrows to a footpath at the point where the Old Inclosures of the village terminated. The footpath then goes between 20th-century housing development until it reaches the busy main road now known as Mill Lane, but which in 1767 was a private road to the Nether Mill. To the west of Lower Leys, and extending southwards to the road and westward to the river, was Dovehouse Close; this belonged successively to the Cooke, Fremeaux and Thornton families. On part of that Close, a short distance up Lower Leys from Green End, a large house was built during the 19th century known as *Fremeaux House*. It is interesting to note that this house uses a similar style of construction to the two cottages we have just examined: exposed stonework on the ground floor, except for brick corners and window openings, surmounted by the same form of cornice with brickwork above. The house faces south; its original main door opened on to the garden, with a gate giving access to the lane.

In Mary Thornton's diaries there are some references to this house, which the family called 'The Villa'. In April 1878 Mary records in her diary taking "Millie and Katie to look at the new building at Duck End, which has the rafters & gables for the roof up." In March 1879 she and her sister Bertha "...took Miss Biedlin over the Villa." This sounds very much as if the house was still unoccupied. In March and in July 1880, she again records people being taken to see the Villa. Then in March 1882 Mary and her mother took a walk "through the river meadow below the Villa to see Hope's Place &c." On 6 August 1890 she refers to this house as *Fremeaux Villa*, which makes it clear that this was the earlier name of *Fremeaux House*. However, it may also have been known as *Fremeaux Cottage*: this was listed in Kelly's directory of 1885 as being occupied by Henry Cooper, and the 1881 census says that he was a Public Accountant living at the bottom of Duck End with his wife and a servant.

To its rear, and marking the furthest point of Green End, stands a building which might perhaps have been a coach house with some accommodation for a coachman or groom. To the right of that, i.e. to the north, is a cottage of stone, numbered 1a, originally thatched, and having a more recent brick extension to the west. Walking eastwards up Green End, the first property encountered is the 20th century property that became the Rectory. Until this property was built, there was a gate here giving access to a field and the brook (the continuation of the spring at the Kings Well) that ran down to the river. There is a very attractive view of the south elevation of the cottages in Hope's Place from here, looking between the Rectory and the adjacent property; their dormer windows and tiled roofs are best appreciated from this vantage point.

King William IV

Next to the Rectory is a dwelling that must represent the conversion of at least two cottages and some other buildings; according to sale particulars of November 2002 it has four reception rooms, four bedrooms and a wide gateway giving access to a garage. There are two more cottage conversions before reaching the public house *King William IV*, the western extension of which stands on the site of another old cottage. The structure of this building contains several examples of the herringbone pattern of stones, sandwiched between brick courses, referred to earlier; but here the patterns are more sophisticated, sometimes pointing outwards from a central point and sometimes inwards from each end. This style of decoration may be an indication that the present building was built by the Thornton family. (See *Endnote 2* for further details.)

The popularity of the name *King William IV* for public houses was owing to the fact that this king was instrumental in the introduction of the Beer Act of 1830, which rebated the tax on beer. According to a notice in the bar of the present *King William IV*, William Parbery (who was the present writer's maternal grandfather) held the licence until 1898, when he took on the *Old Five Bells*; this had been named after the number of bells in the church tower, the sixth bell being added in 1911. Alfred Wallace Page then ran the *King William IV* until 1931, when Herbert Clarence Horner (the present writer's father) took the licence for the Northampton Brewery Company, and held it until the end of 1938.

Hope's Place and Church Cottage

Proceeding from the *King William IV* in a northerly direction towards the church, on the left are some late 20th-century houses and then the row of cottages in Hope's Place, several of which have

The dormer windows of the cottages in Hope's Place, viewed from Green End. (Photo by the author).

small dormers above the eaves on their north elevation. Alec Brooking saw the eastern end of Hope's Place before the end cottage was demolished and rebuilt differently; he drew attention, in his photographic volume, to part of a moulded stone window surround that was almost completely obscured by the construction of that end cottage. His evidence indicates that there are at least portions of original structures in Hope's Place that may date from the 18th century or earlier. The census of 1851 shows only one dwelling in what it calls 'Holt's Place', between Duck End and Parson's End.

Next is the old bakehouse, known as *Church View*, now, after a number of years of dereliction, converted into modern accommodation. When it was put up for sale in November 1918, along with 30 other properties in Kingsthorpe, it was described as "a brick built and slated dwelling house with living room, parlour, four bedrooms, small yard and WC; with bakehouse attached, and stables, loft, cart shed, barn and pig-stye". The bakehouse and the flour loft were accessed on the north side of the building, where the loft door has been retained. Further modern development has taken place to the west of this property.

Facing the old bakehouse is the L-shaped *Church Cottage*, somewhat spoiled by the erection of a garage in front of it, but still a very attractive building. It has a south-facing wing built of coursed stonework, with an oriel window (not original) at attic level in its eastern gable; the other wing is clad in painted timber, with bay windows to both floors and its own entrance door, with a tiled canopy running along this elevation. Brooking describes the south-facing wing as sandstone, with the gable end rising above a late tiled roof. The chimney near the centre of the house (since replaced with a metal flue) shows the other gable end of the original structure. He thought that the height had been increased at the eaves, as evidenced by the different stone at that point. But there is no evidence

King William IV public house in Green End. (Photo by the author).

195

of this at the front, and the gable end appears to be entirely original in structure; certainly there is a slightly different stone used in the upper courses of the north elevation, but this does not seem to be related to later changes in height. Brooking suggested that the sash windows, with boxing showing, indicate a probable date for this wing of around 1750 or earlier. For the east-facing wing he suggested a late Victorian date, the bay window being identical to those in Alexandra Terrace, dated at 1903.

Of course the most significant, most ancient and most admired building in the village is the church of St John the Baptist, which has stood on its mound at the heart of the community for almost a thousand years. A first simple structure, perhaps built of wood, may have been here in Saxon times; the central portion of the present structure is certainly early Norman, but it has gone through a long process of evolution since then. A detailed description will be found in a separate chapter.

Vicarage Lane

In 1859 it was decided by the Vestry to stop the footpath at the east end of the church and to "enclose the present footpath"; this pre-

45 and 47 Vicarage Lane. (Photo by the author).

32 and 34 Vicarage Lane. The upper storeys of these cottages, with the dormer windows, as well as the entrance porches, are 20th century additions. (Photo by the author).

36 Vicarage Lane. The very attractive Georgian frontage is a later addition to an older stone cottage. (Photo by the author).

44 and 46 Vicarage Lane. The entrances to these cottages are at the rear - possibly because they were opposite to the entrance to the Rectory! (Photo by the author).

The converted Glebe Farm buildings at the end of Vicarage Lane. (Photo by the author).

sumably refers to the path that runs at the west end, now called Church Passage, along which this walk continues into Vicarage Lane (originally known as Parson's Lane). Facing one here is the overflow graveyard, the land for which had formed part of the Great House Close owned by Sir George Robinson. The decision to purchase was made at a Vestry meeting on 5 March 1863, and a Church Rate of 1/- in the £ was approved to cover the costs. The Great House Close was where the Morgan family mansion once stood; it comprised the land enclosed by Vicarage Lane, Cow Yard, Knights Lane and The Green.

On the left of Vicarage Lane is a row of four 19th-century brick cottages, and then some groups of early 20th-century dwellings. The first of these was originally a shop; at its rear in the first half of the 20th century was a farmyard with pigsties.

Well Yard

Then comes what must be one of the best-preserved older build-

Well Yard House, with the door of Griffin Cottage to the right. This doorway was moved around 1800 from the east gable end facing the road. (Photo by the author).

Well Yard House, the east elevation. Its doorway was originally where the ground floor window is now. (Photo by the author).

ings in Kingsthorpe; it now consists of two dwellings in Well Yard: *Well Yard House* and *Griffin Cottage*. These two very attractive houses (originally one, and still shown as one on the 1884 OS map) were proposed for demolition in 1971, but were fortunately rescued from that fate and restored to good habitable condition. *Well Yard House* is built of local stone; its two- and three-light mullioned window openings have drip mouldings to the three windows in the gable end (one of which is above eaves level) and to other ground floor windows.

A Grade II listed building, it is described as a "second half of 17th century vernacular house of two storeys and an attic. The main room has a chamfered stone chimney piece." Its steeply pitched roof indicates that it was originally thatched; it is now slated and there are two roof lights on the south. It was built with its gable end towards the road in order to allow the passage of farm carts, and Brooking thought that it was once known as *Grange Farm*. Attached to its west end is another Grade II listed house, currently known as *Griffin Cottage*, which is of very similar structure but lacks the stone mullioned windows; it was apparently built without any windows, the current wooden windows being later additions. It would seem that it was a late 17th- or early 18th-century extension to *Well Yard House*, providing kitchen and storage facilities. Its south elevation lines up with its neighbour, but the north elevation is at a slight angle. According to the report prepared by the Northampton Civic Society in 1971, its moulded stone door surround was moved, at the time of the extension, from the east gable end facing the road, where a window was inserted in its place; the evidence for this can be clearly seen. The present doorway to *Well Yard House* is a relatively modern insertion.

Another, smaller cottage is attached to the west end of *Griffin Cottage:* No.12 (currently The Cottage), which has a less steep fall to its roof and no stonework to door or windows. This was clearly erected at a later time than its neighbours, perhaps as much as a century later. Beyond this there used to stand a row of four cottages, facing east, but these have been replaced by modern development. A photograph of 1974 shows that they were of stone and slate construction, each having a casement window on the ground floor and a sash window on the first floor.

'Parson's End'

On the northern side of Well Yard stood a terrace of five early 19th-century coursed rubble stone cottages, now converted into two dwellings; these are Grade II listed buildings. Beyond these is an attractive 19th-century brick built cottage of three storeys (No. 45) set further back from the road. It has a central doorway, with seven windows forming an 'H' pattern. And then (No. 47) a late 17th- or early 18th-century stone house, also Grade II listed, which has kneelers to the stone copings of its gabled side elevations; it originally had

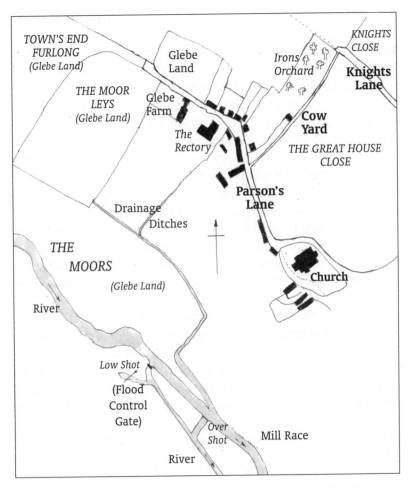

A sketch map of Parson's Lane at the end of the 18th century.

a thatched roof. It has an attic window in the south gable and a modern dormer at the rear.

On the other side of Vicarage Lane is another varied group of properties. Numbers 32 and 34 are coursed stone cottages with slate roofs, on three floors, with gabled dormers formed from a continuation of the front wall above the eaves. The front doors are set in gabled stone porches. The gabled dormers and front porches were not present in Alec Brooking's photograph of c.1967, when these properties more closely resembled numbers 44 & 46; he thought that different stone was then in evidence at all three floors, suggesting a successive raising of the front elevation from one to two and later to three stories. Comparing their present appearance with that of 1967, it is clear that the height above ground of the first and second floor windows has been increased - hence the dormers.

Adjoining them is a brick and slate house, No. 36, with large Georgian style sash windows, two on the ground floor to the left of the painted wooden door surround and hood, and three on the first floor. This property, *Dolphin Cottage*, was described in sale particulars in 2003 as late 18th century; the accompanying photographs showed that it is stone built at the rear. Next to this is a pair of Victorian houses, then a much smaller stone built cottage (No. 42), with the top of its first floor windows level with the bottom of those of the previous pair (38 & 40). Numbers 44 and 46, also built of stone, have entrances at the rear and are on three floors. They each have two windows on each floor, but without the use of dormers. The land on which they were built (probably in the late 18th century) belonged to the Rector in 1767; since they were built opposite the entrance to the Rectory, this may explain why they had their entrances at the rear.

Returning now to the other side of the road, next to No. 47 once stood the Rectory with its large garden surrounded by a high stone wall. It was actually the residence, across several centuries, for the Rectors of St Peter's, Northampton, with Kingsthorpe and Upton. It officially became a Vicarage in 1850, but its older name continued in use for a number of years after that. It was eventually demolished in the late 20th century. However, good photographic evidence of its appearance has enabled reconstruction of its complex history; a detailed description, together with information about some of the Rectors who lived there, will be found in the following chapter.

The Rectory was a commodious L-shaped building, the earliest portion of which cannot now be dated. In 1950 it ceased to be used as the Vicarage and was let in flats for a time, when it was known as *The Grange*. It was then demolished by a local builder, Keith Barker, to make room for some tasteful modern development; he discovered a date stone for 1632 and a roof timber bearing the date 1812, indicating at least two extensions. Its name is commemorated in Vicarage Close, on the north side of which are dwellings converted out of the farmhouse and, east of that, a barn belonging to the old Glebe Farm. By 1855 the farm buildings had fallen into disrepair, and a faculty was obtained in that year for the necessary improvements to be carried out.

Serjeantson (1904; pp.38, 113) says that the rectors of St Peter's lived at the Rectory in Kingsthorpe, usually officiating there and leaving St Peter's to be run by a curate. In 1850, when Kingsthorpe was separated from St Peter's as an independent parish, a new dwelling house had to be provided in Northampton for the rector of St Peter's. But the rectors did not always reside at Kingsthorpe; several of them were absentees, leaving the services to be carried out by a curate. This is shown by examination of the details of the various rectors between 1500 and 1850, as described by the Rev H I Longden in his book on the Northamptonshire and Rutland Clergy. It is also confirmed by an advertisement in the Northampton Mercury of 4 January 1747/8 for the letting of the Parsonage House at Kingsthorpe.

As stated by a witness in the footpath dispute of the early 19th century, James Fremeaux settled at Kingsthorpe in or about 1769 and rented the Parsonage House, where he and his family lived for five and a half years; he continued to pay rent for it and kept a servant there until 1786. It was from the Rectory in 1784 that Peter Fremeaux went for his accustomed swim in the river and so met his death by drowning:

> On Tuesday last, an Inquisition was taken by Robert Abbey, Gent. on the Body of Peter John Fremeaux, Esq., of Kingsthorpe, who was unfortunately drowned in the River, as he was going to bathe, according to his usual practice; when the Jury brought in their verdict: Accidental Death. (Northampton Mercury, 5 April 1784.)

At the very end of Vicarage Lane is a large field extending northwards, now used for horse grazing, which in 1767 was awarded to the Rector as 24 acres of Glebe land. Prior to that, it formed part of the open field system and was known as Towns End Furlong, or Parson's Townsend Furlong. This is the sole remaining portion of the ancient open fields of Kingsthorpe. The original strips or lands into which the furlong was divided can still be distinguished, particularly when the sun is low in the sky. Measurement of the width of some of these lands gives an average of 34 feet (about half a chain), which compares well with the widths recorded in a survey of the Robinson estate in Kingsthorpe in 1727. The southern boundary of this field is marked by an old stone wall, curving away towards the west and the river, and then by a hedge with a drainage ditch under it. The area to the south of this wall and hedge was an ancient inclosure known as The Moor Leys, which was bounded on the west, and thus separated from the river, by the North Moor Meadow - the northern half of The Moors. The drainage ditches in this area were once part of the system of 'common gutters' referred to in the local laws of 1547, which specified penalties for those who failed to keep them clear and free-flowing.

ENDNOTES

(1) Thomas Wakefield, cordwainer of Kingsthorpe, owned these cottages, or their predecessors, in 1734; he and his wife Frances occupied one cottage and John Walker the other. Thomas died, and his will was proved in April 1735. He left the property (along with other lands in Kingsthorpe) to his widow for life. When Frances died (her will being proved in November 1748), she left the property to her kinswoman Mary Dixon, daughter of Charles Dixon (Dickson) of Westminster, Merchant. Mary Dixon married James Bowker, a gentleman of London, in 1749 or 1750. He died in 1768, and his widow inherited the property.

In October 1827 there was an auction sale at the Cock Inn, Kingsthorpe, of a

'Dwelling House, near the Green, with Barn, Brewhouse, Garden and Orchard - about one rood - and a Close of two acres at the rear. Occupied by Chas. Gardner at an annual rent of £13:13:0. Also a cottage in tenure of James West - yearly rent £3:10:0. The estate has been in the possession of the present owner and her mother, Mary Bowker, for 80 years and upwards...'

Charles Gardner purchased this property at the auction for £560. It was conveyed to him by a Lease and Release on 15 & 16 February 1828 by

Charlotte Frances Bowker, daughter of Mary Bowker deceased - the latter being the widow of James Bowker. In this document Charles Gardner is described as a musician. On 18 February he mortgaged the property for 1,000 years to secure a loan of £400 from Mary Dunkley of Kingsthorpe, a widow. The mortgage deed is endorsed by Mary Dunkley with a receipt, dated 25 July 1833, for £415 - being principal and interest in full - acknowledging payment by Thomas Reeve Thornton, and undertaking to assign the mortgage to the latter when required. But the next document in this collection reveals that Charles Gardner had died in 1829. Probate was granted on 26 September 1829 in respect of his will, dated 5 January 1828, in which he describes himself as a clothier, and devises everything to his wife Elizabeth. T R Thornton of Brockhall, Lee Thornton of Park Street, London, and Thomas Dawes of Brockhall, a butler, were witnesses to the will. Finally, these properties, including the close of 1a.3r.19p., were conveyed by Elizabeth Gardner of Brockhall, widow of Charles Gardner deceased, musician, late of Kingsthorpe, to T R Thornton. At that time the Curate of Kingsthorpe, Rev Woodward, was living there, and Henry Turner leased the close. Thus, by this roundabout route, the cottages, outbuildings and land became part of the estates of the Thornton family. It may be that the cottages were rebuilt, or at least altered, by the Thorntons in the 19th century in a style similar to Fremeaux House.

(2) According to the records of the Thornton estate, in 1864 Mrs Rebecca Parbery was paying rent of £3:3:0 for a "cottage (Inn) and premises" as well as £16 for a "dwelling and orchard with land, in all 2a.1r.17p." In 1868 the same source states: "Mrs Rebecca Parbery's holding contains messuage, brewhouse, barn, garden, orchard and appurtenances containing by estimation nearly 2½ acres." This must have been the property now known as 25 Green End; its description is the same as the property conveyed to T R Thornton by Charles Gardner's widow. This is confirmed by the mention of the footpath in an entry dated May 1871 in the previously quoted Thornton notebook:

> Rebecca Parbery's W orchard wall 6 yards down and 18 want rebuilding: height from footpath 9 feet and 4½ within.

Rebecca was a widow, her husband William having died in 1861. The census of that year shows him as the head of two households: a house then known as (44) Duck Lane, where only four of his children lived, and (56) Duck Lane, a Beer House, where he carried on his business of Publican and Pork Butcher. (The numbers in parentheses refer to entries on the census return; they do not indicate the number of properties in Duck Lane.) In the

1871 census Rebecca is a 'Beer House Keeper' living at the 'King William' in Duck End. Her son William, described as 'Shoemaker and Grocer', also lived in Duck End along with his wife and three young children. There were other Parberys living in Duck End (as well as elsewhere in Kingsthorpe) as shown by the census returns and by the records of the Thornton estate, which owned a number of cottages there at that time.

In 1873 Rebecca paid a total of £11 rent up to Lady Day; then she paid £4:4:0 for the half year up to Michaelmas for the King William and £2:16:0 for a close or field. Since she paid £8:8:0 p.a. instead of £3:3:0, this *may* indicate that the property had been rebuilt, and the fact that the census refers to the 'King William' indicates that it was a public house then, as opposed to a cottage used as a beer house. These rents remained the same until, in November 1875, William Parbery began to make the payments. Rebecca (or Rebekah as it is sometimes spelled) had obviously retired in that year, and the 1881 census shows her living in a cottage two doors down from the King William IV; the cottage in between was uninhabited. William, a Beer House Keeper, was then living at the public house; perhaps a further indication that it may have been rebuilt by then is that his wife and seven children also lived there.

In March 1882 Mary Thornton records in her diary that her mother gave William Parbery notice to quit at the following Michaelmas; this presumably relates to the cottage that now forms part of Green End Cottage. Perhaps it was following the end of his tenancy that the cottage was altered.

Historical Diversion:
KINGSTHORPE RECTORY AND SOME OF ITS INHABITANTS

The Rectors of St Peter's with Kingsthorpe and Upton lived at a Rectory or Parsonage House in Kingsthorpe. This was situated at Town's End or Parson's End, the end of what was then known as Parson's Lane and is now Vicarage Lane. When Kingsthorpe became an independent parish with its own Vicar in 1850, the Rectory eventually became known as the Vicarage; it continued in the occupation of various incumbents until 1950. It was then let in flats for a few years, when it was known as The Grange, but was eventually demolished in 1969 to make room for some attractive domestic development. The present Vicarage Close marks the northern boundary of its garden.

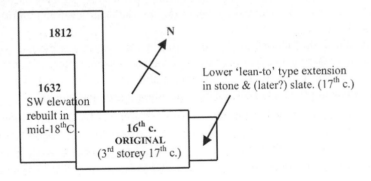

Prior to its demolition, the Borough Engineer & Surveyor's Department took a series of photographs of the old Vicarage, prints of which are in the possession of English Heritage, National Monuments Record, at Swindon. These reveal a most interesting building with a complex architectural history. Its appearance was probably unknown to many people, apart from those who actually visited it, since it was not clearly visible behind its high stone walls.

The hypothetical history of the Rectory is as follows: it began life as a symmetrical stone and thatch building of two storeys and a cellar, with its front facing north-west. Judging by features that

The old Rectory, or Parsonage House, from the north-east. It originally had only two floors, and the right hand wing was added in two later stages. (Picture courtesy of Northampton Borough Council).

remained in the rear elevation, it must have dated from the 16th century, but some extensive modifications were made to the front elevation at a later date, when the roof was tiled. This may have taken place in the early 17th century. The Hearth Tax return for 1674 states that the Rev Reynolds had nine hearths, but the original building had only two chimney stacks, which were unlikely to have supported so many hearths. But there is clear evidence that the early building had been extended: during the 20th-century demolition, a date stone for 1632 and a roof timber bearing the date 1812 were discovered. The sketch plan (not to scale) indicates the probable growth-phases of the building.

The date stone of 1632 was found in what had been the north-west gable wall of that extension, and it also bore the name of Samuel Clerke, who was the Rector at that time. The photographic evidence indicates that this early extension to the south-west of the original building must have been much modified, particularly its south-west

The old Rectory, south-east elevation. This clearly shows a mixture of dates and styles of window. (Picture courtesy of Northampton Borough Council).

elevation, in the 18th century. The same photograph clearly shows where the later (1812) extension was made to the north-west. At the same time, this wing of the house was extended north-eastwards towards the original front door, thus obscuring part of this elevation.

From the evidence of the photographs, the original building had its front elevation, which was of ashlar construction, raised in order to provide a third storey with dormer windows to three attic rooms. There was a difference in the colour of the stones forming the para-

pet and the north-east gable verges; an attic window was also inserted in this gable. Below this a 'lean-to' type two-storey extension was
built of coursed rubble, with a single roof fall towards the north-east.
The upper windows of this were of 17th-century type, with square
lead cames. The front of the original main building had a central door
with a tall window to the north-east, providing light to the staircase.
At some stage, this window-opening was extended to the ground so
that another door could be inserted. Upstairs there were presumably
three symmetrically-positioned windows with square lead cames,
although the windows on the ground and first floors to the south-
west of the door disappeared within the 1812 extension.

The rear elevation of the original building had a mixture of windows, some in strange positions, but none of them to the third storey.
At least one of the windows appeared to be of the 16th century, with
stone mullions and diamond shaped lead cames, though others had
obviously been 'modernised' at various times during the 17th, 18th
or even 19th centuries.

The extension made in 1632 (and modified in the 18th century)
was a little offset from the building line of the original. Its roof had a
much shallower slope, so its ridge was noticeably lower, and it had a
chimney stack at each gable. Of course, this roof may not have been
the original, but part of the later modification. The photograph of the
south-west elevation indicates a date in the second half of the 18th
century. Its sash windows were clearly of this date, and some were
set in recessed arches – very similar to those designed for
Kingsthorpe Hall by John Johnson in 1774, although those at the
Rectory were probably earlier than that. One large window on the
ground floor extended right down to the ground, so that the lower
sash could be lifted to give access to the garden. The glass panes in
the sashes of this window were large, extending the whole height
and divided by only one glazing bar in each sash. The glazing bars in
all these windows were narrow, and this, combined with the size of
the panes just mentioned, points quite clearly to the mid-to-late 18th
century at the earliest.

The 19th-century work extended this south-western elevation further to the north-west, with another large window giving access to

The old Rectory, south-west elevation. The right-hand portion of this wing was originally built in 1632, and a further addition made in 1812; the butt-joint can be clearly seen. (Picture courtesy of Northampton Borough Council).

the garden, but this time using 'French Doors'. This building was butt-jointed up to the quoins of the earlier one, so the line was clearly visible all the way up to the side of a new window on the first floor. An additional chimney stack was built on the new north-west gable, the older one thus serving as further evidence of the modifications. Internally, this resulted in a very thick wall between the older rooms and the new ones. At the same time, this portion of the L-shaped Rectory was widened to allow corridor access to the rooms in the new extension. Complex roof structures were avoided by extending a flat lead-covered roof towards the north-east, with the new wall rising to a parapet; this was the cause of leaks when snow melted on this roof, so later occupants had to sweep it clear, gaining access by means of the south-western-most dormer window.

From examination of Serjeantson's invaluable research of the

Rectors of St Peter's with Kingsthorpe and Upton, it seems unlikely that any of them lived at Kingsthorpe before the 16th century. William Bretteyn was Rector from 1534 to 1552, but he had many other preferments and appears to have lived in Westminster. In the Kingsthorpe PRs there is a burial on 29 May 1547 of "Bennett Davy, Parson & Priest". There is no other record of him as Rector but, following William Bretteyn, we have Edmund Davye (note the surname) who was Rector 1552-1559; he desired to be buried "in the Chapel of the Church of St Peter's." In 1561 William Roote was said to be "Rector: No degree: Priest: Learned: Resides there: Has no other benefice." The will of Sir John Harryson, ('Sir' was a normal title for a priest at this period) Rector of Brampton, dated 12 July 1557, was witnessed by "William Root, Curate of Kingsthorpe"; so he was presumably promoted to Rector on the death of Edmund Davye in late 1559. It is likely that he lived at Kingsthorpe, but in his will he asked to buried in the chancel of St Peter's.

The records of other Rectors provide no real evidence of residence until we come to Dr Samuel Clerke, who became Rector in November 1608 on the presentation of Francis Morgan of Kingsthorpe. He also held the position of Rector of Winwick, along with St Peter's, from 1614 until his death in 1641. His first wife bore him 14 children and Serjeantson tells us that "The parish registers of Kingsthorpe contain frequent references to the baptisms, marriages, and burials of Dr Clerke's large family." Examination of the PRs confirms this: baptisms begin in September 1616, followed by eleven more from October 1617 to February 1634, all being children of Dr Samuel Clerke and his wife Margaret. She clearly died as a result of that last birth and was buried a few days later. In September 1635 he married Mrs Katherine Sympson in Canterbury Cathedral, and there are three more baptisms recorded at Kingsthorpe between 1638 and 1640. Not all these children survived, of course: five burials of Margaret's children are recorded, and two of the three children of his second wife. There is also a burial, in February 1618, of Stephen Graves, "servant to Mr Sam Clerke DD".

So here is a Rector who clearly resided in Kingsthorpe, and he had a large family that required a large house and servants. It was during his tenure that the Rectory was extended, no doubt to house his growing family. Perhaps it was also he who added the attic rooms, for nursery and servant use, and the two-storey north-eastward extension. Unlike most Northamptonshire clergy of the time, Dr Clerke was apparently not a poor man. His will, dated 5 March 1641, has been lost, but it is quoted in the minute book of *'The committee for sequestrations sitting at Northampton for the Parliament, 1644'* which shows that he held several closes and pastures in the parishes of Norton and Welton; these would have produced additional income.

Robert Hill was the next Rector, being instituted in April 1641. He apparently resided here, for there are six baptisms recorded of children of Robert and Joane Hill between 1644 and 1649. Mrs Hill's burial is recorded in December 1650, and H I Longden (vij 15-17) records a second marriage, to Mrs Elizabeth Fichreoffery (Fitzgeoffrey?) of Northampton, at All Saints church on 2 June 1655. He also says that Robert Hill was probably buried at Kingsthorpe in 1658, his will having been proved in that year (PCC 576 Wootton). Serjeantson (p.96) suggests James Williams as the next Rector, on the basis of a mention of him in the Augmentation Books in the Lambeth Palace Library, where he is described as a "minister of the gospell att St Peter's in Northton" in an entry dated February 1654/5. But it seems most likely that this indicates his position as a Curate there: see below.

Edward Reynolds, who paid Hearth Tax on nine hearths in 1674, was Rector from 1658 (the year of Robert Hill's death, be it noted!) to 1698. He also had a large family of six daughters and seven sons, twelve of them recorded in the parish registers of Kingsthorpe along with details of five of their marriages. Philip Atkinson, Rector from December 1698 until his death in 1702, also appears to have lived here; there is a baptism recorded at Kingsthorpe in March 1701 of "Lewis Bulkeley, the son of Philip Atkinson, Doctor of Divinity and rector, and the Honble. Catherine his wife." Welbore Ellis became Rector in 1702, but resigned his living in 1705, when he became Bishop of Kildare.

The details of the next two incumbents seem to have little to add to the history of the Rectory, and they were probably both non-resident, as indicated by an advertisement in the Northampton Mercury of 4 January 1747/8 for the letting of the Parsonage House at Kingsthorpe. It describes it as "fit for a gentleman's family" and included among other things a brew-house, stables, dove-house, and a pond stocked with fish.

Richard Reynolds was Rector from 1706, and he held the position, along with all his other preferments, until his death in 1744. He was Bishop of Bangor from December 1721 and subsequently of Lincoln from 1723. He died in Westminster and was buried in Buckden, Hunts, so he was clearly not often seen in these parts during the later years of his incumbency. Edward Patterson was Rector of St Peter's from 1744 until his death in April 1750, and it was during his term of office that the above advertisement appeared.

During the years 1750 to 1850 there were only two Rectors: Edward Lockwood 1750-1802 and Robert William Baxter 1802-1850. In 1750 the Rev Mr Lockwood was appointed to the rectories of Hanwell in Oxfordshire and St Peter's in Northampton, and was granted a dispensation allowing him to hold both livings. He held them both for the next 52 years until his death at the age of 82. He was married three times, twice to heiresses, and was the father of nine children, six of whom survived him. Baptisms are recorded at Kingsthorpe from 1753 to 1764, and in the April of that year his first wife, Lucy, was buried. There are no further entries in these parish registers, so he may well have been non-resident soon after the death of Lucy.

He was instrumental in the process of inclosure of the common fields of Kingsthorpe in 1766-7, as a result of which he was awarded 17% of the total land involved; he was granted permission to let this out to tenants. James Fremeaux came to live at the Rectory with his family in 1769 or 1770, and in February 1770 the Rev Lockwood married for the second time. According to one of the witnesses called in a footpath dispute in the early 19th century, Mr Lockwood was "a man of considerable fortune worth £5,000 per annum, and resided in London...and that the Parsonage House was for many years occupied by one of his sons." The Peterborough Diocesan Records say that he lived on his own estate near Epping in Essex, that he was over 80 years of age and unable to perform his duties as Rector; those duties were undertaken by the Curate, Mr Tufnall, who lived in Northampton. Mr Lockwood was excused appearances at Bishops' Triennial Visitations to Northampton from 1795 onwards; but he did not always appear on earlier occasions, being excused in 1774, 1777, and 1783.

The above gives strong indication that it was Mr Lockwood who modified Samuel Clerke's extension at some time between 1750 and 1770. The final extension, from the evidence of the timber dated 1812 (which also bore the name W Gore, who was a carpenter from Dallington) was carried out during the tenure of Rev R W Baxter, the last Rector of St Peter's to reside at Kingsthorpe.

In 1850 Kingsthorpe became an independent parish with its own Vicar, and the Rectory became the Vicarage – although still referred to as the Rectory for some years, as indicated by the diaries of Mary Susan Thornton from 1874 onwards. In 1950, during the incumbency of the Rev Andrews, the parish acquired a new Vicarage in the shape of a large attractive brick and tile-hung house at the bottom of The Leys, overlooking the Green and the church; the Thornton family had originally built this 'Villa' in 1888. When the Team Ministry was implemented in 1973 the Vicar, the Rev Wolstenhulme, became known as the Rector once more, and his dwelling thus became known as the Rectory. But this house became too large and too expensive to maintain, so a new, more modest Rectory was provided in Green End in 1979 by enlarging an existing modern dwelling.

WALK NUMBER THREE

This walk begins at No.1 The Green, east of the King's Well, across the triangular green. This is the first of a terrace of three similar stone-built cottages, but No. 1 is double fronted. The front elevations of these three were obviously rebuilt at some time in the early 19th century, judging by their large sash windows. Details of their history will be found in *Endnote 1*. The terrace continues with an older stone cottage on three floors, which appears to have been converted from two original cottages of the 18th century.

The bungalows opposite were part of a development in the 1930s known as the Green Estate, on land that once formed part of the old Great House Close; the two-bedroom bungalows were let at 10/2d per week. Alec Brooking says that, following an outcry, Mr F H Thornton of Kingsthorpe Hall stopped further development; he gave the

No.1 The Green. The original structure can be seen in the side elevation, the frontage having been rebuilt with large sash windows. (Photo by the author).

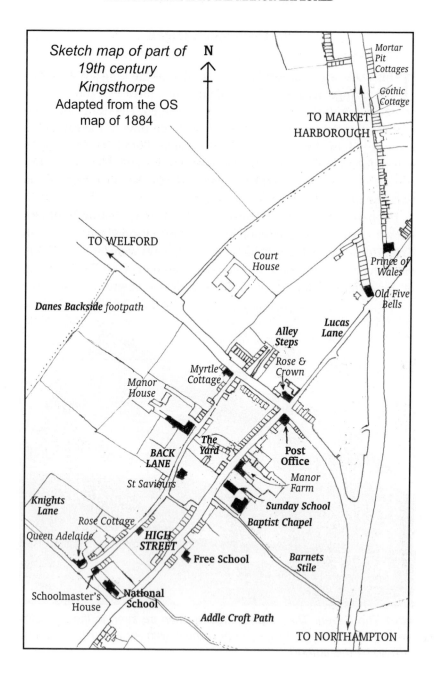

Sketch map of part of 19th century Kingsthorpe
Adapted from the OS map of 1884

remaining portion of the field to the Village as a gift. This land was later used for the new C of E Primary School, and the children had the benefit of a pleasant setting for the early years of their school life.

High Street

On the corner of Knights Lane is the old National School, the original portion of which was built in 1840. It then comprised two classrooms and central living accommodation for the Master. A later extension in the same style was added to the east in 1892, and the building had further additions in the early years of the 20th century. Following the opening of the new school in 1962, the building was used as a youth centre for a number of years. At the time of writing it is being carefully restored to its late 19th-century form externally and converted internally to living accommodation. To the north, on the corner of Knights Lane and Manor Road, stands the Master's House that was built in the second half of the 19th century, when the accommodation in the original school became totally inadequate. This house was sold off in 1968.

High Street, looking east, at around 1900. The cottage that was then 16 High Street is on the left of the picture. (Picture courtesy of Alan J Clarke).

22 and 24 High Street. There is clear evidence of the raising of the eaves of number 24, probably when the thatch was replaced with slates. (Photo by the author).

26 and 28 High Street. (Photo by the author).

16 High Street at around 1890; this was the home of John Parbery, house painter and photographer. (Picture courtesy of Robert Hounslow).

Opposite the old school is the entrance to Addlecroft Path, which takes its name from that of the land lying between High Street and the main road. The area was known as Haddlecroft or Addlecroft; this name may perhaps be derived from one of the meanings of 'addle', barren or empty, since the land lies mainly on a north-facing slope. To the right of this path, and further up the slope, stands Addlecroft House, built in the late 19th or early 20th century. On the left side of the path (Old Yew Court), and to right of the gateway to the house (High Green), can be seen the remains of old stone pits; it seems likely that these were originally quarried for the building of cottages in High Street; they are mentioned by Diana Sutherland on page 60 of her fascinating book *Northamptonshire Stone*.

Proceeding in a north-easterly direction up High Street, which was clearly the most densely populated part of the old village, it is clear that the original properties here have undergone much conversion, demolition and rebuilding during the past century or more. The 25-inch OS Map of 1884 gives a picture that is very different from what is there today; but some interesting remains are still visible in this area.

Further along the south-east side can be seen an attractive terrace of (early 19th century?) cottages, numbered 13-19. They are constructed of roughly squared stone with slate roofs, front doors that originally opened into the parlours, and sash windows with flat arches formed by stone lintels. Then there is the converted remains of the old Free School, currently known as *High Point*. This was apparently the third school building on the site, and dates from 1870; it could be mistaken for an old chapel. Part of its original gable front can be seen, but its elevation to the south-west gives a better impression of its original structure. Crossing over The Rise and passing the modern development (25-29), numbers 31-37b form a pleasant terrace of Victorian houses with bay windows. At the end of this terrace is the footway known as Barnet's Stile, on the other side of which is the Baptist Chapel, opened in 1835 and enlarged in 1892; a Sunday School was opened next to the Chapel in 1881.

On the north-west side of the road, above the old National School, numbers 6-14 appear to be a Victorian terrace, followed by modern dwellings. But number 22 is an older two-storey house of sandstone, with its symmetrical front elevation covered with painted stucco. Its gable end has a parapet with kneelers, and the remains of the chimney stack contains old bricks. Its windows are not original, and may once have been sashes. Number 24 is a two-storey house with a much steeper pitch to the roof, which was originally thatched but is now slated. Part of the gable parapet is still visible to the north-east, but it disappears towards the eaves, indicating a lifting of the front elevation at the time it was slated; this is confirmed by the use of brickwork, above the lower stonework, to raise the level of the upstairs windows and the eaves. The three sash windows that remain are probably late 18th century, the fourth having once been a shop window. Number 26 is built of brick, with the lighter coloured headers making an attractive pattern. The windows have flat brick lintels; the

Right: 49 High Street, the south-west gable. This includes an attractive pattern produced by the use of triangular stones. (Photo by the author).

Below: 49 High Street, elevation to the street. There is some evidence here that it may originally consisted of two cottages, perhaps merged when they were re-roofed. (Photo by the author).

Kingsthorpe Post Office in the late 19th century. William Kelsey, whose name appears over the doorway, was listed as sub-postmaster in 1884 but not in 1898; it may be he who is standing outside the door in this picture. (Picture courtesy of Robert Hounslow).

doorway is arched, and probably not original. Number 28 appears to be of similar style but with a wider frontage, which has been rendered, so the structure is not visible. Numbers 30-38 form what appears to be another Victorian terrace ending at Danes Passage, a footway that links High Street to Manor Road; it was named after one of the main 19th-century land owners in the village. This is followed by a row of modern dwellings, 38a-38d and 40a.

Stable Court

On the other side, next to some more modern development, is number 49, which used to be *Manor Farm*, and now has its entrance at the rear in Stable Court. The gable that faces south-west is of a most interesting and attractive construction, consisting of narrow courses of small stones alternating with much wider courses of large stones; but the latter are not only square or rectangular, but very frequently of triangular shape, laid with their points alternating upward and downward. The pattern thus produced is not absolutely precise, but sufficiently uniform so as to give a very distinctive appearance.

The north-west elevation to High Street indicates that number 49 was originally two houses; certainly there are two types of stonework and two types of window openings, and the division corresponds with the chimney of old brick. The wall of the south-west portion of the frontage is mainly of well squared rubble laid to courses; it contains one ground floor window with its original stone mullions, though they are now very thickly painted over; another window with a wooden lintel could once have been a doorway. The north-east portion is of coursed rubble, and its lower windows have flat arches of stone voussoirs. All the upper windows have wooden lintels. The roof is of slate and there is a toothed cornice at the eaves, formed of brick headers with concave quadrant mouldings. The north-east gable is of rubble, and shows signs of alteration at some period; it originally formed one side of the entrance to the old stable yard, which was bridged over at first floor level. The rear elevation, around the corner in Stable Court, has a tall first floor window with a semi-circular top with correspondingly shaped glazing bars. The present house is L-shaped, with its entrance door in part of the old stables, which are constructed of a mixture of stone and brick. This example of vernacular architecture (possibly dating back to the late 17th century?) deserves to be a Listed building. To the north-east of Stable Court are some remaining portions of an old high stone wall with pantile coping.

The Yard

The remainder of High Street on this side consists mainly of a terrace of 19th or early 20th-century houses. On the other side numbers 40-44 have brick elevations to the road, but the gable ends of this group are of stone, with old brick used in the stacks. At the side of 44 there was once an entrance to a Yard containing four small cottages. Next to this entrance was a small garden and then numbers 46-52, but these have now been replaced with modern dwellings. It appears from some lawyer's notes that Joseph Litchfield, a 'Dissenting Minister', once occupied the original number 46 here; for details, see *Endnote 2*. The Rev. Joseph Litchfield was the pastor of Kingsthorpe Baptist Church from 1848 to 1891; he was also Master of the Free School from 1852 until 1888. Numbers 56-62 are obviously old, but their structural details are no longer visible at the front; however, their rear elevations are of coursed rubble with small windows, and may be 18th century.

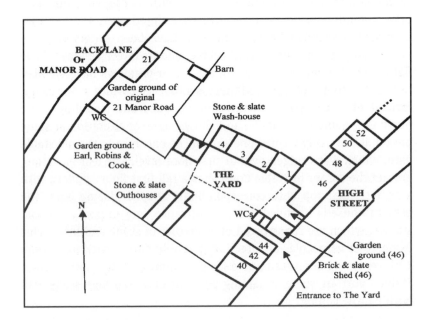

Sketch plan of The Yard
The Yard had an entrance passageway between 44 & 46 High Street. This sketch plan is based on the OS map of 1884 and some lawyer's notes relating to the estate of the Danes family c.1909.

Welford Road to Harborough Road

At the top of High Street, at the junction with Welford Road, to the north are two pairs of attractive buildings constructed of a combination of stone and brick, with some decorative half-timbering. On the other corner of High Street is an empty plot where the Post Office used to stand during the 19th and early 20th centuries; further to the south along Welford Road are some 19th-century business premises of three storeys, with a warehouse door on the first floor.

High Street used to continue on the other side of Welford Road, through to Harborough Road; during the 18th century this portion was known as Johnson's Lane. The building of a petrol station has now offset the entrance to this part of High Street, but prior to this the first property on the north-west side was the *Rose & Crown* public house. The short terrace of Victorian dwellings that stood beyond it is still in existence; the flat arches to their windows and doors have alternate red and blue bricks as their voussoirs, and the doors have fanlights. At the junction with Harborough Road is the public house that was known for many years as *The Old Five Bells*, and kept in 1830 by Robert Lucas; this part of High Street was known as Lucas Lane during the later 19th century.

Across the main road, in the acute-angled junction of Boughton Green Road and Harborough Road is another public house, the *Prince of Wales*. This is mentioned in Wright's Directory of 1884, with William Thomas Flavell as the publican. In the decades following the Inclosure (1767), the frontages running from this Inn along both these roads were sold off for housing development, so there are many 19th-century houses in this area.

To the north of the junction of High Street and Harborough Road, on the west side of the latter, there is a terrace of eight two-storey cottages (86-100) in sandstone, with slate roofs and brick stacks, probably dating from the late 18th or early 19th century. They have wooden window lintels to the first floor and flat arches of stone voussoirs to the ground floor. At the southern end a later brick cottage has been added. At the north end of the row is a stone house on three floors, number 102, with later artificial stone surrounds inserted to the windows and doorway. Attached to its rear is what could

The terrace of cottages to the north of the High Street/Harborough Road junction. (Photo by the author).

Cottages, or old workshops, to the rear of 102 Harborough Road. (Photo by the author).

have been two small stone cottages, or possibly workshops, with small sash windows to the first floor.

Boughton Green Road

On the north side of Boughton Green Road, just before the more modern development begins, is a three-storey house, number 89, with its front elevation of ashlar construction; no doubt the stone was obtained from the quarry that used to exist to its rear. At the top of the hill stands the attractive *Hill House*, built of brick, with three floors at the front but only two in the rear wing, the windows being taller there. This house was once known as Dunkley's Lodge. The remains of one of Kingsthorpe's old windmills stands on the other side of Boughton Green Road; it was turned into a house around 1900 by Mr Thomas Wilson. This is a Grade II Listed Building, officially described as follows:

Early 19th century tower windmill, altered and no longer used as a mill. Coursed rubble battered tower of three storeys with parapet hid-

Hill House, Boughton Green Road, once known as Dunkley's Lodge. (Photo by the author).

ing roof. Modern casement and sash windows. Additions to east and west of whitewashed brick and roughcast with Welsh slated roofs, one storey and one storey and attic.

Harborough Road

On the east side of Harborough Road, at the back of the Prince of Wales, stands what used to be some small cottages, but which are now one dwelling. A wall plate states that these were once called *Newland Cottages*, standing in Newland Square. Continuing from here in a northerly direction is an enormously varied collection of dwellings. Along with some terraces of 19th- or early 20th-century houses, there are several groups of stone cottages with flat window and door arches of stone voussoirs, some with quite wide flush sashes indicating early 19th-century construction. The sashes of 139 & 141, for example, are four panes wide, rather than the more usual three. Next to them is *Stoke House* (145) of early 19th-century ashlar construction with three stone bay windows to the front elevation and a long extension to the rear of stone and of brick. Examination

Newland Cottages, Harborough Road, next to the Prince of Wales. (Photo by the author).

230

139 and 141 Harborough Road. Note the wide, flush sashes, indicating early 19th-century construction. (Photo by the author).

Stoke House, Harborough Road. Its southern portion is integrated with number 141. (Photo by the author).

Gothic Cottage, Harborough Road, with quaintly decorated barge-boards to its twin gables. (Photo by the author).

The terrace of cottages which once stood on the western side of the Harborough Road, where Wallbeck Close now stands. (Picture courtesy of Alan J Clarke).

154 Harborough Road, which has its gable end to the road. (Photo by the author).

of the frontage of this house clearly shows that the south end, with its bay, are of the same construction, and integrated with, numbers 139 and 141; only the northern part, which contains the front door and two bays, are of ashlar construction. The four cottages that used to be 147-153 have been converted into two dwellings, 147 & 151, by blocking up two door openings, and they now have modern tiles to the roof. Then there is the detached house called *Gothic Cottage* (155), also early 19th-century, with its twin gables at the front and quaintly decorated barge-boards. Numbers 139, 141 and 145 to 155 on this side of the road are Grade II listed buildings with group value.

Just before reaching Chalcombe Road stands a cottage (175) that Diana Sutherland *(Northamptonshire Stone* p.70) says is built of the famous white Kingsthorpe freestone, also used for Kingsthorpe Hall and other buildings in the area. She also believes that the row of cottages opposite, now demolished, and parts of No. 154 were also constructed in this material. Beyond Chalcombe Road lies much modern development, but there is one, originally isolated, detached stone

*Wardington Court, previously known as the Court House, and origi-
nally as Court Farm. (Photo by the author).*

Wardington Court, north elevation. (Photo by the author).

house (now number 247) with a slate roof and stone stack, its front is in ashlar, with a stone bay. The gable ends have attic windows, and to the south there is a later ground floor extension.

Crossing the road, to the south of Glan-y-Mor Terrace is the *Fox & Hounds* public house; its north gable is stone, with a panel proclaiming its early ownership by the Northampton Brewery Co. To the south of this there once stood the terrace of cottages mentioned above, set well back from the road with their gardens in front; but these were demolished in the 20th century to make way for the modern housing of Wallbeck Close. Then there is a symmetrical fronted two-storey cottage (154) facing south, with its gable end to the road, constructed of ashlar at the front and squared stone otherwise. It has gable parapets and stone voussoir flat arches to the ground floor windows and door. There is a lower extension to the west, which may have been formed from the remains of the other cottages that used to extend in that direction according to the 1884 OS map. This plot of land, 33 perches in extent, was granted to B and T Cuffley in 1767.

To the south of the cottage just described is the Recreation Ground, across which one can return to Welford Road. The Thornton family once owned the land between these two roads and, on 21 November 1912, 21 acres between Harborough Road and Welford Road adjoining the *Court House* were sold to the Northampton Corporation for a Recreation Ground. The *Court House* is now *Wardington Court*, but in the mid-19th century it was *Court Farm*, referred to by George James de Wilde in his *Rambles Roundabout & Poems*. In 1767 this farmhouse was in the ownership of Richard Wood; the Thornton family subsequently rebuilt it, and it was then either leased out or occupied by members of the Thornton family. Irvine Walter Douglas was listed as resident at Court House in 1885, according to Kelly's Directory.

Alley Steps

Turning left, past the entrance to *Wardington Court*, is Kingsthorpe Clinic, where seven cottages stood in the 19th century, and then there are the steps that give access to a pair of bungalows (14 & 16). At this point in the early 20th century there stood twelve cottages in what was known as Alley Yard or Alley Steps. As the name implies,

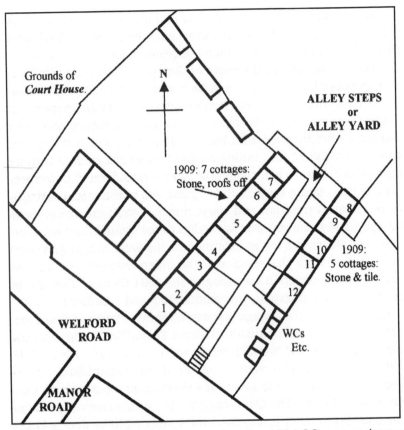

Grounds of
Court House.

N

ALLEY STEPS
or
ALLEY YARD

1909: 7 cottages:
Stone, roofs off

7

6

5

4

3

2

1

8

9

10

11

12

1909:
5 cottages:
Stone & tile.

WELFORD
ROAD

WCs
Etc.

MANOR
ROAD

A Sketch plan of Alley Steps based on the 1884 OS map and some lawyers' notes of c.1909.

these dwellings were also approached by steps from Welford Road; there were two facing terraces of seven (to the north) and five (to the south) at right angles to the road. The 1884 OS map shows nine properties in the northern terrace. In her diary for 1878, Mary Susan Thornton, of Kingsthorpe Hall, records a number of visits to Annie and Eliza Warren at 'Up Steps'; no doubt this was yet another name for these cottages.

Manor Road

On the other side of the road is the entrance to Manor Road (previously known as Back Lane). At its junction with Welford Road can be seen, on the north side, the 2½-storey *Myrtle House*, 41 Welford Road, previously known as *Myrtle Cottage* and, according to a recent owner, built in 1752. The angle of its roof clearly indicates that it was initially thatched. A photograph of 1962 shows that there were then two cottages, but the northern one, since demolished, had only one window on each floor. Evidence of the existence of that cottage remains in the north gable of *Myrtle House*, which lacks a gable parapet and has exposed purlin ends; it may be that the two cottages were converted from an earlier large house. In 1962 the roof of these cottages appears to have been of corrugated material. Attached to them at that period were two other, later cottages; a large one of stone and slate construction, with sash windows downstairs and casements upstairs; and a smaller cottage of brick and slate, with one casement window downstairs and a sash window upstairs.

On the south-east side of Manor Road stands a cottage that obviously incorporates some old structure, but is now rendered in such a way as to obscure its original elevation. Examination of the 1884 OS map indicates that there have been some significant alterations in this area. Then there are some 19th and 20th century dwellings as far as number 21, next to the entrance to Danes Passage. The large detached house now numbered 21 was originally *St Saviour's Home*; In Kelly's Directory of 1894 and 1898 Miss L Ensor is described as the Lady Superior. The Home was still listed in 1903; see *Endnote 2.*

On the north-west side of Manor Road stands a very attractive terrace of four cottages (numbers 2-8). These are of roughly squared rubble, with slate roofs. Brick was used around the door and window openings, with curved brick arches over each. The end cottages have large sandstone quoins. Next to these cottages stands Manor House (number 10), now the Presbytery of St Aidan's Roman Catholic Church; the church was built in 1964 on what had been part of the orchard and garden of Manor House. This used to be the farmhouse of the Danes family, who owned much land and property in the area, as well as in Northampton; they played a significant part in the life

The terrace of cottages, numbered 2 to 8, Manor Road. (Photo by the author).

Manor House, south elevation. This was once the farmhouse of the Danes family. (Photo by the author).

of the Parish, particularly during the 19th century. In the early 20th century the house came into the ownership of the Perkins family, whose members also played significant parts in Kingsthorpe's history. It is built of roughly squared rubble laid to courses, with some string courses of darker stone. Alec Brooking says of this property:

A two-storey house (c.1820-30?) in sandstone with a hipped roof in slate. The chimney stacks do not have early brick. The thickness of the walls and timber beams across the ground floor ceilings suggest an earlier dating, but there are no authorities for this. The west elevation has two bay windows (balanced either side of a door similar to the front door), whilst to the north there is a terrace of cottages and barns adjoining the house and now one with it. In the gable end of the barn is a date stone '1843', but it is not obvious whether this applies to the house also. Another date stone '1825' is now let into the boundary wall behind the R C Church built in the grounds of Manor House. History of this not ascertained.

Modern concrete tiles have, sadly, replaced the slate roof. The northern stone outbuildings actually consisted of storage rooms, servants living quarters, granary, dairy, &c. In the gable wall of these

Manor House, west elevation. (Photo by the author).

there were once two holes allowing barn owls to nest in the roof timbers; where grain was stored there would be vermin, and barn owls would help to control these. The holes have now been filled with brick, so their position can still be noted. The date stone in the boundary wall also includes the initials C D, presumably for Charles Danes the elder.

Modern dwellings now occupy the remainder of the north side of Manor Road, but the south side still has some older cottages. Numbers 23-33 are of stone, with brick edges and arches to their openings, and 35-43 are of brick construction. Particular mention must be made of *Rose Cottage*, (45) which dates from 1647; it has its windowless rear wall to the road and its front, now rendered and much modernised, faces south-east. Tradition has it that this cottage was used in the 19th century as a Dame School; see the chapter *The Infant Schools*. Then there is a pair of 20th-century houses built in a central european style. Adjoining the old Master's House, mentioned earlier, are four cottages (55-61) that were rebuilt in the 20th century; they have stone elevations to the front and modern brick extensions to the rear.

On the opposite side, at the junction with Knights Lane, stands the *Queen Adelaide* public house, which was apparently built in the 18th century (1760?). Its gable ends used to rise above a slate roof, but it now has a modern tile roof; its casement windows have wooden lintels. In the outer wall of its car park indications have been retained of the entrances to a row of cottages that once stood next to the inn. Cornelius Love kept a beer house here in the early 19th century; he is listed as a beer retailer in Kelly's County Directory of 1847, but he had to supplement his income by making shoes and butchering. He apparently slaughtered cattle in the yard at the rear. He described himself in the trade directories as a publican in 1861 and as a beer retailer in 1869 and 1877. In Wright's Directory of 1884 Thomas Love in listed as a publican at the *Queen Adelaide*. In Kelly's Directory of 1903 Richard W Love of Manor Road was listed as a beer retailer, so this public house stayed in the same family for at least three generations.

The Queen Adelaide public house, at the junction of Knights Lane and Manor Road. The building probably dates back to the mid-18th century; in older photographs its gable ends rose above a slate roof, and it may originally have been thatched. It seems to have begun to be used as a beerhouse, run by Cornelius Love, around 1815. (Photo by the author).

ENDNOTES

(1) Number One The Green, previously 1 High Street.

The history of this row of cottages is rather interesting. The collection of deeds relating to them begins with an Indenture dated 29 September 1725, when the properties consisted of a house, a shop, a dairy and a meal-house. It is not clear whether these deeds refer to the whole row of cottages, but it seems most likely that only the first three are involved – particularly since No.1 is double fronted. Further Indentures are dated 21 March 1736/7 and 15 September 1752; the latter refers to Josiah Kenning, a shepherd, and his son Robert Kenning, who was being apprenticed to learn 'the art or Mistery of Woolcombing.' The next document, from 1782, shows that the properties then consisted of three tenements, with the shop having been converted into a stable, the dairy having become a tenement, and the meal-house was a comb-shop for use by the owner, Robert Kenning, a Woolcomber; he always signed himself 'Robart Kinning'.

Then there is Robert Kinning's last will and testament, dated 6 February 1801, in which he gives his wife Ruth all his goods, chattels effects and personal estate, together with a life interest in the four properties. These were in the several occupations of Elizabeth Robins and William Howard in the eastern-most two properties, and Elizabeth Potter and Robert himself. Following his wife's death, the two western-most properties, bounded on the west by the Parish Workhouse of Kingsthorpe, were to pass to Robert's son-in-law William Craft. The other two properties *'together with eight yards in width of the garden ground behind the same to be measured from the wall which divides the said garden from a close in the occupation of William Stanton'* were to pass to his son-in-law Thomas Craft once he attained the age of 21 years. There is a copy of the Weston Favell Parish Register entry for the baptism of Thomas, son of Henry and Ruth Crafts, on 26 May 1782, certified by the Rector of that parish and dated 23 April 1801. There is also a note of *'The measure of Mrs Kinning's garden: Sir George's piece, 4 poles; Thomas's piece, 4 poles; William's piece, 6 poles.'*

The next document in the sequence is a 4-part Indenture conveying the properties in trust from Thomas Craft and Mrs Markham to John Barrett and his trustee. Then in July 1812 John Barrett conveyed the properties to William Trasler of West Haddon and his trustee, John Trasler of Kingsthorpe. The final deed records the conveyance on 21 December 1813 from the last named to Robert Trasler of Northampton, a Baker, and his trustee, Joseph Trasler of Kingsthorpe, also a Baker. But there is an interesting note on the outside of this last conveyance that says:

By an Indenture dated 7 August 1903 made between (1) John Mackaness of the one part and (2) Wm Henry Freise Brown of the other part, one of the messuages within described and being No. 1 High Street, Kingsthorpe was conveyed from (1) to (2).

At that time, of course, there were no bungalows opposite, and these properties were counted as the beginning of High Street. They presumably became part of The Green when the estate was developed on the other side of the road.

(2) 40-52 High Street, & The Yard

Numbers 40-52 were once owned by the Danes family. A description of the estate of Geo. Danes, deceased, dated 1908/9, refers to eight cottages *"Now seven: 40-52 High St. [and] a small cottage added to Litchfield's"*. From the sketch plan in the same document it appears that the Rev Litchfield occupied No. 46, which was somewhat wider and had two storeys & an attic, with cottage No.1 in the Yard at the rear attached to it. The entrance to the

Yard, with its four dwellings, was between 44 and the garden of 46. In 1909 the occupants of 40-52 were given as Jelly, Freeman, Mitford, Earl (formerly Litchfield), Ager, Plackett, and Green (respectively), and the occupants of three dwellings in The Yard were Tindall, Cook and Robins.

The same document recites the property devised in trust for the deceased Geo. Danes by his father, Chas. Danes deceased. From this it appears that Mr Litchfield had previously occupied a white stone and slate cottage *"standing nearly opposite to the deceased's messuage or farmhouse."* This cottage later became known as 21 Manor Road, but clearly not the present number 21, which is a large detached 19th century building. According to the notes about the Danes estate, the white stone cottage stood to the north-east of the latter. When the cottage was demolished, along with others nearby, there may have been some renumbering. The 1851 census shows the Rev Litchfield, with his wife and young daughter, occupying a house in Back Lane – later known as Manor Road.

THE CHURCH OF ST JOHN THE BAPTIST

THE actual origins of the parish church of Kingsthorpe are buried in the mists of time and beneath the additions and reconstructions made to the fabric since. Although the earliest portions of the present structure are Norman, there was almost certainly a church here in Saxon times. This may originally have been a simple wooden structure, perhaps replaced in the early Norman period by stone walls forming a nave and chancel, the latter possibly having an apsidal sanctuary. The roof at this time would have been of timber and thatch. The initiative for its building would have come from St Andrew's Priory, to the north of Northampton, the lands of which abutted the southern parish boundary of Kingsthorpe – or Torp as it was then known. A priest from that priory would have served the church; the population of the village at that time (less than 150 according to the information afforded by the Survey of 1086) could not have supported a resident parish priest.

What remains of that early stone church? Some portions were discovered when the building underwent a massive restoration in 1863. The three bays of the nave, and two bays on the north of the chancel, are clearly Norman. But, upon removing the plaster and whitewash from the wall during that restoration, the upper parts of two very early round-headed windows were discovered in the north and south walls over the eastern piers of the nave, and portions of similar windows were found over the north and south piers in the chancel. These openings were only four inches wide on what had once been the outside wall, but splaying inwards to a width of 3 feet 4 inches. It would therefore seem that these had once formed part of the walls of an earlier church.

Whether this earlier church was Saxon or early Norman has been a matter of some dispute, but experts say that these window open-

Kingsthorpe Church interior: The inside of the original north wall, showing two (later) Norman arches with one of the ancient window openings between them; further to the east can be seen the old entrance to the rood loft. (Photo by the author).

In the north aisle, between two early Norman arches, part of the exterior of an earlier window. (Photo by the author).

245

Looking from the chancel towards the north west, part of the interior of an early window. (Photo by the author).

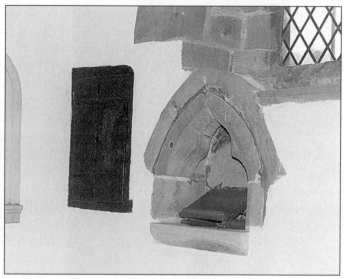

Piscina and old aumbry cupboard in the south aisle. (Photo by the author).

ings are not characteristic of Saxon work. Soon after the Conquest of 1066 the Norman Baron Simon de St Liz claimed the Patronage of the living of St Peter's, Northampton, with Kingsthorpe and Upton: so it is possible that these early remains date from that time.

Later in the Norman period, around 1170, the Patronage was given to St Andrew's Priory. Serjeantson and Wolstenhulme suggest that at this time the church was enlarged by the addition of north and south aisles to the nave and part of the chancel. However, R J Thorneycroft, in his most useful work, suggests a more likely sequence of chapels being added to the north and south of the chancel around 1170, followed about a decade later by the construction of north and south aisles to the nave. The construction of the chapels would have been carried out by breaking through the western end of the chancel walls and constructing two arches on each side. This would have been done gradually, supporting the upper portions of the walls to avoid removing the roof; the church could thus remain in use during the period of construction. This work would have produced a church that was cross-shaped in plan.

The existence of altars in these chapels is revealed by the remaining piscinae, which would have been to the side of each altar. A piscina is a shallow basin, recessed into the wall, which drains into the ground; it was used for disposing of the water used in cleansing the sacred vessels after Mass, and was normally situated to the south of an east-facing altar. In the case of the southern chapel, the piscina, now in the wall of the south aisle, would have been in the appropriate position for an east-facing altar. However, it seems to have been moved further eastward at some point in its history, as does the one in the north aisle; Serjeantson seems to agree with this suggestion. This appears to be the oldest piscina in the church. It was modified at a later time by the addition of a hinged door, perhaps to be used for storing the consecrated oils used in certain sacraments.

The slightly later construction of the aisles would have been carried out in a similar manner to the construction of the chapels, with round Norman arches being formed in the old external walls; the south aisle was a little narrower than the one to the north. A porch was apparently constructed at the south door at this time. At around

1220 the two bays on the south side of the chancel were rebuilt in Early English style with pointed arches, and the Norman pillar between them re-carved with four clusters of three shafts each. The corresponding bays on the north side were not changed, and are still Norman. At around the same time the east end of the sanctuary was extended further to the east.

In the early 14th century (Thorneycroft), or the late 13th century (Wolstenhulme), the east walls of the north and south chapels were moved eastwards in line with the main sanctuary. They were linked to the sanctuary by a large arch on each side. The church was then almost rectangular in plan. If the altars of the original two chapels remained in use, then there would have been five altars in the church at this period. The piscinae still existing in these eastward extensions prove that there were altars there in any case. In the new south chapel, almost certainly dedicated at that time to the Blessed Virgin Mary, next to the piscina there is an ancient locker with hinged door; Wolstenhulme suggests that this may date from the same period, and that it may have been an aumbry for storage of the Holy Oils.

The number of chapels can perhaps be gleaned from the legacies in ancient wills, which indicate altars dedicated to the Holy Trinity (probably the high altar); Our Lady (in the south chapel); St Katharine (in the north chapel); All Souls; and St John (but was this St John the Baptist?). In the 1545 will of John Smyth, who styled himself "priest of Kingsthorpe", he desired to be buried "in Our Ladye chapell within the church of Kingsthorpe." And he gave "unto Our Ladye Aulter & Seynt Nycolas Aulter within the same church a flaxen sheet to make thereof ij alter cloths unto ye said aulters." He was a local man, son of Thomas Smyth of Kingsthorpe by his wife Annys. He was clearly not the Rector, but may have been a curate or else the priest associated with Bacon's Chantry; see below. It is interesting to note that, in the Church Survey of 1637, there was still a reference to 'St Nicholas Chapel'. There was also a dedication to St Christopher, but this may have been an image of the saint that stood, according to a Manor Court Roll of 1390, "by the altar of St Katharine".

In 1471 John Bacon founded and endowed a chantry here, "for a chaplain to sing for ever at Our Lady's altar". In 1535 the income of

This pillar in the south aisle, originally Norman, was re-carved around 1220 with four clusters of three shafts; at the same time, the bay on each side of it was rebuilt in Early English style. (Photo by the author).

the chantry was £4, and a certain John Howell was the chantry priest. The priest was to pray for the souls of John Bacon, his father and mother, and of his wife Agnes. The King's Survey of 1548 found that the value of the chantry lands was then £6.5s.0d, of which the chantry priest received a stipend of £3.10s.4d. The value of the ornaments was put at 3/4d, indicating that this was not a richly decorated chapel in its own right, such as we see in some of our cathedrals; the priest was to celebrate at Our Lady's altar, and the chantry foun-

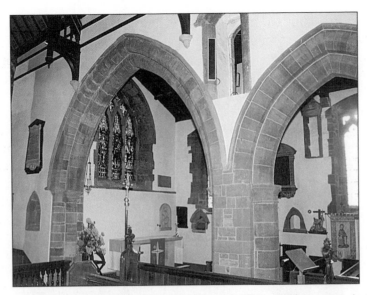

View from the chancel looking south east. The south access to the rood loft can be clearly seen, and beyond, in the south wall of the Lady Chapel, are the old aumbry cupboard (tucked right into the corner), two piscinae, and (higher up) the decorated niche. (Photo by the author).

The access to the rood loft, as seen from the south aisle. (Photo by the author).

250

dation was intended to provide income to support that priest. Such endowments were not uncommon, and the provision of additional clergy in this way was of great benefit to many parishes. As a chapel to St Peter's church in Northampton, Kingsthorpe may otherwise have had only a curate at that time, perhaps shared with Upton.

In the mid-14th century the chancel arch was moved eastward by one bay and the screen and rood loft erected. The rood loft was a platform on top of the screen; it supported the rood, or crucifix, which would have had images of the Blessed Virgin and St John on either side of it. The priest would have gone up to the rood loft in order to preach a homily. The roof was also raised at this time and a clerestory constructed above the nave walls, with four windows on each side. Around this period two square headed windows were built into the south wall of the south chapel and aisle. The top of the piscina in the Lady Chapel actually projects slightly into the opening of the eastern-most window; this may be seen as poor planning, but at least the builders had their priorities right in not damaging the piscina. Between these two windows, and quite high up, is a niche with a richly moulded canopy; Wolstenhulme conjectures that it may have once contained a statue, but it surely would have been lower down in that case. Perhaps, like the piscina, it too has been repositioned at some stage. Certainly it does not look like part of the access to the rood loft.

Wolstenhulme says that the east windows of the two aisles and those of the north wall, along with the north door, date from the mid-14th century; an exception is the window in the present vestry, which is probably around 1400. He also believes that the south wall was moved outwards at around this time, to form a continuous line with the chapel wall; but Thorneycroft says that this was not carried out until 1863 – as indicated by the architect's drawings!

The tower and steeple were added to the west end in the late 14th or early 15th century, and a crypt and new sanctuary were constructed to the east. The tower was built in sandstone, but was protected later by the addition of a cladding of Kingsthorpe freestone; hence its light colour. The steeple has been repaired and partly reconstructed on a number of occasions, owing again to the softness of the original sandstone. The crypt, at one time used as a charnel house, can only be entered from the churchyard. It is just over 15 feet in length and breadth and ten feet in height; it has a central pillar with stone vaulting supporting the floor of the sanctuary above. The latter was thus raised higher than the floor of the chancel and accessed by four steps, just as it is today. Piscinae at each side of these steps indicate the previous position of the main altar.

The complete restoration undertaken in 1863 involved the rebuilding of the three Norman bays on the north side of the nave, along with the whole clerestory; also, the north-east corner of the tower and the west end of the north aisle, including the window, were rebuilt where damage had been caused by settlement of the tower. The arch between the nave and the chancel was demolished, and a new one built in the original position: one bay to the west. The wall of the south aisle, together with the porch, was demolished and rebuilt in line with the south wall of the Lady Chapel. The east gable of the clerestory was rebuilt, and new roofs were constructed for the south aisle, the nave and part of the north aisle. The floor of the sanctuary was repaved with patterned ceramic tiles; a low stone wall was built at the entrance to the choir; the west end gallery was removed; and the old box pews were replaced with those that can be seen today. The Thornton family contributed over £2,000 towards this restoration, the total cost of which was £22,000.

During this work an aumbry or Cross Locker was discovered in the east face of the block of masonry in the south aisle that indicates the position of the Norman chancel arch. The external opening of this recess was 5 ft. 6 ins. high and 10 ins. wide, and was closed by a rudely formed door in two lengths, hung with hook-and-band hinges. The interior was roughly formed rubble work coated with plaster. In 1863 this opening was walled up, and the door and hinges removed, but the external features have been preserved.

When the clerestory was rebuilt, with three windows on each side, one original square headed window was re-fixed at the east end of the south side and the others were made according to its pattern. The new chancel arch was not made to match the older structures, but is typically Victorian Gothic. The six small shafts sustaining the inner

Two square headed windows, built into the south wall of the south chapel and aisle around the mid-14th century. (Photo by the author).

Niche and monuments in the south aisle. (Photo by the author).

The old Cross Locker in the south aisle, discovered in 1863; the interior has been filled in. (Photo by the author).

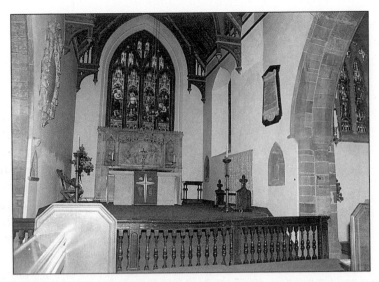

The Sanctuary: note the two older piscinae, just beyond the early 17th century altar rails; these date from the period prior to the eastward extension of the Sanctuary. (Photo by the author).

An old piscina at the south side of the entrance to the Sanctuary. (Photo by the author).

The remains of a piscina at the north side of the entrance to the Sanctuary. (Photo by the author).

254

order or arch are of red Mansfield stone, and the voussoirs of the outer order are alternately of Ketton and red Broughton stone.

The pulpit dates from the early years of the 17th century, and the altar rails from the first half of the same century. Three of the 'poppy head' bench ends on the Sanctuary Servers' seats are the work of mediaeval wood carvers, and worth close examination; the remainder are the work of 19th century craftsmen. For a more detailed description of the decoration and furnishings of the church, including numerous internal modifications and re-orderings carried out during the 20th century, one cannot do better than consult the excellent and most readable A4 booklet produced by R J Thorneycroft, to which is owed much of the above description, and which is available in the church. The Victoria County History also contains a good architectural description.

In 1985 a new building was added to the north side of the church in order to provide a meeting room, office, kitchen and toilet facilities. Built of stone, and in the style of a chapter house, it blends in extremely well with the older structure of the church.

Memorials

In the north aisle:

1914-1919 War memorial, recording 91 names, together with a War Memorial Window.

Further along towards the east there is a stone memorial for John Danes, d.1791, and Simon Danes, his son, d.1771.

In the Vestry there are the following:

A stone memorial for five members of the Boddington family buried in a vault just outside the north wall of the church: Susannah, d.1847; Harriott, d.1848; Maria, d.1852; Emma, d.1865, and Frances, d.1873. These were daughters of Thomas Boddington of Clapton, by his wife Maria Catharina, daughter of James Fremeaux.

Stained glass window: Anne Thornton, d.1911.

Memorials for the Fremeaux family in the Vestry include:

James Fremeaux d.1799
Margaret Fremeaux d.1801 (Widow of James).
Peter John Fremeaux d.1784 (Son of James)
Susannah Fremeaux d.1797 (Widow of Peter John)
The following daughters of James Fremeaux:
Margaret Fremeaux d.1802
Gertrude Joanna Portington d.1803
Adriana Constantia Fremeaux d.1812
Elizabeth Fremeaux d.1826

The following Rectors of St Peter's, Kingsthorpe & Upton have memorials in the Sanctuary:
North wall:
A white alabaster memorial for Dr Edward Reynolds, Rector 1658-1698, and his wife, Frances. Serjeantson mentions several other slabs in the floor of the chancel in memory of their children.
South wall:
A white marble memorial for Robert William Baxter, Rector 1802-1850.

The following Vicars of Kingsthorpe are remembered:
In the Lady Chapel is a stained glass window to the Rev John Hulbert Glover, Vicar 1856-1885. The Litany Desk is a memorial to the Rev E L Tuson, Vicar 1885-1918. The Lectern is a memorial to the Rev J P de Putron, Vicar 1918-1936.
The East Window was given by the Rev J H Glover in 1884 in memory of his wife.
The window on the south side of the Sanctuary was added in 1904 in memory of Mary Susan Thornton (d.1901), and was given by her mother, Anne (to whose memory is dedicated the window in the north wall of the Vestry).
The reredos was erected in 1891 in memory of the Rev William Thornton of Kingsthorpe Hall, who died in 1881; it was donated by Anne, his widow. It is of white alabaster and was executed by Messrs Brindley & Farmer, who were also responsible for the

The 1863 arch at the entrance to the Chancel. The voussoirs of the outer order, being alternately of Ketton and red Broughton stone, can be clearly distinguished. (Photo by the author).

reredos in St Paul's Cathedral.

Other members of Kingsthorpe families have memorials as follows:

In the Lady Chapel:

On the south wall a black and white marble memorial to Mabel Morgan, who died 1 February 1664/5, together with some members of her family.

Above the Morgan monument is a plain oval white marble tablet to Dame Mary Robinson, the daughter and heiress of John

Above: Old carved 'poppy heads', on benches on the south side of the Chancel. The right hand one is a later, 19th century, production.
Left: One of the old carved 'poppy heads' on a bench in the Chancel; it is thought to represent the head of a lion. (Photo by the author).

Morgan. She died in 1734, aged 24.

In the south aisle:

A floor slab on the north side to Francis and Elizabeth Morgan, who died in 1704 and 1706 respectively. Its brass plate has been removed and is now attached to the east face of the block of masonry in the south aisle next to the remains of the old Cross

Locker mentioned earlier. Closely adjoining the Morgan slab, according to Serjeantson, "is a slab, much defaced" to the memory of Walter Faunt and his wife Mabel, née Morgan, who died in 1695 and 1698 respectively. He says that Bridges records a third inscription, now destroyed: it was in Latin and commemorated Edmund, son of Francis Morgan, and Mabel his wife.

Thorneycroft mentions a brass plate to Mrs Hester Farmer, who died in 1713/14, which Bridges places in the Sanctuary. This has also been attached to the wall at the side of the old Cross Locker.

On the south wall of the Tower there are four more memorials, and there are five consecration crosses built into its walls, four on the north and one on the south; but these are now hidden behind shelving and cupboards.

In Bridges's time (1720) there was to be seen "near the steps of the communion table" a slab marking the burial of Lady Margaret Lane, who died 22 April 1669. A stone in the nave still bore the name of Lane in Serjeantson's time, and he thought it was to the memory of Bridget, a daughter of Sir Richard and Lady Lane, who married Francis Cooke of Kingsthorpe, and died in January 1665/6. Bridges also mentions another stone in the nave, to the memory of Francis Cooke, but the inscription even then was no longer legible. These two slabs can still be seen, and the name 'Lane' is clearly discernible on one of them.

The porch

In the south porch is a wooden cupboard with glazed front, for the loaves of George Cooke's Bread Charity, inscribed:

Mr George Cooke gave in ye year 1690 the Interest of a Hundred Pound to be gave in Bread, Every Sunday to 12 Poor People of this Parish for ever.

The cupboard beneath the inscription now contains the church notice board. Further details of the Bread Fund, along with other endowments and legacies for the benefit of the poor, can be found in the chapter entitled *Charities for the poor*.

The altar, and behind it the alabaster reredos of 1891 dedicated to the memory of the Reverend William Thornton. (Photo by the author).

The Churchyard

This contains some interesting tombstones of people who once played their part in the life of the parish, but most of these memorials are of the 19th century. Photographs of a century or more ago show many more stones than are visible today; it is said that some were laid flat and grassed over, but there is no confirmation of this assertion. There is a burial vault on the north side of the church, which used to be accessed by steps from the east end of the north aisle (now the Vestry); it houses the remains of members of the Boddington family, for whom there is a memorial stone in the Vestry covering the years 1847-1873. The graveyard to the north, long since closed, also contains memorials bearing well-known names; a survey of these memorials was carried out some years ago, and is available for inspection at the County Record Office.

The Bells

The church would have possessed a Sanctus bell, to be rung at the consecration of the bread and wine during Mass, from at least the 15th century. But the earliest mentions of other bells, contained

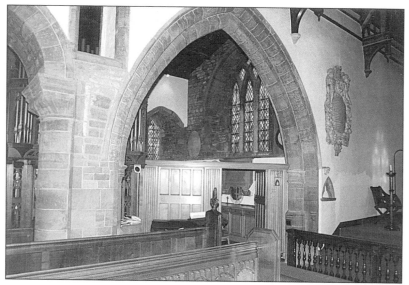

The Vestry arch. (Photo by the author).

The interior of the Vestry, with various monuments attached to the walls. (Photo by the author).

mainly in legacies for their ringing or repair, do not specify the number. In 1552 the inventory showed that there were four bells in addition to the Sanctus bell. All but the latter were confiscated by King Edward VI's Commissioners, along with a silver chalice and a number of vestments and altar cloths.

Five new bells were hung in the tower during the 17th century, two in 1621, and the others in 1622, 1671 and 1680. The sixth, a new treble bell, was given by the Rev E L Tuson in 1911 to mark the coronation of King George V, and the bells were then re-hung in a steel frame. In 1951 they were tuned and re-hung on ball bearings.

RECTORS OF ST. PETER'S NORTHAMPTON
WITH ST. JOHN THE BAPTIST KINGSTHORPE
AND ST. MICHAEL'S UPTON

The following list varies somewhat from those previously published, since it goes back to Serjeantson (1904), pages 73-102, which contain the results of his exhaustive research into the subject. Earlier lists (i.e. before 1904), as well as those published since, showed some omissions and some confusion between Old Style and New Style dates. (For information on dating see the chapter entitled *Currency, Measurements & Abbreviations*.) Serjeantson's additions are marked with an asterisk, and the Old/New Style dates, where applicable and where known, are included. Some notes are provided below giving further information gleaned from the research of Rev H I Longden.

John, son of Ranulph *
c.1190 Henry, son of Peter *
1220 Thomas de Fiskerton
1222 Robert de Bath
1243 John de Houton (Archdeacon of Northampton)
1258 William de Altavilla *
1266 William de Windsor (Deprived
Feb 1290/1)
1291 William de Windsor (Reinstated
March 1290/1)
1294 Hugh de Novo Castro
1297 Ralph de Haggele   (24 March 1296/7)

1306 John de Leeke (28 Feb 1305/6.
Archbishop of Dublin 1311)
1311 William de Bevercote(s) (Chancellor of
Scotland until 1335)
1347 Richard Aunsel
1350 William de Boulge (25 Feb 1349/50)
1358 John Ferers (14 Feb 1357/8)
1361 William Wenge de Castlebitham
1371 Thomas de Duffield
1393 Thomas de Morton (15 Feb 1392/3)
1425 John Verney (12 Feb 1424/5)
1428 Robert Fitzhugh (Bishop of London
September 1431)
1432 William Okeburn (19 Feb 1431/2)
1433 John Smythe
1433 Thomas Leversegge
1444 John Thornhill
1476 Robert Prudde
1487 Thomas Palmer (4 Jan 1486/7)
1494 Robert Hundesworth (16 Feb 1493/4)
1503 Richard Watson
1507 Edmund Collerton
1514 Robert Bright
1534 William Bretteyn (4 March 1533/4)
1552 Edmund Davye (Note 12)
1560 William Roote (29 Jan 1559/60) Note 4.
1563 Richard Burdsall
1577 William Nowell (12 Jan 1576/7) *
1591 William Stocke (16 Jan 1590/1) *
1603 Thomas Bellamye (3 March 1602/3)
1607 John Cocke (26 Jan 1606/7)
1608 Samuel Clerke (See Note 8)
1641 Robert Hill
1649 Henry Arnold (See Note 3)
1654 James Williams * (See Note 1)
1658 Edward Reynolds (See Note 6)
1698 Philip Atkinson * (See Note 2)
1702 Welbore Ellis (Bishop of Kildare 1705)
1706 Richard Reynolds (Bishop of Lincoln
1723) See Note 7.

1744 Edward Patterson
1750 Edward Lockwood (See Note 9)
1802 Robert William Baxter

INCUMBENTS OF ST JOHN THE BAPTIST KINGSTHORPE

1850 John Wightman
1854 Samuel Price Davies
1856 John Hulbert Glover
1885 Edward Luxmoore Tuson
1918 John Percy de Putron
1936 Maurice Lionel Couchman
1946 Donald Finch Andrews
1966 Arthur James Wolstenhulme
1987 Michael Robert Henry Baker
1996 Timothy Short

NOTES

These notes supplement the list of Rectors, giving personal details about some of them; information is also provided about several other priests associated with Kingsthorpe, where this seems relevant or of interest. Unless stated otherwise, the source of what follows is H I Longden's catalogue of the clergy of Northamptonshire and Rutland from 1500 to 1900.

1: Attention must be drawn to a doubt concerning the Rectorship of James Williams in 1654, which Serjeantson (p.96) bases on a mention of him in the Augmentation Books in the Lambeth Palace Library, where he is described as a 'minister of the gospell att St Peter's in Northton' in an entry dated February 1654/5. H I Longden in his catalogue, vol. vii, pages 15-17, says that Robert Hill, the previous Rector, married his second wife, Mrs Elizabeth Fichreoffery (Fitzgeoffrey?) at All Saints, Northampton, 2 June 1655. He was still living in 1658 and was probably buried at Kingsthorpe in that year, since his will was proved in 1658 (PCC 576 Wootton). So perhaps James Williams was simply a Curate at St Peter's.

2: ATKINSON, Philip: Rector of St Peter's 26 December 1698. Died 1702. Issue: Lewis Bulkeley, christened at Kingsthorpe 30 March 1701; mother: The Honble Catherine.

3: ARNOLD, Henry: He was an intruder at Kingsthorpe in 1649. Intruders were Puritan ministers thrust upon parishes that were thought to be too faithful to the Bishops.

4: ROOTE, Sir Wm: In 1546 he was Curate of Moulton; he was then Curate of Kingsthorpe, where he witnessed wills 1549-58. He witnessed the will of Sir John Harryson, Rector of Brampton, 12 July 1557 as 'Curate of Kingsthorpe.' Installed as Rector of St Peter's 29 January 1559/60, and was still there 30 August 1561.

5: HARTE, Sir Robert: He was recorded as Chantry Priest at Kingsthorpe in 1526. Longden does not mention any other Chantry Priests, but John Howell was the Chantry Priest in 1535, according to Serjeantson (1904), page 165.

6: REYNOLDS, Edward: Son of Edward Reynolds, Bishop of Norwich; born 27 May 1630. Rector of St Peter's 15 October 1658. Prebendary of Worcester 1660; Archdeacon of Norfolk 1661. He married Frances Alston of Pavenham, Beds. Issue: six sons and five daughters. His wife was buried at Kingsthorpe 17 September 1722. He died 28 June and was buried at Kingsthorpe 1 July 1698.

7: REYNOLDS, Richard: Son of Richard Reynolds of Leverington, Cambs. Born there 1674. Rector of St Peter's 23 November 1706. Dean of Peterborough Cathedral 20 November 1718 until 1721, then consecrated Bishop of Bangor, and Bishop of Lincoln two years later. On 22 July 1722 he ordained John Woodford as a Deacon at Kingsthorpe. Died 15 January 1743/4 in Charles Street, Westminster. His 7th son, Conyers, was christened at Kingsthorpe 1 January 1708/9 and buried there 4 January 1710/11. Two other sons were christened at St Peter's in 1712 and 1713.

8: CLERKE, Samuel, DD: Born 14 December 1582. Installed as Rector of St Peter's 2 November 1608, and as Rector of Winwick 14 July 1614. Chaplain to Prince Charles in 1616. Master of Wigston's Hospital, Leicester, 1620. Married first to Margaret Peyto; issue: eight sons and six daughters. She was buried at Kingsthorpe 9 February 1633/4. According to Northants Notes & Queries (Vol 5, p 57) he then married

Mrs Katherine Sympson, a widow, of the Precincts of Christ Church, Canterbury, on 13 September 1635 at Canterbury Cathedral, by Licence dated the previous day. Issue: two sons and one daughter. His will was proved by his eldest son Samuel on 27 May 1641 (PCC 61 Evelyn).

9: LOCKWOOD, Edward: 5th son of Richard Lockwood MP. Born 6 January 1720. Brother of St Katharine's Hospital 30 May 1750. Married (1) 29 August 1752 Lucy, daughter and co-heir of William Dowdeswell of Kingham, Oxon. She died 4 April, buried at Kingsthorpe 13 April 1764. Issue: three sons, the first dying at two weeks old. Married (2) 23 February 1770 Elizabeth, only daughter and heiress of Joseph Percival of Stapleton, Gloucs. She died 7 November 1770. Married (3) 3 November 1772 Judith, daughter and heiress of John Bedingfield of Caistor, Norfolk, and widow of Sir John Rous, 5th baronet, of Henham Hall, Suffolk. She died 10 September 1794 and was buried at Lambourne. Edward Lockwood died at Portman Square, London, on 22 January 1802 and was buried in Lambourne Church, Essex. One of his sons, John Cutts Lockwood, was Curate of Kingsthorpe in 1789 and Vicar of Yoxford, Suffolk 1793-1816.

10: SMYTH, John: In his 1545 will he styled himself "priest of Kingsthorpe"; he may have been a curate or else the priest associated with Bacon's Chantry. He was a local man, son of Thomas Smyth of Kingsthorpe by his wife Annys. Some of his bequests and desires have been mentioned in the description of Kingsthorpe Church. He also made bequests to "Robert Co[o]ke my kinsman & Agnes his wife."

11: MORGAN, Edmond: He was the son of Francis Morgan of Kingsthorpe, christened there on 5 October 1615. He was Minister of Upton in 1648 and Rector of Gayton in 1656. He died, unmarried, 9 February 1681/2 and was buried two days later at Kingsthorpe. He desired burial in the parish church of Kingsthorpe "near my dear mother..." To his nephew Francis Morgan he gave his house in Kingsthorpe and lands there and in Dallington. He left £50 to erect a monument to his mother, Mabel Morgan. He also made provision of 20/- yearly for ever for a sermon in All Saints church, Northampton, on the day the conflagration happened in the town, out of the rents of a close lying in the North Field of Kingsthorpe next to Boughton Meere.

12: The PR records the burial, on 29 May 1547, of "Bennett [i.e. Benedict] Davy, Parson & Priest." This may indicate that there were two more Rectors between William Bretteyn and Edmund Davye. Note that the last Master of St David's Hospital before the Reformation was - Benedict Davey.

PATRONAGE

The Patrons of St Peter's church with Kingsthorpe and Upton were carefully researched and recorded by Serjeantson (1904; p.157 & footnote), who lists the Prior and Convent of St Andrew, Northampton, as the first Patron. Henry III took the patronage from the Priory in 1266, and then, by a charter dated 26 August 1329, Edward III granted to the Hospital of St Katharine, in London, the perpetual advowson and patronage of St Peter's, with the chapels of Kingsthorpe and Upton annexed. From time to time other persons were granted the patronage, for a limited period, by the Hospital. In 1476 John Holcot and Richard Isham were joint patrons when Robert Prudde was instituted, and Sir John Alen presented William Brettyn as the new Rector in March 1533/4. Following that, Francis Morgan of Kingsthorpe was granted the patronage for 90 years; his widow, Ann, continued to exercise this right, followed by other members of the Morgan family of Heyford and Kingsthorpe. The Hospital of St Katharine was again Patron when Robert Hill was instituted in 1641; they remained so for all subsequent Rectors with the exception of Richard Reynolds, whom Queen Anne presented in 1706.

CHURCH BUSINESS ADMINISTERED BY THE VESTRY

One of the ancient functions of the church not mentioned in the local documents is the practice of sanctuary-seeking. The Rev R M Serjeantson published, in 1913, details of Sanctuary-Seekers in Northamptonshire. He took the details from several Assize Rolls, including the record of a General Eyre for the County of Northampton, held in 1329, which covered a period of at least 30 years. The practice began in Saxon times whereby criminals could seek Sanctuary in churches or churchyards. After forty days they could, in the presence an agent of the Crown, confess their crime, swear to abjure the realm and submit to banishment. They then had to travel to a named port, dressed in a white robe or in sackcloth, and take the first available ship. Their only hope of returning was by means of a King's Pardon. The following details appear on page 429 of Sarjeantson's book:

[KINGS]THORPE: Richard of Horton for fear of arrest took sanctuary in the Church of Thorpe and there confessed that he was a thief and abjured the realm. His chattels were worth 19d.

KINGSTHORPE: Henry Bertam [Bertram?] for fear of arrest took sanctuary in the Church of Thorpe. He confessed divers thefts and abjured the realm. His chattels were worth 2s.8d.

KINGSTHORPE: Simon Bate of Brampton killed Richard, son of John Fraunkeleyn, in the fields of Kingsthorpe. He fled forthwith and took sanctuary in the Church of Kingsthorpe, where he confessed that he had committed the murder and abjured the realm. His chattels were worth 3s.4d.

The Vestry Meetings

Nearly 500 years later than those records of sanctuary seekers, the earliest minutes of Vestry Meetings begin in 1808; but they record only the letting of the Town Close and the Poor's Close, otherwise known as Bush Close, details of which will be found in the chapter *Charities for the poor*. It is only with the meetings of the Select Vestry from 1823 onwards that more detail begins to appear in the minutes – and sometimes too much; for instance in that year, and from 1833 to 1835, there are recorded the various allowances made to, and withdrawn from, poor persons in the parish.

The responsibilities of the Vestry at this time were wide ranging, including as they did the work of Local Government; but this chapter is concerned only with those matters affecting the church itself. The Easter Vestry, usually held on the first Monday following Easter, had as its main task the appointment of Parish Officers for the following twelve months – give or take a few weeks, depending on the date of the next Easter. These officers included the Churchwardens, one of whom was selected by the incumbent and the other by the people, and two Overseers of the Poor. Other officers appointed by the Vestry were the Constables; the Surveyor of the Highways or Waywarden; a

Pinner to round up stray cattle; and, when the collection of levies or rates became too onerous, a salaried Rate Collector. The duties and responsibilities of these officers are summarised in the chapter *Historical Overview* in the Local Government section. The Parish Register at one point contains some notes of the appointment of Churchwardens:

Vestry 1708 April 8: Churchwardens: Stephen Hawkes, Wm Morris Jnr. chosen by the parishioners. Ric. Reynolds Rector: Hatton Atkins, Edward Fitzhugh.

Vestry 1709 April 27: Rector chose: John Stephenson. Parishioners chose: Wm Wallis & Edwd Fitzhugh.

Vestry 1710 April 13: Rector chose: John Cooch. Parishioners chose: Hatton Atkins & Wm Green.

From the late 16th or early 17th century there is a list of Churchwardens and other officers, on the reverse of which appears an Order relating to taxes and levies. There are two lists of officers side by side, which may relate to two different years, and they include the following: Constables, Churchwardens, Townes men, Overseers of Highways, Thirdboroughs and Headboroughs. Headboroughs and Thirdboroughs are terms that sometimes refer to deputy constables, but they can also refer to representatives of tithings. In Anglo-Saxon times each inhabited area was divided into tithings: these were associations of ten households that were held jointly responsible for the behaviour of each member. The system was known as Frankpledge, and at the manorial Court Leet a 'View of Frankpledge' reviewed the working of these tithings.

It was also the responsibility of the Vestry to set the rate in the £ of each levy, whether it was a Poor Levy for the Overseers expenditure, a levy for the upkeep of the roads, or a Church Levy for the Churchwardens, who had responsibility for the maintenance and improvement of the church. There were normally two Churchwardens, but (as noted above) occasionally three or even four seem to have been appointed. They kept a careful record of all their expenditure in a ledger, and this formed the basis for the one or two church rates levied each year. Any unusual or large expenditure had to be approved by the Vestry, and major repairs or improvements often necessitated an additional levy.

An example of this occurred on 31 July 1833, when it was noted that more accommodation was needed in the church and it was agreed unanimously that the Gallery should be extended at the west end. The Rector would cover the expense himself. On 12 June 1834 we learn that Mr Page of Weedon Bec, employed in building a new Gallery, proposed ceiling the church roof, washing and colouring the walls, cleaning and varnishing the pews, etc. for £42. The Rector would pay a proportion of this, and it was agreed to cover the balance with a Church Rate of 4½d in the pound. In May 1840 a rate of 6d in the £ was agreed to pay for repairs to the church roof on the south side and repairs to the tower.

During 1844 refreshments for the Confirmation candidates were approved, and a platform for the accommodation of the Sunday School children in the church was considered. A rate was to be determined which would cover any necessary work. The plan proposed by Mr Woodward, the Curate, was accepted and specification and estimates were to be obtained. The Rector would contribute £5, and a rate of 2½d per £ would be collected. Benjamin Cuffley's estimate of £16.18s.6d was accepted in due course. In October a bill for £19.17s.0½d for roof repairs from Mr Bond the Plumber was deemed unreasonable: Mr Law of Northampton inspected the work and valued it at £12.15s.9d, and Mr Danes was instructed in December to pay this amount to Mr Bond.

A note on 13 April 1857 indicates that the Parish Clerk's salary was to increase from 3 guineas to £6; but the following year an objection was raised that the Clerk's salary and 15/- coals were not payable out of a Church Rate, presumably because they were not repairs.

In December 1858 the question of enlarging the churchyard was discussed, and it was proposed that part of the Village Green be enclosed for this purpose. This was not acceptable, so a variety of other propositions were considered over the next few years. In 1859 it was decided to stop the footpath at the east end of the church and to enclose the present footpath. The question of the extension of the churchyard was raised again on 4 December 1862; then on 1 January

1863 it was stated that "an addition to the Burial Ground is immediately necessary". On 5 March 1863, after hearing the Churchwardens' report, it was proposed to purchase some land from Sir George Robinson lying to the north of the present churchyard, on the other side of the road. All previous proposals were rescinded and a Church Rate of 1/- in the £ was approved to cover the costs.

On 29 May 1862, the plan for the complete restoration of the church had been presented by Mr W Slater and approved in its main features. The work would be done provided the necessary funds could be obtained, so a subscription committee was formed. No further mention is made in the minutes relating either to the restoration of the church or to the extension of the churchyard, but both are recorded in the Churchwardens' Accounts.

The following fees, payable at Kingsthorpe, were approved on 14 December 1865:

Banns: 2/6d.   *Marriage:* 2/6d;   Parish Clerk: 1/6d;   *By Licence:* Minister 10/-; Clerk 5/-; *Certificates:* 2/6d.

Burials: Clerk's fees, including tolling the bell twice and digging an ordinary grave, 6 ft. for an adult: 5/-; 10-15 years: 4/-; under 10 years: 2/6d. No additional gratuity in any form was to be demanded. Fees for gravestones: flat 20/-, upright 6/8d. There were to be no burials in future under the floor of the church. There was no fee at Churchings: the offering made by a woman at Churching was purely voluntary and was added to the offerings made at Holy Communion.

On 18 February 1869 the vital question was asked: How was money to be raised in future for church purposes, since the law regarding Church Rates had been altered? Suggestions included annual voluntary subscriptions and the letting of the sittings. It was agreed that the debt for the bells be met by voluntary subscription, and future expenses by collections on the third Sunday of each month.

On 19 May 1870 consideration was given to the proposal to attach a Village Clock to the Church Tower. The Trustees of the Town Land would provide £50 towards the cost, which was estimated at £100, and subscriptions would (hopefully) provide the balance. A Clock Committee was formed, which met the next day; Mr Cumberpatch was appointed Treasurer, and the Churchwardens, Mr Wood and Mr Ashby were to canvass the parish for subscriptions. At a committee meeting a week later it was decided to obtain estimates from local Northampton clockmakers. Two possibilities were proposed: A clock with a skeleton face and 6 ft hands or an ordinary face with 5 ft hands. The Clock Committee met again on 11 July 1870, when five estimates were considered. It was agreed that a skeleton dial clock would be best with a dial about 10 ft in diameter. A sub-committee was formed to examine the estimates and report back. On 23 July the sub-committee submitted two estimates, those of Renshaw and Wilby, to the Clock Committee for a final decision. One week later that committee gave a majority vote to Wilby.

At the usual Easter Vestry on 1 April 1872, Mr Barrett and Mr W Cox were elected as Sidesmen, the first time this office had been mentioned. At a Vestry on 21 November 1872 it was decided to charge a fee of one guinea (£1.05p) for the burial of a person from outside the parish. The fee for a brick grave or an enclosure in masonry was set at two guineas. Although the Incumbent was entitled to these fees, they would be applied to the Churchwardens' collection for church purposes. A complaint had been made about the Clerk/Sexton regarding burial fees: T Hayes was sent for and reminded that he must keep strictly to the scale of fees on the list in church. For this he must as a minimum toll for 20 minutes and ring for 10 minutes for a death, and toll for 30 minutes for a funeral.

The problem of raising sufficient funds for church expenses was again discussed at a Vestry on 10 April 1877, attended by 21 persons. It was agreed that offertory collections would be taken up on the 2nd and 4th Sundays at each service, instead of just the 3rd Sunday. The sittings in church were to be allocated by person instead of by families. The Churchwardens were to fill up empty sittings when services had commenced, and they were to break up the mass of boys and lads in the north and south aisles! A plate would be used at offertories rather than the bag (perhaps for greater visibility?). The second service during the summer months would be in the evening rather than the afternoon. It was also suggested that the choir should be enlarged and strengthened if possible.

At the Easter Vestry on 6 April 1885, attended by well over 200 persons, the Churchwardens' Accounts were explained and passed, and Officers chosen for the next year. J Trasler was selected for another year of office as the Vicar's Churchwarden. For the office of Parish Warden, Mr Banks obtained 95 votes and Mr Green 84; so a poll was arranged for the next day between 12 noon & 7pm. A note indicates that the Ratepayers of Semilong were entitled to vote, along with occupiers whose rates were paid by the owners; but lodgers were not entitled. The result of the poll was: Mr Banks 511, Mr Green 191. This illustrates the amount of public interest taken in such elections at that period.

On 30 March 1891 two Churchwardens and four Sidesmen were selected. The meeting approved the erection of a Reredos under the East Window and voted their thanks to Mrs Thornton for her munificent offer. These meeting were now becoming more business-like, as indicated by the number of accounts laid before the meeting: Churchwardens; Parochial Charities; Parochial Committee & Sanitary Authority; and the accounts of the Trustees of the Manor & Town Charity (presented by Mr E M Browne). At the 1892 meeting it was indicated that the accounts of the Free School Charity ought in future to be laid before the Easter Vestry; it was noted that the Free School (originally endowed by a member of the Cooke family) had not been operating for the past 18 months. It was also noted that the Churchyard would have to be enlarged soon or a cemetery provided.

At the Easter Vestry on 7 April 1896 the following charity accounts were presented: Bush Close, Bread Fund, Prichard's, Baxter's and the Manor Lands. The church insurance was to be increased to £3,000. Further consideration was to be given to the possibility of a Church Council. On 20 April 1897 it was reported that Bush Close, the Bread Fund and the Prichard charities had become Parochial Charities, and the Urban District Council had appointed Trustees to administer them. Baxter's Charity remained an Ecclesiastical Charity in the hands of the Vicar.

In 1899 there was some discussion about moving the Sunday evening service from 6pm to 6.30pm. It was decided to ring the bells on the Queen's Birthday, and to pay the ringers 2/- each. In 1904 the

proposed decoration of the East End of the church and repairs to the
Tower were discussed. Several deficits in church income in recent
years were attributed to the opening of Holy Trinity church and to
the use of more gas, coke and coal for the increased number of services. In 1907 the insurance of the church was increased to £4,000.

In 1908 it was unanimously resolved to draw the attention of the
Magistrates of the Borough and County to the prevalence of Sunday
gambling in public places, and the great nuisance caused thereby to
residents in the neighbourhood. In 1910 it was reported that the
spire and tower had been restored during the past summer at a cost
of £177.11s.6d, and the clock repaired at a cost of £11.7s.6d. In 1911
the minutes record the provision of a sixth bell, when the bells were
re-hung, to commemorate the coronation year of King George V. In
1912 it was proposed to introduce incandescent burners to the existing gas lighting brackets. (Until then, light had been provided by gas
flames.) The church insurance was increased by £2,000. In 1913 the
offer had been accepted of a new stained glass window in honour of
the late Vicar, Rev. J H Glover.

In 1914 a new Diocesan Scheme of Finance was introduced, for
which Kingsthorpe's quota was £14.12s.2d. In 1915 this was
increased to £15; it was to be raised by means of a 5% commission
on all other church collections. In 1917 it was reported that the
church collections totalled £267.6s.5d, of which £164.0s.8d were special collections; the balance was allocated to church expenses. The
church windows had to be darkened during the previous year, in case
of air raids. On 4 December 1917 a set of 37 Hand Bells in a strong
wooden box was handed over to the Vicar. In 1918 it was resolved to
repair the bell frame in the tower and to re-gild the clock dial and
hands. A committee was to consider what form a village War
Memorial might take, and in 1919 a meeting was summoned to consider a War Memorial for the church. Also in that year, the Church
Army were to be invited to take over the Church Institute and work
it as one of their Social Centres. (This is the first mention of the
Institute in these minutes.)

The first appearance of ladies at the Easter Meeting occurred in
1921, when two 'Mesdames' appear among the attendees. The fol-

lowing year there were eight ladies, and in 1923 twelve ladies were present. The church insurance was increased in 1921 to £10,000. In 1923 it was recorded that the accounts had been submitted to the Parochial Church Meeting in January; this was the normal procedure from then on.

In 1924 the Easter Vestry was held at the Institute; eleven men and seven women attended. (The Institute continued to be the venue until 1933, following which there is a gap in the record until 1946.) In 1925 there were 18 women and 21 men present. A vote of thanks was accorded to Mr Thornton for allowing the use of the Infant School (the old Town House) at a nominal rent of £1 per annum, for use as a Sunday School. The Easter Offering that year was £26.5s.3d. It was agreed to give the church a 'Spring Clean'. The Parish Charities continued to be distributed as usual at this period. In 1931 £49 from the Free Will Offering was granted towards the expenses of the Institute. In 1932 and 1933 the Institute accounts were presented; in 1933 it was proposed to install an Emergency Staircase there.

Following the gap in the minutes, the record begins again on 25 April 1946, when the meeting took place in the Day School. From 1947 through to 1963 the meetings were held at the Institute, and in 1964 and 1965, when the record ends, in the Day School. In 1958 it was proposed that funds should be raised by a Finance Committee for a Church Hall and a house on the Sunnyside Estate; a new Institute; and repairs to the Organ: all at an estimated £18,000. In 1961 and again in 1964 the setting up of a Stewardship Campaign was reported upon. The main business of these meetings otherwise was the election of Churchwardens and Sidesmen.

CHURCHWARDENS' ACCOUNTS

From the 16th century there are two pieces of paper containing lists of payments that are very difficult to decipher. One of these refers among other things to a variety of repairs to the church, such as glazing windows and mending the church gate; also, cleaning the church, payments for bread and wine at Midsummer and Michaelmas (29 Sept), and a "payment to a certain Goodwife for washing the church linen."

From the early 17th century comes a list of names and amounts of money, though whether these are disbursements or receipts is not clear. Since the 'Over Mill' and the 'Nether Mill' are mentioned it could be a list of levies collected, but there are a few obvious payments at the end. 74 names appear on the list followed by "paid at Ester...for bred & wine 17s:2d. Paid at Crismas last for bred & wine 4s:6d. Paid at Ester last for bred & wine 17s:8d."

Then, from the 18th century, there is a ledger containing the records (usually in detail) of the Churchwardens' annual expenditure, beginning on 29 May 1781 and ending with the accounts for 1931/2. Churchwardens were elected at the Easter Meeting, so the Parish financial years varied somewhat in length, depending on the date of Easter. The details of the first year recorded in this ledger are set out below.

Money paid in 1781 by Thos West, Churchwarden		£	s	d
May 29	To a Ringing Day		2	6
	To Oil for the Clock		2	6
June 3	To Bread & Wine for the Sacriment [sic]		3	11
June 4	To a Ringing Day			6
June 14	To Thos Harris for new Bell Ropes	1	2	0
June 25	To Richd. Wells [Clerk] a quarters pay		7	3
July 9 & 13	To Carridge [sic] three Load of Old Lead to Northampton		15	0
July 20	To Carridge of two Load of New Lead from Northampton		10	0
	To Carridge of Lime & Sand		2	0
Sep 22	To a Ringing Day		2	6
Sep 29	To Richd. Wells a Quarters Pay		7	3
Sep 30	Bread & Wine for Sacriment		3	11
Oct 23	To the Briefs		2	4
	To the Court Fees		6	0
	To the Visitation	1	1	0
		5	8	8

In the second half of the financial year, (between 25 Oct 1781 and 27 April 1782) Wm. Danes recorded similar items, together with the following:

	£	s	d
Paid Thos. Allin by Bill	49	17	5½
Paid Benjamin Cuffley by Bill	18	12	1½
Paid John White by do.	2	5	1
Paid Willm. Johnson by do.	1	13	7
Received by Levy	80	4	9½
Due to the Parish from last Year	2	6	5¾
	82	11	3¼
Total expenditure	81	4	5
Due to the Parish	1	6	10¼

The heavy expenditure during the year 1781-2 was obviously owing to the renewal of some of the roofing leads. In 1783-4 Jerom Green and John Cumberpatch expended £17.1s.1d. This included such items as:

20 load of cheppens [chippings] for the Church Yard	6/8d
Ale for gravelin [sic] the Churchyard	2/8d
Lock for Church Chest	3/-
Paid to Wm. Gardner for washing Surples	
& tabel Linnen & cleaning the plate	3/-

In 1784-5 a new prayer book for the Clerk cost 11/-. A new set of Bell Ropes each year usually cost just over £1. In 1785-6 there was more work to the roof leads, with the accounts of Thos. Allin, Daniel Cuffley and Wm. Johnson being settled. The total expenditure was £55.5s.3d, and the Levy was £54.4s.3½d. In 1786-7 the following items were included:

Paid at Mr. Dines for six & thirty Dinners & Beers	1 16 0
Farmers Dinners & Liquers at the Visitation	1 1 0
Paid at Mrs Barritt's Visitation	1 1 0

In 1787-8 Ann Wells (Clerk) received 7/6d per quarter, an increase of 3d. Wm. Gardner washed the linen six times, for which he was paid 6/6d plus 6d for cleaning the plate. Twice yearly Visitations still cost £1.1s.0d each. One recurring item was "Oil for the Clock": this must have been for the chiming mechanism, since there was no clock face on the outside of the tower until this was authorised by the Vestry in 1870.

In July 1789 "Dinners & Ale" cost £1.11s.0d. In 1792 Wm. Gardner was paid 15/- for ringing the bell: he was presumably the Sexton. In 1795-6 £2.15s.0d was being paid for "40 Dinners & Ale" and £3.5s.9½d for "Ale to the Church Work".

On 3rd June 1802 the Churchwardens were instructed to repair the middle aisle of the church. In that year £1.12s.9d was paid for "Beer for the workmen"; £1.10s.0d for wine for the Sacrament; and a half-year fee for Wm.Gardner of £1.2s.6d. In 1809 four bottles of wine cost £1. In 1810 Mr Cheshire was paid £67 for repairing the spire; 3/1d was paid to John Fitzhugh for "Ale for the workmen at the Church"; and Wm. Gardner's annual salary was £3.3s.0d. From the evidence of subsequent entries, the recurring item of 2/6d for a "Ringing Day" appears to be the cost of beer for the Ringers. (Present-day campanologists please note!)

In August 1811 the previous year's accounts were, for the first time apparently, "examined and approved of (Errors excepted)" by the Rector, Robert Baxter BD; C A Danes; and Wm. Green. Expenses for the Bishop's Visitation in 1813 amounted to £4.4s.0d, and items such as "Parchment 2/6d" and "Strings for the Bass 2/6d" appear. In 1820 someone was paid 5/- for "Tolling the bell for his Majesty" (George III died in that year). The same amount had been paid in 1818 for tolling for "the Princes" in May and "for the Queen" in October. A similar item appears in April 1827 "for the Duke"; then, on 9th July 1838, 5/- was paid to the ringers to celebrate the coronation of Queen Victoria.

The purchase of coal and faggots for the church stoves appears for the first time in January 1823, although an item in April 1824 says "For lighting the stoves 2 years last Christmas & for scuttles 10/-"; also "For candles 1/-". Most services were held in daylight, but presumably a little light was required on dark winter days for those reading prayers or scripture passages; candles were also used on the altar. The purchase of coal appears regularly from then onwards, priced in 1836 at 15 pence per hundredweight (112 lbs), and fees were paid for taking down and cleaning the stoves in the summer.

Brushes or brooms were purchased for church cleaning, and in 1837 "half a dozen of besoms" cost 1/-. In that year the dinner for Confirmation candidates cost £2.6s.9d.

On 1st March 1863 the following entry appears:

Commencement of the Restoration of the Church.
E Slater Esq Architect. R Cosford, Contractor. Mr Thompson, Clerk of the Works.
Mark Cumberpatch & Wm. Trasler Churchwardens.
Re-opened November 19th 1863 with full Choral Service

The Church Rate levied that year totalled £262.5s.6½d.

Then appears the following:
1863: Burial Ground Expenses.

Paid: Sir George Robinson, ½ acre of land	£100	0	0
Sir George Robinson's Solicitor		14 15	0
Mr Tomalin Junr., Bill		34 10	2
Messrs Hayward, Surveyors		3 7	6
Johnson, for Walling		25 12	8
T Goff for carting stone		8 16	0
Labour		8 11	0
Mr Wood for lime		8	8
Mr Tomalin Senr. for stone		23 5	0
Gates		5 16	10
Clover seed		3	5
Keys for gates		1	2
Consecrating Church Yard		20 18	0
Bill for Gates		14 15	0
Bill for Gravel		1 0	0
Paid Labour		3 1	0
[Total]	£265	1	5

The new Burial Ground was consecrated by Dr Jeune, Bishop of the Diocese, on 30 July 1864. At that time Charles Danes was the Choirmaster & Organist; the first Harvest Festival was held on 14 September with a full choral service, using the united choirs of Kingsthorpe and Dallington.

Friday, 23 March 1866 was a Day of Humiliation for the Cattle Plague. There were three services, including two sermons. Evidence from the accounts of the Kingsthorpe Manor & Town Lands Charity shows that a Cattle Plague Rate was levied in 1866, presumably to assist those who were financially affected by the disease (which may have been Anthrax).

In February 1869, since it was no longer legal to levy Church Rates, the Vestry decided to defray future expenses by taking up a collection on the third Sunday of each month, presumably at both main services. In 1870 the expenditure of £1.1s.0d for insurance of the church appears for the first time. Included in the expenses for 1873-4 was "one gallon of petroleum: 1/10d"; but no details are mentioned regarding its use.

The financial situation of the church was clearly unsatisfactory at this time: until 1868 a Church Rate had been levied on each property in the parish, set at a level that would produce sufficient funds to defray the past year's expenses; payment of this rate was compulsory. But now that the income of the church depended upon the generosity of its members, expenditure often exceeded the funds available. This meant that donations were often requested in order to make up the deficits.

The Parish Church was lighted with gas for the first time on Christmas Day 1887; the pendants had been designed by the Northampton church architect Mr M H Holding. The cost of installation was £112, which was raised by the proceeds of three concerts, a bazaar held at the Vicarage, and a number of donations. This installation meant that quarterly gas bills became payable, totalling nearly £10 in the first year.

On 9 August 1901, for the Coronation of Edward VII, the ringers were paid £2.10s.0d; this was twenty times as much as was paid for a ringing day a century earlier. By 1904-5 the Organist was being paid £26; the Organ Blower 10/-; and the Sexton £10 per year.

During 1909-10 repairs to the spire and tower were carried out: the top of the spire, the north window, and the north-east and north-west buttresses of the tower were rebuilt; and loose or decaying stones in the spire made good; the total cost was £192.10s.11d. During 1911 the Bells were re-hung and the oak fittings replaced with steel, the cost being raised by subscriptions. A new bell was also added, which was the gift of the Vicar, Rev. E L Tuson. The bells were rung for the first time at the Coronation of King George V on 22 June. In the accounts for 1915-16 The County Fire Office charged an additional premium of £2 because of possible air raids. In 1916-17 a special collection of £19.5s.1d was taken up for curtains and shades for the windows and gas pendants on account of air raids. The turnover that year was £123.19s.1d. In 1917-18 the total insurance premiums were £5.10s.0d, including £1 for aircraft cover.

The year 1918-19 saw an increase in the number of special collections:

	£	s	d
Lord Roberts Memorial Fund	7	4	2
Organ recital for St Dunstan's Home	2	15	0
Harvest Festival offerings divided between the General Hospital and the Holloway Prisoners of War Fund	17	6	2
Mission to Seamen	7	10	0
St Dunstan's Home	6	3	9
Red Cross Committee	3	11	9

In the following year the outgoings included:

Central Church Fund	14	19	1
Waifs and Strays Society	4	9	9
Diocesan Fund	13	5	0
General Hospital (Harvest Festival offerings)	14	6	5
Choir Treat	6	17	3
Save the Children Fund	18	10	0
Sunday School Fund	7	19	2
Society for the Propagation of the Gospel	9	9	7

The above payments are a clear indication of the fact that Kingsthorpe was by then not just a country parish, but part of a much wider world. It also indicates the increased level of prosperity found in at least a section of the community. Turnover for the year 1919-20 was £227.14s.4d.

On 10 October 1920 the stained glass window and oak tablet in memory of the Kingsthorpe men fallen in the Great War 1914-1918 was unveiled by General Lord Horne. In 1920-21 Wednesday evening services were introduced during Advent and Lent. Special offertories were then quite numerous, including such objects as the Fabric Fund, Sunday Schools, Red Cross, the Sick and Needy, the Hospital, and the missions. By 1922 the Organist was paid £8.10s.0d per quarter, and the Organ Blower £1 per Quarter. In 1919 and 1920 the choir rendered Stainer's *Crucifixion* on Palm Sunday, and again in 1922 on Good Friday; in 1921 they sang *The Way of the Cross*.

During 1923 the restoration of the Tower, estimated to cost about £2,000, was commenced: Messrs Law Harris & Co. were the Architects and Messrs Henry Martin Ltd. the Contractors.

The turnover for the year 1924 was £294.14s.2d. In 1926 the payment for the restoration of the tower was completed – paid for out of a separate fund, of course. £54.14s.0d was spent in the same year out of the Organ Fund. During 1929 a new Heating Apparatus was installed in the church at a cost of £290.17s.5d.

The final entries in the ledger are the accounts for 1932; to enable comparison with the expenditure of 150 years previously (1781-2 transcribed above), here are the details:

INCOME		£	s	d
Brought forward from 1931		24	9	0
Collections – including special collections		290	8	4
Total		314	17	4

EXPENDITURE				
Feb 15	H Parker: gas mantles		6	0
	Sunday School Funds	5	19	0
Mar 12	E F Moore: printing	1	1	0
	The Church House – Donation	2	2	0
Mar 15	G T Durant: coke	4	1	2
Mar 16	Church Missionary Socy.	4	13	8
Mar 23	Repair bell rope		1	6
Apl 1	Mr Warren: Organist	8	10	0
	Mr Wallace: Sexton	6	5	0
	Mrs Parker: Cleaning church	3	10	0
	Mr Blennerhassett – Organ blowing	1	0	0
Apl 7	Jerusalem & the East Mission	2	0	0
Apl 11	Chas Oakley: printing		19	0
Apl 18	Visitation fee		16	0
Apl 17	Choir Surplice Fund	14	9	1
Apl 23	Oil for bells		1	9

Date	Description	£	s	d
May 1	Diocesan Quota (part)	5	6	10
May 3	N'ton. Gaslight Co.	2	19	3
	G T Durant: coke	3	12	8
May 18	Choir Outing Fund	5	0	0
May 20	Universities Mission to Central Africa	3	19	0
June 12	P'boro' Cathedral Restoration Fund	5	14	9
June 26	N'ton. General Hospital	7	16	7
July 1	Mr Warren: Organist	8	10	0
	Mr Wallace: Sexton	6	5	0
	Mrs Parker: Cleaning church	3	10	0
	Mr Blennerhassett – Organ blowing	1	0	0
July 2	Queen's Institute of District Nursing	6	16	6
July 25	H Parker: gas mantles etc.		12	2
	Church Fire Insurance Policy	9	0	0
	Employer's Liability Insurance		10	0
July 27	Work done in Churchyards	6	2	6
July 28	N'ton. Gaslight Co.	1	18	1
Sept 1	Sweeping stoke-hole chimney		2	0
Sept 12	R Harris & Son: printing	1	1	0
	Messrs P Phipps: Communion wine	1	4	0
	Messrs Arlidge & Son – stationery		10	0
Sept 16	G T Durant: coke & coal	6	6	7
Sept 20	Chas Oakley: printing	1	6	0
Sept 28	N'ton. General Hospital	14	18	9
Oct 1	Mr Warren: Organist	8	10	0
	Mr Wallace: Sexton	6	5	0
	Mrs Parker: Cleaning church	3	10	0
	Mr Blennerhassett – Organ blowing	1	0	0
Oct 8	Carting water		3	6
Oct 12	Missions to Seamen	9	2	1
Oct 22	Repair bell rope		3	6
Nov 5	N'ton. Gaslight Co.		19	5
Nov 22	H Parker: gas mantles etc.		6	6
Nov 29	British Legion	7	2	7
Dec 7	Draught proof tubing and fixing		4	11
Dec 14	Mrs Walden: washing surplices	1	0	0
Dec 21	R Harris & Son: stationery	1	7	6
Dec 22	G T Durant: coke	1	12	5
Dec 24	Annual sub. - Rural Decanal Conference		10	0
	Soc. For the Propagation of the Gospel	7	11	1
	Messrs Phipps & Co – Communion wine	1	4	0
	Childrens' Endowment Policy	2	8	8
	Sunday School Fund		12	0
	Sick and Needy	18	19	2

Easter Offering	19	18	8
2 cheque books (May & Oct)		8	0
Mr H J Hill: winding clock	2	10	0
N'ton. Gaslight Co.	2	9	4
Messrs Starmer Shaw & Son: Tuning Organ	3	15	0
Union Chaplaincy Fund	2	3	0
Choir Surplice Fund	3	2	0
1 broom		1	0
Messrs Cleaver Ltd – Installation of water	11	0	0
Mr Warren: Organist	8	10	0
Mr Wallace: Sexton	6	5	0
Mrs Parker: Cleaning church	3	10	0
Mr Blennerhassett – Organ blowing	1	0	0
Carried forward	18	5	4
Total	**314**	**17**	**4**

THE FOUNDATION OF NEW PARISHES

Due presumably to the increasing population of Northampton, a proposal was made on the occasion of the death in 1850 of the Rector, the Rev R W Baxter, that Kingsthorpe should be severed from the Rectory of St Peter's. It was to become a separate Parish for Ecclesiastical purposes and a Perpetual Curacy and Benefice. It had an annual value of £500 from Glebe Lands and Surplice Fees, and there was, of course, "a Rectory House and offices fit for the Residence and hitherto occupied by the Incumbent of the said Rectory". The Patronage and right of nomination was to remain with the Master and Brothers and Sisters of the Royal Hospital or Free Chapel of St Katharine near the Tower of London, whose Chapter approved the proposal on 9 February 1850. The Order in Council (No. 20) was approved one month later.

The next alteration to the parish was in 1877, when a new and separate parish was carved out of Holy Sepulchre and Kingsthorpe parishes to form the parish of St Paul in the Semilong area. In her diary, on 22 June 1877, Mary Susan Thornton records that the Rev Hugh Somerville Gedge came to live in St George's Terrace and began his work as the Vicar of St Paul's. She also says that the last time the School at Semilong was used for church services was Sunday, 9 December 1877; the new 'Iron Church' (a temporary building constructed of corrugated iron) was opened the following weekend. The official documentation says that 'certain persons' (undoubtedly the Thornton family) had given an endowment of £1,045, which would provide a payment of £34.16s.8d to the future incumbent in May and in November each year. The Rev Glover, Vicar of Kingsthorpe at the time, gave a piece of Glebe Land next to the river and adjoining Semilong Lane, 11 acres in extent, which was intended to provide a further grant of £50 per annum to the incumbent.

In 1894 a new parish, that of St Matthew, was formed in the Kingsley area of Kingsthorpe parish; the approval of the church by the Ecclesiastical Commissioners was sealed on 22 November 1894. The Rev J R Hussey had been appointed Curate in Charge of the district in 1889, when services were initially held in a small Infant School. A temporary iron church was opened on Palm Sunday of that year, on land given by the Thornton family. Mr Pickering Phipps gave another piece of land and built the permanent church in memory of his father (also named Pickering Phipps). Building work began in August 1891, the foundation stone being laid one month later. The finished church was consecrated in September 1893, and the Rev Hussey was instituted as Vicar.

Holy Trinity parish was formed in 1900, and was named in honour of the Hospital of the Holy Trinity, otherwise known as St David's. The Ecclesiastical Commissioners approved the church on 28 September 1909, following its consecration in July of that year.

In 1939 St David's church was built as a daughter church, and opened in 1940. It was formed into a separate parish in 1967, but as part of the implementation of the Team Ministry in 1973 it once more became part of the major parish.

St Mark's church at White Hills was built as a dual-purpose church and hall in 1950 and dedicated in 1980 to serve as a District Church.

NONCONFORMISTS IN KINGSTHORPE

NONCONFORMISTS have a long and important history in the Kingsthorpe area, the earliest recorded Meeting House here having been licensed in 1702. This chapter transcribes what is recorded about those Meeting Houses; it mentions the influence of Philip Doddridge; it gives a brief description of the Baptist Church; and finally, to complete the religious picture, it mentions the more recent history of the Roman Catholics and Methodists in Kingsthorpe.

Nonconformists or Dissenters of one type or another existed from the English Reformation onwards. These were people who, for various reasons, preferred to worship in ways that differed from the established church, the Church of England. Following the third Act of Uniformity in 1559, people were to be fined twelve pence for every absence from church; by the end of Elizabeth's reign such fines had been increased to £20 per month. In view of such penalties, it is not surprising that many nonconformists kept their personal views quiet and attended the parish church. Those who declined to attend were known as Recusants, although from 1570 onwards this term was usually applied to Roman Catholics, otherwise known as Papists, who dared to adhere publicly to the 'Old Religion'.

Then there were those who considered that the established church did not practice Christianity in close enough accord with the principles of the New Testament. Some believed that there should be no interference in religion by the state; others held that only adult believers should be baptised. Such nonconformist sects were persecuted until the passing of the Toleration Act of 1689, which gave them the right to have places of worship together with their own preachers and teachers.

An Ecclesiastical survey, known as the Compton Census, was made in 1676: the results for Kingsthorpe gave figures of 570 Conformists,

6 Non-conformists, and no Papists.

Non-conformist Meeting Houses

Meeting Houses for Dissenters were licensed from 1689. Persons associated with Meeting Houses in Kingsthorpe between 1699 and 1852 (excluding 1708-1736) are listed in the *Meeting Houses Index* at NRO as follows:

1702	Beriiga[?] Cooper	Carpenter
1704	Wm Garrett	
1737	John Marriott	
1740	John Johnson	
1774	John Dines	Occupier
1774	Chas Fitzhugh	
1774	John Johnson	
1774	Richd Manning	
1774	Richd Wood	
1774	Thos Wood	
1822	Jeremiah Perrin	A certain barn in the occupation of Jeremiah Perrin.
1826	Wm Stanton	Owner
1835	Stephen Manning	A new erected Building on the premises late belonging to Stephen Manning [i.e. The Chapel.]
1835	Richd Sibley	Owner

The following registrations of Meeting Houses for Protestant Dissenters were submitted to the Archdeacon or to the Bishop of Peterborough:

10 September 1787: House of Chas Johnson. Signatories: Thomas Lee, John Roe, John Ealey, George Bradshaw.

17 May 1799: House in High Street. Signatories: Abraham Abbott, Richard Manning, Thomas Green, John Wood.

5 November 1802: House belonging to Wm Buckler. Signatories: William Buckler, Thomas Dunkley, Mary Yeomans, Joseph Slinn [mark].

9 May 1804: House occupied by Wm Tarry. Signatories: Susanna Yeomans, William Tarry [mark], Samuel Johnson, Richard Johnson.

2 June 1807: House of Thos Parbury. Signatories: Isaac Lilly, Thomas

Parbery [sic], William Turrey, George Peach. [Thomas Parbery's wife, Hannah, was baptised into the Baptist Church at Kingsthorpe in October 1823.]

The influence of Philip Doddridge

Philip Doddridge's ministry in Northampton spanned the years 1729-51; he first lived at 34 Marefair on the corner of Pike Lane, and later moved his home and academy to the former Northampton residence of the Earl of Halifax in Sheep Street. Support for Doddridge's *Family Expositor* (1738-56) included at least one from Kingsthorpe; this may well have been Elizabeth Cooke (1700-63), wife of Thomas. Although they normally lived at Stoke Newington, the Cooke family still had their residence and other property in Kingsthorpe. Geoffrey Nuttall, in his calendar of Doddridge's correspondence, says that she was also a donor of books to the Northampton Academy. Doddridge's connections with the Cooke family are reflected in his letters; he mentions at least eight visits to the Cooke household between 1731 and 1749. His friendship with Thomas Cooke's daughter-in-law Elizabeth resulted in the Non-conformist emphasis at the Free School at Kingsthorpe when she appointed the first trustees in 1753.

In June 1732 Doddridge, through his preaching in a barn at Kingsthorpe, incurred the wrath of James Wells, Curate at Kingsthorpe 1730-4. The barn in question was no doubt one of those attached to the mansion owned by the Cooke family. An item in the Northampton Mercury of 9 November 1900 says that it was through preaching at Kingsthorpe and getting into an angry discussion with the Curate that Doddridge was cited for keeping his Academy at Northampton without the permission of the Bishop of Peterborough. This disagreement is reflected in Doddridge's letters to Wells during August and September 1732, quoted by Nuttall as Items 375, 377, & 378.

In his letters to his wife Doddridge reports preaching in November 1742, when he "walked to Kingsthorpe in the Deep Dirt" and baptised several children, and preaching at Kingsthorpe again in December and in February of the following year.

Early Baptists in Kingsthorpe

From 1768 Abraham Abbott, of Kingsthorpe, was a member of College Lane, and he later became one of the deacons; he died in December 1820. Eight persons baptised at Moulton by the Rev. William Newitt formed the first Baptist Church in Kingsthorpe, independent of College Lane, in March 1823; they were joined by a number of members of the College Lane Church, in Northampton, who lived in the Kingsthorpe area.

But well before this time Kingsthorpe had been an important preaching station from College Lane during the pastorate of Dr. Ryland. The Rev John Collett Ryland was born in 1723; he joined the Baptist Church in 1742; moved to Northampton in 1759; and was Minister at College Lane until 1785. He was actually ordained on 18 September 1760. He left Northampton for Enfield, Middlesex, in 1786. He died on 24 July 1792 and was buried in the College Lane church on 29 July. His son, John Ryland Junior (1753-1825), was co-pastor and then minister at College Lane 1781-1792; his letter of release was dated 24 November 1793.

During his pastorate Dr John Collett Ryland preached more often at Kingsthorpe than at any other village. He recorded preaching there, often on Sunday evenings, between 1770 and 1786. John Ryland Junior was regularly preaching in the area from the age of 14, and by 1776 was preaching an average of four times each week. So it may well have been the son, not the father, who preached in Kingsthorpe from 1777 onwards.

Kingsthorpe Baptist Church

This is not intended to be a detailed history of the Baptist Church in Kingsthorpe. But its influence on the spiritual life of the community was of such importance, second only to the Parish Church, that the first century following its formal foundation deserves to be dealt with in some detail. In 1808 the dissenters at Kingsthorpe were not satisfied with the preaching of the then minister of College Lane. So the pulpit at Kingsthorpe was supplied by John Chown, a member of the family that had been involved in the foundation of the Baptist Church at Moulton. Mr Chown's ministry lasted only until Lady Day

The Baptist Chapel in the High Street, opened in 1835. (Photo by the author).

1809. The pulpit was then supplied on alternative Sundays by a Mr Smith of Guilsborough and by students of John Sutcliffe's Academy at Olney. Mr Chown returned to Kingsthorpe in 1814 and continued as pastor until 1821.

The pastor from 1822-1824 was Mr Hewitt; it was during his ministry that the formal separation from College Lane occurred. (Was this, perhaps, the same person as the Rev William Newitt, mentioned above under *Early Baptists in Kingsthorpe*?) The next recorded pastor was the Rev George Ashmead, who came to Kingsthorpe in 1837. Between those two pastorates the congregation had met in the "two rooms", and there is also mention of the "old place of worship" (which may be different). The first proper Chapel was opened in High Street in 1835, and it forms the central part of the chapel that stands there today.

Mr Ashmead's ministry lasted from 1837 to 1847, when the Rev Joseph Roberts came to Kingsthorpe; but he died a few months after his settlement. In 1848 the Rev Joseph Litchfield became pastor of Kingsthorpe until 1891; (born in 1814, he died at Kingsthorpe in 1892). Three years after his settlement he was offered the Mastership

290

of the Free School, a position he maintained until 1888. There is no doubt that the additional income enabled him to remain at Kingsthorpe, and enabled the Church, though apparently somewhat weak at that time, to retain his dedicated ministry. The Rev J T Brown made a lovely remark on the occasion of the erection of a tablet in memory of the Rev Litchfield, when he said of him that he was

> "...no ordinary man. He was very simple, unobtrusive and quiet in his habits, choosing to walk in retired paths, and moving in those without noise."

The Rev Joseph Litchfield, pastor of Kingsthorpe Baptist Church from 1848-1891 and master of the Free School 1851-1888. (Picture courtesy of Peter Valentine).

In 1872 a site next to the Chapel was purchased for the building of a Sunday School; this was opened by the Rev J P Chown of Bloomsbury in December 1881. The Sunday School had been founded in 1813 and had met in 'Kelseys Yard School Cottages'. It is not known where this was, but it seems possible that it was a cottage in The Yard, off High Street: a description of the estate of Geo. Danes, deceased, dated 1908/9, refers to seven cottages "40-52 High St. [and] a small cottage added to Litchfield's". From the sketch plan in the same document it appears that the Rev Litchfield had occupied No. 46, which was somewhat wider and had two storeys and an attic, with cottage No.1 in the Yard at the rear attached to it. The entrance to the Yard, with its four dwellings, was between 44 and the garden of 46 High Street.

Wright's Directory of 1884 is quite informative about religious matters: it says that Sunday services at the Baptist Chapel were held at 10.30am and 6pm, and there was a meeting on Mondays at 7.30pm. Mr Biggs played the Harmonium and the Chapel Keeper was William Jeffs. In 1891 the Rev G W Robert became pastor, and shortly afterwards a scheme to enlarge the chapel was completed. The main building was carried back about twice its original length, and an entrance porch of Duston stone was built. The interior was re-seated with pitch-pine pews; a new rostrum and new floor of wood blocks completed the alterations. The opening ceremony was held on 8 September 1892. Rev G W Robert left Kingsthorpe in 1896 and was succeeded by the Rev F Neal, who was pastor until 1902. The Rev R E Letheren was pastor from 1903 until 1907; the Rev G H Robinson from 1909 to 1916; and the Rev S Somersall Black from 1917 to 1928.

In November 1909 a large upstairs lecture room, with a vestry and two large classrooms below, were opened. The Centenary celebrations of the Church took place in 1923 and the organ was installed in June of that year. A fund was then opened to enable the purchase of the Church's first Manse, 33 St. Paul's Road. This was to remain the Manse for only a short period of time, for in 1929 it was sold and a new Manse, 105 Queens Park Parade, was purchased.

For a more detailed description of the history of this church, see: Noon, Frank E & Valentine, Peter (1973); *Kingsthorpe Baptist Church, Northampton: Ter Jubilee 1823-1973: A Brief History*. A copy can be found in the Northamptonshire Local Studies Collection.

Roman Catholics in Kingsthorpe

Although there were no Papists in Kingsthorpe in 1676, according to the Compton Census mentioned earlier, there were certainly Catholics living in the village during the first half of the 20th century; but they had to go to the Northampton Cathedral at the top of Primrose Hill to attend services. In 1956 a Mass Centre was established, using an upper room in outbuildings at the rear of the old Rose & Crown public house, at the corner of the Welford Road and High Street, for the celebration of Mass on Sunday mornings. But with about 150 people attending, the floor of the room was found to be unsafe; so in 1959 the Mass Centre transferred to a room in

Kingsthorpe Hall, at that time used as a Community Centre. The Rose & Crown had been purchased with the intention of building a church on the site, but a proposed road-widening scheme prevented further progress, and an alternative site was found in Manor Road. This had once been the farmhouse, orchard and outbuildings belonging to the Danes family, and had later come into the possession of the Perkins family – another well-known Kingsthorpe name. A fund was opened to provide finance for the permanent church, and Bishop Leo Parker laid the foundation stone of St Aidan's Church in May 1963. The old farmhouse, known as Manor House, became the Presbytery. The church, designed by the architect Sebastian Comper (son of Sir Ninian Comper), was opened in 1964, with Fr Christopher Roberts as its first Parish Priest.

Methodists

On 12 December 1894 the Kingsthorpe Local Board approved plans for the building of a Wesleyan School Chapel in Queens Park. Newspaper files state that the Gold Street Wesleyan Methodist Chapel in Northampton opened a new school chapel on a site in Osborne Road on the Queen's Park Estate in May 1895.

In the later 20th century the Methodists of Kingsthorpe converted a disused cinema on the Welford Road into a chapel with meeting rooms &c. The chapel in Osborne Road then became a Gospel Hall.

Other places of worship

Kelly's Directories of 1898 and 1903 say that there was a Free Gospel Hall in Garfield Street, but no trace of this can be seen today. There is, however, a building set back from the other houses in Lincoln Street which might once have been a chapel; at its rear (visible from the Asda car park) it has only one window; this is at first floor level, and has a semi-circular top. The building appears to have been converted to a dwelling house by the addition of bay windows to the front elevation and a chimney external to its gable wall. The minutes of the Kingsthorpe Local Board, meeting on 11 October 1893, record the approval of building plans for a Mission Hall in Lincoln Street.

ENTERTAINMENTS AT KINGSTHORPE

THERE was once a tradition of holding May Games here, according to Bridges; the Lord and Lady of the games were appointed by the Bailiff after evensong on Easter Sunday. But these games had been discontinued long before Bridges's time, following an accidental death. Baker says that there were occasions in the past when a quintain was erected on the Green; apparently the last time this was done was in 1722, as part of the celebrations following a marriage. In the Northampton Mercury of 22 May 1749 there appeared an announcement concerning an entertainment at The White Horse on Tuesday 30 May. The prize of a silver-laced hat of about 25/- value was to be played for, or rather fought for, at Singlestick; this was a form of fencing using a stick with a basketwork handle. There were also six pairs of buckskin gloves, which were to be wrestled for. Gentlemen attending were to enter their names between 2pm and 4pm that afternoon and agree the wrestling arrangements among themselves.

Whitsuntide Festivities at Kingsthorpe

At Whitsuntide in 1850 the Monday and Tuesday were given over to a selection of amusements; these apparently attracted several thousand people from Northampton over the two days, according to the Northampton Mercury of 25 May of that year. The event seems to have been initiated the previous year by William Parbery, landlord of the *King William IV*, and he was joined in the enterprise by George Waterfield of the *Mason's Arms* (now Kingswell Cottage). At the top of the village, at the *White Horse*, the Bowling Green was available and there were some tea gardens. On the Green there were "revived rustic amusements on a liberal scale". On the Tuesday, for instance, there were a variety of races: sack race, blindfold race, and wheelbarrow race; also "swarming the pole for a fine leg of mutton" and "boys eat-ing hasty pudding" for the prize of a hat. There was another pole-swarming event at Cornelius Love's beerhouse (now the *Queen Adelaide*), and it seems that both legs of mutton were secured by the same person, who had developed a method of climbing the pole with the help of a piece of rope; the onlookers were not amused!

Kingsthorpe Horticultural Show

In the Northampton Mercury of 13 July 1867 there was a long report about the Kingsthorpe Horticultural Show, held in the grounds of Kingsthorpe Hall, now known as Thornton Park. The tenant at that time was Miss Frances Boddington, and she opened the gardens and shrubberies for public access on these occasions. The Perkins family, being local Nurseymen, were represented by numerous exhibits, and there was great interest in an exhibition of wild flowers. This event was an annual attraction, organised by the Kingsthorpe Horticultural Society; in later years it was held in the grounds of St David's, courtesy of Lady Winifred Robinson.

At the Half Way House

During 1875 posters appeared in the area advertising a "great walking feat of 240 miles in six successive days". This feat was to be performed by a 76 years old 'Pedestrian' named Mountjoy. On Monday 30 August he was to begin his walk from Mr Plumb's, *The Half Way House*, Kingsthorpe Road, to *The Coach & Horses*, George Row, and from there to *The World's End* at Ecton; he would then return to his starting point. The circuit was to be traversed three times on each of the six days. As if that were not sufficient: "In the Ground at Mr Plumb's the veteran will perform his GREAT FEATS at six o'clock in the evening". These feats consisted of walking half a mile and then walking backwards for half a mile; picking up 30 stones, placed on the ground one yard apart, one at a time and bringing each one back to a basket placed near the first stone. He would then pick up 20 eggs (also placed one yard apart) with his mouth, and without his knees touching the ground, and put them in a bucket of water. All of this was to be done in 45 minutes.

The poster stated that 'the Veteran' had twice walked a record distance of 79 miles a day for six successive days; this was from Norwich to Yarmouth and back, twice a day. Tickets "to see the Old Man perform each evening in the Grounds" were 6d each, and could be obtained at *The Half-Way House*. The Grounds referred to in the poster were the Pleasure Grounds, or Albert Recreation Grounds, associated with *The Half Way House*. The poster itself forms part of a collection of such items, along with many newspaper cuttings, relating to Pedestrianism and other athletic contests.

The Assembly Barn

The Barn near to Kingsthorpe Hall was put into use as a social centre by the Thornton family. In July 1877 the family was considering how to make use of the Barn for the benefit of the local community, and the Rev William Thornton had several meetings in this connection. Later that year it was opened for the use of the men and boys of the village; it was in use every Saturday, with anything up to around 50 attending, and every Monday and Wednesday with about half that number. This continued until the family went to the south of France for the winter of 1880-81, where the Rev Thornton unfortunately died. The Barn was eventually re-opened on Saturday, 25 November 1882 when, as the Rev Thornton's daughter Mary recorded in her diary, "between 50 and 60 came from 8 till 10 o'clock". It was then to be open three nights a week, Monday, Wednesday & Saturday, as of old.

It is likely that this Barn was the one nearest to the Hall, since the other was converted into 'Home Farm' at around this time; but there is no certainty about this.

KINGSTHORPE BOWLING GREEN CLUB

The information about this Club is contained in the five NRO documents CAM 1049-1053, which consist of record books kept by the Club between the years 1771 and 1852. On the cover of the first of these books is inscribed 'Bowling Green', and on the back cover 'White Horse...Kingsthorpe.' The Bowling Green itself was part of the estate of the Robinson family; it was just across what is now Kingsthorpe Grove from the Inn known as the *White Horse*. This was not, of course, the present building but its predecessor. (See George James deWilde's reminiscences about the *White Horse* in the chapter *Rambles Roundabout*.) The members were professional gentlemen such as attorneys, physicians, merchants, clergy, and landed gentry mainly from the surrounding area, not only from Kingsthorpe. Meetings were held from May to October each year; lists of members were entered in the records, sometimes accompanied by nicknames.

The club was as much a Dining Club as an opportunity for a game of bowls, since the meetings included an extended meal at the *White Horse*, evidently accompanied by much drinking. No doubt many business and financial projects were initiated at these meetings, and the members were not averse to a wager: on one occasion about the eventual cost of the London-to-Birmingham Rail Road; at other times about bowling prowess; but often about such trivial matters as the age of the waitress.

Eventually a set of rules was formulated for the club, with conditions for membership, the attendance of guests, and the payment of subscriptions, fines, and so on by the members. As the years passed meetings became less frequent and less well attended, and charges had to be increased accordingly. The record ends abruptly, without any explanation, in 1852, a year when there had been 20 members and only five meetings. Although the members of this Club – or Society as they often liked to call it – were for the most part not Kingsthorpe residents, the records are of interest from the point of view of social history. They illustrate the life-style of the gentlemen of the area in the late 18th century and the first half of the 19th, a period when a large proportion of the residents of Kingsthorpe were experiencing great poverty. They also illustrate the facilities and popularity of the *White Horse* at that period.

The first list of members consisted of 19 names, but by September 1773 this had increased to 43. James Fremeaux and his son Peter were members during the early years. In 1778 there were 34 members listed, some of them with aliases such as 'Yankee Doodle' and 'Rump & Dozen'. A variety of colourful and amusing notes is inscribed in the records, relating to such things as the weather, the excellence (or otherwise) of the dinner, or the number of bottles of port lost in wagers. In 1799 the members were paying 2/6d each meeting for their dinner and green fees; absentees had to pay 1/6d to the landlord.

It should be noted that the wine drunk on these occasions was not table wine but port at 3/6d a bottle. There are many notes regarding the provision of venison. It appears that Lord Northampton and Lord Spencer each provided venison for the Club every year. On 31 July 1800 there is a reference to Lord Northampton and the expectation of venison to be had at the next meeting. On 14 August a request was submitted to know when the Gentlemen wished to have the 'Althorpe Venison'; it was agreed to have it at the next meeting and ladies were to be invited.

On 9 May 1805 it was reported that the landlord had been making losses, presumably in the previous season. It was decided that subscribers would be made responsible for arrears of payments in respect of people that they had proposed. But that did not solve the landlord's problem. So it was agreed that subscribers would pay 2/- for non-attendance and that the Dinner Ordinary would be increased to 3/-. Five years later a further increase was agreed, when Ordinaries would be 4/- and non-attendance forfeits 2/6d. The charge for Tea would be 1/6d. Typical bills for that year (1811) were £5.12s.6d, £4.12s.9d (this for 7 persons), £5.18s.9d, and £7.7s.4d. More than half of each of these amounts was for drinks.

An 'extraordinary meeting' was held on 8 December 1808, when one of the members furnished a haunch of doe venison. This was so successful that meetings were held in subsequent years on the Thursday nearest to 8 December. In 1810 Lord Northampton's venison was ordered for Wednesday 8 August; and Lord Spencer's venison was consumed on 23 August, when 9 ladies and 13 gentlemen were present. The bill for the dinner on that occasion came to £13.14s.6d, of which at least £7 was for drinks.

In May 1824 an amended set of *Rules & Regulations of the Bowling Green Society* was proposed which included the following:

● Meetings: from the first Thursday in May, every three weeks until the first meeting in October.

● Subscribers pay 4/- for the Ordinary and 1/6d for tea (if taken). If no more than three at dinner, then 7/6d out of fines towards the bill. 2/6d for the waiters on ordinary days & 5/- on venison days.

● 2/- each day for Greenage. Absentees pay 2/6d each time to the Landlord.

● President for the Day would be fined a bottle of wine if he was not present by 3.15pm, at which time Dinner was to be on the table. He was fined the same if the bill was not called for by 5.30pm.

In 1828 there were 14 members and two honorary members. Sir George Robinson (6th baronet) was counted as a member, but never attended meetings. That year there were eight meetings, with venison provided by Lord Spencer, Mr Cartwright and Sir George Robinson.

An indication of how much drinking took place can be gained from the bill for 22 September 1831, when there were nine present and the cost of dinner was £1.16s.0d; wine £2.2s.6d; perry & porter 5/6d; fruit 12/6d; and servants & greenage 4/6d. Average per capita consumption of port was in excess of one bottle at most meetings; on 20 August 1835, when ten members were present, they drank four bottles of champagne and eight bottles of port.

In October 1843 a meeting of the *Kingsthorpe Old Bowling Green Society* was held to see if better regulations could be adopted "with a view to fuller attendance of members". It was agreed that there would be five meetings each year, on the fourth Thursdays of the months of May, June, July, August & September. The landlady was guaranteed payment for at least seven members dining, at 4/- each, even if less were present. In 1845 members met on one Tuesday each month for the purpose of drinking tea, but consumption of port and sherry continued at other meetings at an average of one bottle per person. Port now cost 5/6d per bottle, from which at least twelve glasses could be poured.

On 23 September 1852 eleven members dined for £2.4s.0d; nine bottles of wine cost £2.9s.6d; waiter & greenage 7/6d; and dessert 14/6d. The record ends abruptly at this point without expectation or explanation, but presumably because the *White Horse* had closed its doors; it is not listed in Trade Directories of 1854 onwards. A number of blank pages follow, and at the back of this book are records of the subscriptions received and bills paid from 1845 to 1852.

These records also contain details of the attendance at monthly meetings, from 1808 to 1813, of another Bowling Club that met on different dates. Among the members recorded are names that are recognisable as Kingsthorpe residents, such as tradesmen or farmers. Their dinner hour was at 4 o'clock. There are no colourful notes, and their purpose appears to have been simply to enjoy a game of bowls and share a meal together.

APPENDIX 1
LAND HOLDINGS FOLLOWING
THE INCLOSURE OF 1767

The following list has been extracted from the inclosure map and associated documents and then sorted into alphabetical sequence.

Abington Church	8	0	34	
Archbold, John	6	0	21	
Atkins, Joseph	32	1	29	
Atkins, Mrs	12	1	04	
Atkins, Mrs	71	3	18	
Atkins, Mrs				Old inclosure in village
Baker, John & Tilley, John	4	2	36	
Bilson, Robert	2	0	13	
Bowker, James	1	3	19	
Brookes, William				Close?
Bryan, Thomas				?
Causby, John	1	0	03	
Cole, Edward	3	2	00	
Conant, Revd.	58	0	06	
Cooch, Thomas	15	0	06	
Cooch, Thomas		1	34	
Corbit, William	3	1	12	In right of his 1st wife
Corbit, William		1	18	In right of his 2nd wife
Cradock, William			16	Windmill Close
CROWN LAND				Great Walbeck Close, portion, not specified.
CROWN LAND	42	1	30	
CROWN LAND	6	1	23	Town Holme, North Mill
CROWN LAND		1	22	Cradock's Little Holme
Cuffley B & T			33	
Cuffley, Benjamin		2	16	
Cuffley, William		2	09	
Danes, John	22	2	12	
Danes, John	28	0	29	
Danes, John				Knights Close?
Dickenson, Elizabeth	2	1	24	
Dickenson, Thomas	8	0	15	
Ecton, George	1	2	37	
Ford, John	64	1	02	
Ford, John			?	
Ford, John	9	3	18	

Name				Description
Ford, John		3	29	
Fremeaux, James				Dovehouse Close
Fremeaux, James			?	
Fremeaux, James	90	0	11	
Fremeaux, James				Walbeck Close (Later
exchanged with Sir George Robinson)				
Fremeaux, James ?				Little Walbeck Close
Gooday, Revd	9	1	28	
Gooday, Revd				Pond Close; inclosure in the North Field
Gooday, Revd	52	2	37	
Gooday, Revd				Close?
Green, Jerom	27	1	38	
Green, Thomas	50	1	29	
Green, Thomas	1	3	13	
Green, William	3	3	37	
Hill, Richard	12	1	17	
Hill, Richard	24	3	37	
Hill, Richd. & West, Wm	8	0	27	
Hill, Richd. & West, Wm.	2	0	01	
Hollis, George		1	14	
Hollis, George	1	3	19	
Hollis, Thomas	1	3	34	
Hollis, Thomas	17	2	24	
Irons, Moses		3	11	
Johnson, Thomas	1	0	17	
Johnson, William	1	0	30	
Kenning, Josiah				Close
Lambe, Mr	12	0	06	
Lockwood, Revd.	24	0	07	Glebe
Lockwood, Revd.	10	1	09	The Moor Leys, The North and South Moor Meadows; in exch. with Sir G Robinson
Lockwood, Revd.		3	12	North part of Tallis's Holme; do.
Lockwood, Revd.	1	1	02	Do. (Townsend Close) exch. Mrs Atkins.
Lockwood, Revd.				Parsonage House & grounds
Lockwood, Revd.	34	1	11	Great Tythes
Lockwood, Revd.	205	2	04	Great Tythes
Lockwood, Revd.				Old inclosure in the North Field
MAIDEN HOOK		2	22	

Nixon, Rebecca	2	3	12	
POOR'S LAND	14	0	18	
Powys, Thomas	4	1	20	For his Bush Rent
Powys, Thomas	3	2	16	For the open field inc. the road
Robinson, Sir Geo				Cradock's Holmes, North Mill
Robinson, Sir Geo			33	Cradock's Holmes, North Mill
Robinson, Sir Geo				Great Wallbank Close
Robinson, Sir Geo	5	0	24	Town Holme at Tallis's Mill
Robinson, Sir Geo				Tallis's Holmes
Robinson, Sir Geo		2	25	Tallis's Mill
Robinson, Sir Geo				Old inclosures
Robinson, Sir Geo				Edmunds's Farm
Robinson, Sir Geo				The New Close
Robinson, Sir Geo	211	2	03	
Robinson, Sir Geo				Old inclosure in the North Field
Robinson, Sir Geo		3	19	From Eliz. Wills (late Cooper Cardew)
Robinson, Sir Geo			18	'Hog Bank'
Robinson, Sir Geo				Knights Close
Robinson, Sir Geo	1	2	33	Allotment in Haddlecroft
Robinson, Sir Geo				The old Lane mansion & close
Robinson, Sir Geo	1	1	17	Elm Close; Exch. w Hill & West
Robinson, Sir Geo		2	22	Swans Nest, Tallis's Mill
Robinson, Sir Geo				Daves's Warren
Robinson, Sir Geo				Bowling Green
Robinson, Sir Geo				Three Corner'd Close
Robinson, Sir Geo				Old inclosures around his house
Robinson, Sir Geo.				The Great House Close
Robinson, Sir Geo.	5	2	08	The Cock Close; later exch w J Fremeaux
Sibley, Thomas	1	0	25	
Smith, Ann	13	1	36	
Smith, William	7	2	31	
Smyth, Christopher	48	3	06	
Smyth, Christopher	9	3	01	

Stanton, Richard	19	3	23
Stevenson, Edward	7	0	07
Stevenson, John (minor?)	12	1	31
Stevenson, Sarah		2	23
Stevenson, Sarah			Old inclosure in the North Field
Stevenson, Susannah	20	2	22
Stone Pits, 4	2	0	00	½ acre each
Tibbs, Henry	5	2	16
Tibbs, Henry	2	1	14
TOWN LAND	14	2	14
Treslar, Elizabeth	14	2	32
Walding, Catherine		1	21
Wells, Zachariah				Close
West, William	21	3	09
White, John	20	0	13
Wills, Elizabeth (minor)	10	0	31
Wood, Richard	5	2	16	In Semilong Field
Wood, Richard	54	2	14	East of Welford Rd
Wood, Richard				Court Farm Close

APPENDIX 2
POOR RATE LEVY DATED 23 NOVEMBER 1681.
(Extracted from NRO Ref: 189p/270).

Name	£	s	d
Mr Morgan		9s	0d
Doct. Reynolds		10	0
Francis Cooke		10	6
Wm Atkins		4	8
Thos Jenaway		1	6
Clement Darlow		2	6
Henry Milward		2	0
Thos Morris		2	4
Wm Green		2	6
Samuel Ladd		3	8
Edwd Causby		2	11
Rich Hollis		1	6
John Biddles		2	6
John Billingham Jr		1	4
Daniel Jaques			4½
John Wood			4
Wm Brookes			4
John Bilingham		2	0
Wm Bates			3
Wm Dixing [Dixon?]			7
Richd Hollis		1	3
John Billingham		1	9
John Food			2
Mrs Pickmer		1	8
Wm Billingham			7
St Andrews Mill		2	0
Dan Jaques			4
Roger Comberbach			2
John Doxey			3½
John Willson			8
John Curall			2
John Wright			2
Robt. Pickmer		1	8
Thos. Jannaway			11
Henry Milward		1	7
Wm Green		2	4
Samuel Crick		3	2

Name	£	s	d
John Childe			2
Walt Dickenson			2
Wm Dixon			2
Geo Lamly		1	2
Rob Wright			5
John Cooper (Junr)			2
Rich Morris			1½
Rich Moris [sic]			1½
Wm Brooks for ye close			1½
John Wakefield			1½
James Waite			2
Wid: Langford			8
Abington Land			4
Richd Billingham			4
Thos Morris (Junr)		2	10
Robt. Cannel			2
John Bidles		2	3
Henry Cooper			3
Wid: Becket			2
Upper Miller		1	3

	£4	10	10

APPENDIX 3
WORKHOUSE INVENTORY (1805)

In the Kitchen: One round oak table, one square deal table, one oak square table and an oak folding table; this [is] almost new. Four chairs, five candlesticks, one clothes brush. A grate, fire shovel, tongs, poker, a brass fender and fire hanger, two smothers and bellows. One large baking pan. One Dutch oven. Eight little drinking pots, six larger ditto, two salt cellars, one Market basket and a candle box.

Pantry: Three barrels. A deal dresser, one pantion[1], a large wooden bowl, one large wood dish. A tape. One brass cook, one wooden cook, a bread basket, one flour barrel, one decanter. An oak thrall[2]. One dozen [and a] half knives & forks.

Hall: Two long forms, a dough trough, one stool, five spinning wheels, one reel, one long brush, three water buckets, one yoke, one coal riddle, a hand bowl, 14 wooden spoons, 14 wooden dishes, two dozen trenchers. Three earthen[ware] baking dishes, one brass gallon kettle, one ditto of two gallons, one brass tea kettle, a large boiler, a tin kettle. Pot hooks, a washtub, two scuttles, two shoe brushes.

Chambers: (1) Three oak bedsteads, three flock beds, three bed mats, three blankets, three pillows, three blankets [sic], six sheets. [We may now be in a second chamber.] Seven bedsteads, seven bed mats, six flock beds and a feather bed, eight blankets, 13 sheets – six of them new. Seven bolsters, seven coverings, three oak chests, and one tea chest. A hop sieve, a large trunk, a Brewing Copper and lid, a warming pan, a cream pot, a clothes basket, a frying pan, an old armchair, a fire hook and grate. [This is the last page of the ledger, and the inventory may originally have continued on to another page, since lost.]

---

1 pancheon or panchion: a coarse earthenware pan
2 Thrall: a stand for barrels &c.

APPENDIX 4: OCCUPATIONS IN 1777

Here is a list of persons selected for Militia service in occupation order:

Richard Manning	baker
John Treslar	baker
Thos Treslar	baker
John Warner	barber
Robert Bassett	blacksmith
Enoch Dudley	blacksmith
Willm White	blacksmith
Edward Wells	breeches maker
Willm Buckler	breeches maker
John Simpson	butler
John Walker	butler
Bartlet Carr	carpenter (infirm)
Willm Cuffley	carpenter
Daniel Cuffley	carpenter
Joseph Cuffley	carpenter
Wm Spooner	carpenter
Thos Flavel	coachman
Henry Higgins	constable
Willm Danes	farmer
Charles Fitzhugh	farmer
Willm Green	farmer
Thos Green (Snr)	farmer
Thos Green (Jnr)	farmer
Jeremiah Green	farmer
John Johnson	farmer
John Lucas	farmer
Samuel Stanton	farmer
Richd Stanton	farmer
Henry Tibbs	farmer
Thos Wood	farmer
Richd Webb	footman
Willm Cumberpatch	gardner
Willm Garner	gardner
Peter John Fremeaux	gentleman
Simon Danes	labr (infirm)

Thos Freeman	labr
John Gibson	labr
Willm Healey	labr
Jeremiah Boswell	labr
Frances Causby	labr
Roger Cumberpatch	labr (infirm)
Thos Dains	labr
Charles Deacon	labr
Richd Dickens	labr
Jeremiah Ellis	labr
Richd Giles	labr
John Hollis	labr
Richd Lack	labr
Thos Lee	labr
Willm Lucas	labr
Samuel Lucas	labr
Willm Morris	labr
Thos Morris	labr
Willm Parrot	labr
Thos Parrot	labr
Daniel Parrot	labr
George Peach	labr
John Percival	labr
James Percival	labr
Daniel Row	labr
Thos Sibley	labr
Thos White	labr
Samuel Whitsey	labr
Thos Wills	labr
John Wood	labr
Charles Johnson	mason
Richd Pell	mason
Abraham Abbot	miller
Thos Banks	miller
Thos Craddock	miller
Willm Manning	miller
Thos Tallis	miller
Thos Butlin	ostler (infirm)
Robert Ammons	servant
George Arbard	servant

John Barnard	servant
Thos Battling	servant
James Clarke	servant
Joseph Dunkley	servant
Willm Ellis	servant
James Horn	servant
James Jones	servant
Thos Lillington	servant
Saben Luckkuck	servant
Samuel Millard	servant
John Miller	servant
John Reave	servant
Samuel Smith	servant
John Southam	servant (infirm)
Frances Thompson	servant
John Wheatley	servant
George Bradshaw	shoemaker
Richd Capin	shoemaker
Thos Percival	shoemaker
Willm Sibley	sieve maker
John Sibley	sieve maker
Willm Whiting	stonecutter
Thos Abbot	weaver
Willm Cuffley	weaver
John Johnson	weaver
Francis Parbery	weaver
Richd Warner	weaver
Robert Kinnig	woolcomer
Thos Peach	woolcomer
Willm Brooks	woolstapler
Samuel Pipping	woolstapler
Willm Stevenson	woolstapler

APPENDIX 5

OCCUPATIONS AND TRADES IN 1851

Here is a detailed classification of occupations, as found in the Kingsthorpe census for 1851 (as analysed by Alec Brooking):

Gentry	7
Clergy	3

Farmers and agricultural trades (251):

Agricultural labourers	221
Farmer	11
Farmer & Miller	1
Farmer & Innkeeper	2
Farmer, Miller, Baker	1
Farmer, Auctioneer, Lime Burner	1
Gardener	7
Miller	6
Shepherd	1

Crafts and Industries (121)

Textile

Lacemaker	17
Handloom Weaver	1
Plain Sewer	1

Ironwork, Metals and Heavy Industries

Blacksmith	6
Farrier	1
Machine worker	2

Building Trades

Bricklayer	3
Brickmaker	6
Brickyard Labourer	1
Carpenter	15
Lime Burner	3
Painter & Glazier	1
Plumber & Glazier	2

Workers in stone (39 in all).

Quarryman	3

310

Stone Mason	25
Stone Mason & Beerseller	1
Stone Mason's Labourer	4
Stone Sawyer	6
Leather Workers	
Cordwainer	9
Currier	1
Miscellaneous Crafts	
Basket Maker	2
Bonnet Maker	2
Chairmaker	2
Chairmaker & Beerseller	1
Turner	2
Wheelwright	4

Distribution trades, clothing, food, etc. (102)

Baker	6
Beerhouse Keeper	2
Beerseller & Butcher	1
Boot & Shoe Maker	55
Boot & Shoe Closer	5
Boot & Shoe Finisher	1
Boot & Shoe Binder	2
Butcher	3
Confectioner	1
Dealer in Grocery	1
Dressmaker	10
Furniture Dealer	1
Higgler	1
Innkeeper	2
Maltster	1
Shopkeeper	2
Soda Water Bottler	1
Tailor	5
Tailor & Beerhouse Keeper	1
Victualler	1

Miscellaneous, services, etc. (91)

Bone & Iron Collector	1
Book keeper	1

Chair woman	4
Dealer	4
Governess	1
Housekeeper	2
Labourer	6
Labourer on turnpike	1
Labourer (road)	2
Laundress	18
Musician	1
Nurse	2
Ostler	1
Policeman	1
Porter	1
Proprietor of Houses	1
Yeoman proprietor of houses	1
Railway labourer	1
Servant	35
Surveyor	1
Teacher	4
Toll Collector	2

APPENDIX 6: KINGSTHORPE
CHRISTENINGS 1540-1554 inc.

This extract is based on the PR transcript of 189p/1 in NRO Library, and then checked against the microfiche of the PR. It should be borne in mind that the original PR was written on paper, but since this proved inadequate the 'old books' were transcribed on to vellum in 1600, when Izacher Brooks and William Morris were Churchwardens. The paper records were no doubt in very poor condition by then, and this accounts for some slightly unusual entries, which could be taken as, for example, burials or marriages entered amongst baptisms. We have to take what we have at its face value, but accept that it is not complete in all details and probably includes some inaccuracies.

Note: All years in this extract begin on 1 January, using New Style years.

Date	Name	Parent	Notes
1540			
June 3	Joan	Geoffrey Brooks	
June 3	Simon	Ralph Cowper	
Nov 7	[daur]	Richard Pierson	
Nov 9	[son]	John Cowper	
Nov 12	Richard	Richard Andrewe	
1541			
Jan 3	Margaret	Richard Pytman [Pickmer?]	See Burial 21 Oct 42
Jan 27	Margaret	Maud Wright	
Jan 28	Richard	Robert Sylbie	
Feb 7	Agnes	William Malyn	
March 7	William	Thomas Sheppard	
March 13	John	John Abbott	
March? 31	Alice	[——] Byrdsall	May 31?
March 31	William	W[——] Brooks	May 31?
July 6	Parnell, daur of	John Orpyn	
July 12	Anthony	Geoffrey Brooks	
July 13	Richard	Robert Parker	
July 14	Alice	Thomas Stormer	
Aug 12	John	Richard Blunte	

313

Date	Name	Parent	Notes
1542			
Feb 27	[son]	Ralph Byrdsall	
March 20	[son]	Henry Boddymer	Robert? Burial Jun 46
April 15	[son]	William Kynge	
April 24	Joan	Robert Sylbie	
June 17	[daur]	William Dobbyns	
June 18	Richard	Clement Sheppard	
July 3	Simon	George Draper	
July 6	Alice	Thomas Sheppard	
[?]26	Alice	Richard Brooks	
[??]	Alice & Margaret	?Luke Watson	
Aug 13	Alice	William Blunt	* Assumed 1542.
Sept 10	Alice	John Clerke	* This group
Oct 15	Agnes	Anthony Smyth	* entered after
Oct 21	Anthony	Robert Dickinson	* March 1543 (n.s.)
Dec 24	Alice	John Else	
[?] 26	Alice	[?] Nutbrowne	Dec 26? Jan 26 1543?
1543			
Feb 23	Peter	Robert Dickinson	See Oct 21 1542.
Feb 27	Elizabeth	Thomas Watson	
Feb 27	Richard	John Dickinson	
March 9	Alice	William Quenbie	
April 1	Thomas	Thomas Watson	
April 3	Richard	John Dickinson	
April 4	William	John Ellis	
April 15	[daur]	Richard Andrewe	
June 12	Mary	Robert Parker	Entered after 4 April
Sept 1	Robert	Richard Pyckmer	
Sept 9	William	Geoffrey Brooks	
Sept 19	Pheby	James Kinge	
Oct 3	William	Richard Pierson	
1544			
Feb 7	Robert	William Curson	
[?] 9	Pleasaunce, daur of	Henry Ragdall	
Feb 20	William	John Orpyn	
Feb 23	Richard	John Cowper	
March 24	Margerie	Thomas Sheppard	
April 1	Joan	Thomas Cannan	
April 15	Benett, daur [sic]	Mr Williamson	Son? (Benedict)
April 15	John	Mr Morgan	
April 30	Philipp, daur [?]	John Abbott	

May 10	Joan	William Brooks	
Oct 13	Agnes	William Kinge	
Oct 28	Bridget	Robert Dickinson	
Oct [?]	Alice	Thomas Wylson	
Dec 3	Richard	Robert Dickinson	Entered in Mar 45

1545

March 15	Elizabeth	John Clerke
March 17	Joan	Richard Alwood
March 30	Joan	Anthony Smyth
April 17	Elizabeth	Richard Andrewe
May 3	Anthony	Philip Davison
June 22	Joan	Clement Sheppard
Aug 12	Robert	William Brooks

1546

Aug 21	[Daur]	William Brooks
Aug 31	[Son]	John Dickinson
Sept 15	Elizabeth	William Malyn
Sept 15	Margaret	James Kinge
Oct 11	[Daur]	Alice Sheppard
Oct 12	[Daur]	Richard Peirson

1547

Jan 27	[Daur]	John Raylton
March 12	[Nicho]las Williamson	son of Brygett [——]
April 17	[Daur]	Thomas Sheppard
May 12	Agnes	Thomas Wylson
June 11	Richard	William Gyles
June 20	Richard	William Davison
July 24	Henry	Richard Skinner
Aug 5	Simon	R[——] Peke
Dec 19	Amy	Richard Peirson
[?] 21	Richard	William Brooks

1548

March 27	Francis	William Morgan	
Sept 7	Mary	Simon Childe	*Entered in Mar 1549
Sept 8	Elizabeth	[——] Hynde	*Buried 23 May 1549
Sept 11	Thomas	William Fleete	
Sept 30	[Daur]	William Paynter	
Oct 3	[Son]	Thomas Wylson	
Nov 19	?Daniel	James Kinge	

Date	Name	Parent	Notes
Nov 20	[son]	Anthony Smyth	
Dec 3	[Doro]the	Robert Dickinson	
Dec 7	[——]me daur of	William Malyn	

1549

Date	Name	Parent	Notes
Jan 6	Fortune, daur of	William Fleete	
Jan 8	Mary	Robert Astell	Buried 6 Feb 1549
Jan 15	Robert	Henry Ragdall	
Jan 22	Avice, daur of	Anthony Smyth	
Jan 23	Thomas	Thomas Barker	
Jan 24	[——]mys daur of	Robert Porter	
Jan 28	William	[——] White	
[Feb?] 17	Mary	John Cowper, the younger	
[Feb?] 17	Alice	John Hollis	
March 9	Barbara	Mr Williamson	Buried 23 May 1549
March 13	Clement	Robert Houghton	
[Undated]	Alice	Nicholas Tedd [Todd]	*Buried 31 Mar 1548
March 26	Alice	Nicholas Tedd [Todd]	*26 Mar 1548?
May 30	Margery	Thomas Frauncis	
July 14	John	Geoffrey Brooks	Buried 5 Oct 1550
Aug 1	Nicholas	Mr William Morgan	
Aug 6	Mary Coste & Mary Wilson		
Aug 18	Mary Geffes & Robert Dobbyns		
Aug 28	Robert	Robert Dickinson	
Oct 20	Alice	Nicholas Tedd [Todd]	*See above, 26 Mar

1550

Date	Name	Parent	Notes
Jan 3	Agnes	Robert Houghton	
Feb 6	Thomas White & Margaret White	John White?	See Burial 12 Feb
Feb 4	Valentine	Ralph Byrdsall	Presumably Feb 14!
Feb 15	Clement	William Brooks	
March 2	William	John Hollis	
March 9	Joan	Robert Pecke	Peake?
April 18	Mary	Richard Skynner	
May 17	Thomas	John Porter	
Aug 17	Dorothie	Anthony Smyth	
Aug 24	Alice	Thomas Tomlinson	
Aug 25	Mary	Thomas Smyth	
Sept 9	Thomas	William Myller	
Sept 12	John	John Ford	
Oct 1	William	William Fleete	
Oct 24	Elizabeth	Simon Childe	

Date	Name	Parent	Notes
Dec 12	Geoffrey	Thomas Grygges	
Dec 25	Mary	Mr William Morgan	
Dec 25	Joan	Christofer Davie	

1551

Feb 11	Nicholas	Thomas Wylson	
March 2	Robert	Thomas Wright	
March 9	Simon	John Cowper	
March 26	Millicent	John Nicolson	
April 1	Thomas	John Baine	
April 5	Thomas	John White	
May 7	William	Richard Skynner	
May 17	James	Mr Williamson	
June 11	Suzann	Thomas Jeffs	
Nov 12	William	Robert Dickinson	

1552

Jan 27	Brygett	Anthony Smyth	
Feb 15	Amey	Geoffrey Brooks	
April 13	Robert	John Barber	
June 21	Simon	John Ford	
July 24	Elizabeth	William Fleete	
July 25	Alice	John Hurlocke	
July 27	Simon	Thomas Smyth	
July 28	Agnes	Nicholas Tedd [Todd]	Buried 1 Aug 1552
Sept 28	William	John Cowper	
Oct 10	Alice	Simon Childe	
Oct 12	Richard	Thomas Wright	
Oct 22	Charitie, daur of	Mr Williamson	
Nov 29	Simon Bonne, son of John Bone		
Dec 16	Thomas	Richard Banckes	
Dec 20	Thomas	John Watts	

1553

Jan 8	Thomas	John Hollis	Buried 19 Jan 1553
Feb 5	Richard	Thomas Geffes	
Feb 20	Alice	Richard Skynner	
March 11	Agnes	Edward Steven	
March 18	Julyan, daur of	John Peake	
April 12	Agnes	Ralph Byrdsall	
May 10	Anne	John Nicolson	
May 25	Brygett	Thomas Wylson	

Date	Name	Parent	Notes
June 3	William	William Wallis	
July 11	Mary	Henry Bett	
July 15	John	William Myller	
Aug 5	Agnes	Nicholas Tedd [Todd]	
Aug 10	Agnes	John White	
Aug 16	Jane	Robert Dickinson	
Aug 27	William	Geoffrey Brooks	
Sept 3	Audrey	Anthony Smyth	
Nov 5	Thomas	John Hurlocke	Buried 15 Nov

1554

Feb 24	Amey White		
Feb 27	Brygett Martyn		
March 4	Thomas Houghton		
April 3	Thomas Hollis		
May 4	Alice Porter		
May 12	Robert	Richard Burton	
June 7	Amey	John Ridge	
June 28	John	Nicholas Williamson, gent.	
July 17	Amey	William Pretty	
July 28	Amey	Edward Geffes	
Aug 18	Simon	Thomas Wright	
Aug 26	Amey	John Walker	
Sept 3	William	Thomas Morris	
Sept 28	Thomas	John Astell	
Oct 6	Thomas	John Redyall	[Ragdall?]
Oct 8	Robert	Symon Cooke	
Oct 14	Thomas	Thomas Smyth	
Oct 20	Alice	William Fleete	
Nov 5	Agnes	Simon Childe	
Nov 8	Thomas Hurlocke		† See 5 Nov 1553
Nov 12	William	William Jenkins	
Nov 15	Alice	John Ford	
Nov 17	Hugh	John Gylbert	
Nov 28	Amey Davie		† These 3 entered
Dec 1	John Cooke		† in March 1554.
Dec 12	John	Geoffrey Brooks	
Dec 21	Simon	John Hurlocke	
Dec 24	Nicholas	Anthony Smyth	

APPENDIX 7: KINGSTHORPE MARRIAGES
1539-1554 inc.

This extract is based on the PR transcript of 189p/1 in NRO Library, and then checked against the microfiche of the PR. See my note accompanying the Christening extracts. At first sight the sequence of dates and the placing of the year markers in the Marriage Register are quite confusing. In addition, if correlations are made, where possible, between the dates of marriages and the baptism of children, a number of anomalies are apparent. I am not referring to marriages that obviously take place after conception – not uncommon at the time – but to marriages that appear to have taken place some months after baptism.

In trying to make sense of this situation I noted the date of baptism, where available, and based a revised year of marriage on this. This information, together with the fact that most of the early years of the record began with a date in the Autumn – often November – initially made me think that the Marriage Register had been based on a year which began at Michaelmas (29 September). But this would have been very unusual, and would mean that the year 'began' six months earlier than the 'Old Style' calendar used in the Christenings and Burials sections, or three months earlier than our present day 'New Style' calendar. The scribe of 1600 obviously had some difficulty in making sense of what he was working from, but was as faithful as possible to the original. However, I suggest that he made a few wrong decisions that I have attempted to correct in my proposed reconstruction.

I have made two versions of this transcription. The first is in the order of the original – that is, the 1600 transcript – with the year markers as found therein; the second is my suggested reconstruction, which makes sense of the anomalies and shows that the record actually starts in October 1538 New Style.

In any case, we have to accept that the record is not complete and no doubt includes some inaccuracies.

Original entries

Date	Groom	Bride	Remarks
1539			
Oct 18	Thomas Watson	Mary Childe	
Oct 19	Nicholas Banes	Julyan [——]	
Oct 21	Richard Browen	Margaret Cheese	
Jan 25	Richard Awartoffe[?]	Joan [——]	
Nov 15	Thomas Castell	Elizabeth [——]	
June 15	John Reinolds	Agnes [——]	
Nov 15	John Raylston	Joan [——]	
Nov 27	Clement Cowper	Joan [——]	
Nov 29	John Dickinson	Margaret Coles	
1540			
Jan 22	Richard Andrewe	Agnes Dickinson	Baptism Nov 1540
Jan 24	William Quenbie	Izabell [——]	
Nov 21	Thomas Chatton	Jane Latham	
1541			
Nov 25	John Clerke	Margaret [——]	Baptism Sept 1542
Sept 17	Richard Blunt	Elizabeth [——]	Baptism Aug 1541
June 19	William Blunt	Margaret [——]	Baptism Aug 1542
Nov 10	Robert Porter	Agnes [——]	
June 25	Henry Aburne	Alice [——]	
June 29	Richard Coventrie	Margaret [——]	
1542			
Oct 21	John Hornsbie	Margaret [——]	
Oct 26	James Kinge	Hawys Talbott	Baptism Sept 1543
Sept 12	Nicholas Banes	Agnes [——]	
1544			
Nov 23	William Fleete	Joan [Eidon? Aide?]	
Nov 6	John Allen	Alice Webster	
1547			
Nov 24	Richard Stanton	Joan Pey	
Nov 27	William Allen	Joan Pyele	
1548	[Year inserted later, squeezed in between entries]		
Sept 30	Robert Nicolls	Joan [——]	
Nov 8	Thomas Castell	Elizabeth [——]	2nd marriage? See Nov 1539

APPENDIX 7

Date	Groom	Bride	Remarks
1548 *continued*			
Nov 7	Simon Child	Eleanor Hurlocke	Baptism Sept 1548
Nov 27	Thomas Frauncis	Elizabeth [Hunt?]	Baptism May 1549
Jan 15	Robert Porter	Joan [——]	Baptism Jan 1549. 2nd marriage? See Nov 1541
Jan 16	John Cowper	Alice Blee	Baptism Feb 1549 2nd marriage? Bapt. Nov 1540 - perhaps his father's child?
Jan 23	Robert Houghton	Alice [Aske?]	Baptism March 1549
April 30	William [Rawell?]	Alice Sheppard	
May 7	John White	Elizabeth Noye	
1549			
June 26	John Richardson	Margaret [——]	
Oct 20	Thomas Tomlynson	Margery [——]	Baptism Aug 1550
Oct 23	Robert Parker	Alice [——]	
Nov 3	Nicholas Tedd [Todd]	Alice [——]	Baptism(s) & Burial Mar '48
1549	[Entered for second time]		
May 12	Robert Morris	Margery Lee	
May 17	Thomas Barber	Agnes Care	
Oct 11	Geoffrey Brooks	Julyan Alee	Baptism July 1549
Oct 14	Thomas Sheppard	Alice Wytnes	2nd marriage? Bapt Apl 1547
Nov 9	Thomas Jeffs	Joan Coles	
Jan 7	Robert Boughton	Isabel Wright	
1550			
Nov 12	William Pretty	Alice Pettyver	
Nov 21	Thomas Smyth	Elizabeth Sheppard	Baptism Aug 1550
Nov 28	Thomas Launsell	Cicilie Morris	
Nov 30	Thomas Wright	Agnes Empson	Baptism March 1551
1551			
Jan 18	Clement Talbott	Agnes Pretty	
April 14	Thomas Skynner	Elizabeth [——]	
April 24	William Myller	Alice Monsole	
Oct 5	Robert Willowes	Agnes Hopkins	
Oct 7	George Matherson	Alice Hodgkyn	

Date	Groom	Bride	Remarks
1552			
March 29	John Abbott	Catherin Ragdall	
May 31	Thomas Wallis	Margaret Brooks	
June 6	Thomas Mannsfeild	Alice Astell	
Oct 5	Thomas Granborowe	Richd [sic] Sheppard	[Perhaps 'Richeldis'. But sometimes women did have men's names.]
Oct 12	Augustine Crispe	Elizabeth Morgan	
1553			
May 2	John Martyn	Alice Jeffes	
June 21	John Walker	Agnes Wright	
July 15	Simon Cooke	Cicely Ridge	Baptism Oct 1554
July 15	John Ridge	Alice Cooke	Baptism June 1554
Oct 9	Edward Jeffes	Joan Bodymer	Baptism July 1554
Oct 10	Robert Dayne	Ellen Alysandere	
Nov 11	John Gilbert	Joan Leach	Baptism Nov 1554
1554			
July 19	Thomas Barker	Agnes [Cowper?]	
Oct 18	Francis Medcalfe	Alice Tysdall	
Nov 12	Robert Peake	Joan Houghton	
Nov 4	John Walker	Catherin Bass	
Nov 10	Thomas Brooke, junior	Ursula Ridge	[Brooks]

1556 [No entries for 1555]

Possible Reconstruction

Note: The years in my reconstruction that begin at Michaelmas are marked as M/s, whilst those that begin on 1st January are unmarked.

Date	Groom	Bride	Remarks
1539 M/s [1538]			
Oct 18	Thomas Watson	Mary Childe	
Oct 19	Nicholas Banes	Julyan [——]	
Oct 21	Richard Browen	Margaret Cheese	
1539			
Jan 25	Richard Awartoffe[?]	Joan [——]	
June 15	John Reinolds	Agnes [——]	
1540 M/s [1539]			
Nov 15	Thomas Castell	Elizabeth [——]	
Nov 15	John Raylston	Joan [——]	
Nov 27	Clement Cowper	Joan [——]	
Nov 29	John Dickinson	Margaret Coles	
1540			
Jan 22	Richard Andrewe	Agnes Dickinson	Baptism Nov 1540
Jan 24	William Quenbie	Izabell [——]	
Sept 17	Richard Blunt	Elizabeth [——]	Baptism Aug 1541
1541 M/s [1540]			
Nov 21	Thomas Chatton	Jane Latham	
Nov 25	John Clerke	Margaret [——]	Baptism Sept 1542
1541			
June 19	William Blunt	Margaret [——]	Baptism Aug 1542
Nov 10	Robert Porter	Agnes [——]	
June 25	Henry Aburne	Alice [——]	
June 29	Richard Coventrie	Margaret [——]	
1542 M/s [1541]			
Oct 21	John Hornsbie	Margaret [——]	
Oct 26	James Kinge	Hawys Talbott	Baptism Sept 1543
1542			
Sept 12	Nicholas Banes	Agnes [——]	
1544 M/s [1543]			
Nov 23	William Fleete	Joan [Eidon? Aide?]	

Date	Groom	Bride	Remarks
Nov 6	John Allen	Alice Webster	

1547 M/s [1546]

Nov 24	Richard Stanton	Joan Pey	
Nov 27	William Allen	Joan Pyele	

1548 M/s [1547] [Year inserted later, squeezed in between entries]

Sept 30	Robert Nicolls	Joan [——]	
Nov 3	Nicholas Tedd [Todd]	Alice [——]	Baptism(s) & Burial Mar '48
Nov 7	Simon Child	Eleanor Hurlocke	Baptism Sept 1548
Nov 8	Thomas Castell	Elizabeth [——]	2nd marriage? See Nov 1539
Nov 27	Thomas Frauncis	Elizabeth [Hunt?]	Baptism May 1549

1548

Jan 15	Robert Porter	Joan [——]	Baptism Jan 1549. 2nd marriage? See Nov 1541
Jan 16	John Cowper	Alice Blee	Baptism Feb 1549 2nd marriage? Bapt. Nov 1540 – perhaps his father's child?
Jan 23	Robert Houghton	Alice [Aske?]	Baptism March 1549
April 30	William [Rawell?]	Alice Sheppard	
May 7	John White	Elizabeth Noye	
June 26	John Richardson	Margaret [——]	

1549 M/s [1548]

Oct 11	Geoffrey Brooks	Julyan Alee	Baptism July 1549
Oct 14	Thomas Sheppard	Alice Wytnes	2nd marrige? Bapt Apl 1547
Oct 20	Thomas Tomlynson	Margery [——]	Baptism Aug 1550
Oct 23	Robert Parker	Alice [——]	
Nov 9	Thomas Jeffs	Joan Coles	

1549 [Entered for second time]

Jan 7	Robert Boughton	Isabel Wright	
May 12	Robert Morris	Margery Lee	
May 17	Thomas Barber	Agnes Care	

1550 M/s [1549]

Nov 12	William Pretty	Alice Pettyver	

324

Date	Groom	Bride	Remarks
Nov 21	Thomas Smyth	Elizabeth Sheppard	Baptism Aug 1550
Nov 28	Thomas Launsell	Cicilie Morris	
Nov 30	Thomas Wright	Agnes Empson	Baptism March 1551

1551 [or 1550?]

Jan 18	Clement Talbott	Agnes Pretty	
April 14	Thomas Skynner	Elizabeth [——]	
April 24	William Myller	Alice Monsole	
Oct 5	Robert Willowes	Agnes Hopkins	
Oct 7	George Matherson	Alice Hodgkyn	

1552

March 29	John Abbott	Catherin Ragdall	
May 31	Thomas Wallis	Margaret Brooks	
June 6	Thomas Mannsfeild	Alice Astell	
Oct 5	Thomas Granborowe	Richd [sic] Sheppard	[Women did have men's names.]
Oct 12	Augustine Crispe	Elizabeth Morgan	

1553

May 2	John Martyn	Alice Jeffes	
June 21	John Walker	Agnes Wright	
July 15	Simon Cooke	Cicely Ridge	Baptism Oct 1554
July 15	John Ridge	Alice Cooke	Baptism June 1554
Oct 9	Edward Jeffes	Joan Bodymer	Baptism July 1554
Oct 10	Robert Dayne	Ellen Alysandere	
Nov 11	John Gilbert	Joan Leach	Baptism Nov 1554

1554

July 19	Thomas Barker	Agnes [Cowper?]	
Oct 18	Francis Medcalfe	Alice Tysdall	
Nov 12	Robert Peake	Joan Houghton	
Nov 4	John Walker	Catherin Bass	
Nov 10	Thomas Brooke, junior	Ursula Ridge	[Brooks]

1556

APPENDIX 8: KINGSTHORPE BURIALS
1539 TO 1553

This extract is based on the PR extract of 189p/1 in NRO Library, and then checked against the microfiche of the PR. See my note accompanying the Christening extracts. We have to take what we have at its face value, but accept that it is not complete in all details and probably includes some inaccuracies. Some regnal dates occur; Anno 1 Edward 6 began 28 Jan 1547 New Style.

Note: All years in this extract begin on 1 January, using New Style years. I have drawn attention to some of the families that had many burials during this period, thus: Brooks **: Pickmer ***: Sheppard ****.

Date	Name	Remarks
1539		
Feb 28	Alice Wooke	No earlier entries.
March 1	Thomas Cooke	
Nov 3	Ellen Tomlynson	† These were
Nov 23	Alice Wattes	† actually entered
Nov 25	Margaret Wattes	† in April 1540.
1540		
April 7	Agnes Anstie	
April 29	Margaret Pickmer	***
May 3	Alice Else	
May 10	Cicilie Morris	
May 27	Margaret Else	
June 10	Joan, daur of Geoffrey Brooks	** [Recent baptism]
June 17	Elizabeth, daur of John Raylton	
July 3	Joan, daur of John Crofte	
Nov 23	Robert, son of John Cowper	Baptised 9 Nov 1540?
1541		
Jan 20	Mr Maior's child of Northampton	
April 1	Alice Hobbes	
June 19	Richard Bett	
June 30	Margaret Barker	
Sept 17	Joan Child	* Actually entered
Sept 19	Thomas, son of Peter Dickinson	* before January item.

Date	Name	Remarks
1542		
June 10	Richard Else	
June 16	Thomas Coates	
June 19	Simon Mewse	[Mewes]
July 29	Peter Dickinson	
Aug 12	Elizabeth Kylworth	
Oct 21	Margaret & Robert, children of Richard Pickmer.	*** Margaret baptised 3 Jan 1541?
Nov 10	Thomas Creaton	
Nov 12	Ellen, daur of Richard Pickmer	***
1543		
Nov 12	John, son of Richard Phillips	
Nov 15	Thomas Kylworth	
Nov 21	Paul Kylworth	
Nov 22	Richard Pickmer	***
Nov 22	Thomas Pickmer	***
Nov 22	Francis Pickmer	***
Dec 28	Agnes Kylworth	
1544		
Jan 15	Simon Hurlocke	
Feb 19	John Styles	
March 29	Joan Sheppard	****
March 29	Margery Sheppard	****
April 3	Thomas, son of Laurence Wattes	
April 19	Joan, daur of Joan Bayley	
April 20	Bennett, son of Mr Billingham	
April 29	Amy Kylworth	
July 12	Alice Fyssher	
July 19	William Cannan	
Dec 17	Joan Brooks	**
Dec 25	William Brooks	**
1545		
April 3	William Brooks	**
April 15	Richard Godderd	
April 16	Suzann Brooks	**
April 17	Robert Smyth	
April 19	Joan Else	
April 28	William Orpyn	
April 29	Julyan Banes	
May 19	Joan Brooks	**

Date	Name	Remarks
June 1	William Corson[?]	

1546

Date	Name	Remarks
Feb 15	Richard Andrewe	
Feb 22	Margery Roe	
May 4	Thomas Crofoote	
June 20	Robert, son of Henry Bodymer	Baptised 20 March 1542?
July —	William Kinge	
July 29	William Sheppard	****
Aug 29	Robert, son of William Brooks	** Baptised 12 Aug 1545
Nov 15	George Draper	
Nov 15	William Strange	
Nov 21	Thomas Morgan, the elder	
Nov 29	Agnes Allen	

1547

Date	Name	Remarks
Jan 16	Agnes Porter	
Jan 17	Elizabeth Horsbie	
Jan 19	Alice Wylson	
Jan 26	Anthony Dawson	
Jan 31	Elizabeth Asson	[Dawson?]
March 20	William Guy	
March 30	Simon Crofoote	
April 2	John Hopkins	
April 2	John Orpyn	
May 1	Elizabeth Backstaffe	
May 3	Thomas Clyfton	
May 5	Thomas Penn	
May 15	Elizabeth Dickinson	
May 15	William Ball	
May 15	Amy Ellyott	
May 16	Agnes Lott	Anno 1 Edward 6
May 19	Joan Peirson	
May 21	Margery Nicolles	
May 23	Elizabeth Creaton	
May 26	William Bett	
May 28	Agnes Parker	Anno 1 Edward 6
May 29	Bennett Davy, Parson & priest	
May 29	William Peirson	
May 29	Thomas Malyn	
May 29	Alexander Ward	
May 29	Agnes Peake	
May 30	Margaret Brooks	**

Date	Name	Remarks
June 21	Joan Child	Anno 1 Edward 6
Aug 25	Lucy Hurlocke	Anno 1 Edward 6
Oct 27	Mary Sheppard	**** Anno 1 Edward 6

1548

March 31	Alice Todd	Anno 2 Edward 6
May 6	Robert Ward	
May 16	Simon Bacon	Anno 2 Edward 6
May 30	Margaret Ward	
May 31	Alice Goodwyn	
June 1	Richard & Alice Peirson	
June 4	Edward Martyn	
June 8	Ellen Peake	
June 10	Richard Brooks	**
June 17	Henry Gyles	
June 17	Agnes Gyles	
June 19	William Preston	
June 20	Elizabeth Ridge	
June 23	Elizabeth Brooks	**
June 23	Margaret Haynes	
July 15	Edmund Ward	
July 15	Thomas Sheppard	****
July 28	Robert Brooks	** Anno 2 Edward 6
Dec 5	Gilbert Williamson	Anno 2 Edward 6

1549

Feb 4	Richard Smyth	† These three: Anno 2 Edward 6
Feb 6	Mary Astell	† (Bapt. 8 Jan 1549)
March 11	John Hopkins	† but should be Anno 3.
April 23	Fortune Malyn	Anno 3 Edward 6.
May 12	John Pretty	Anno 3 Edward 6
May 23	Elizabeth Hynd	Anno 3 Edward 6
May 23	Barbara Williamson	Anno 3 Edward 6
June 24	Mother Pettyver	Anno 3 Edward 6
June 25	Thomas Knight	
June 28	William Brooks	**
July 6	Joan Sheppard	****
July 6	Joan Brooks	** Anno 3 Edward 6
July 11	Hawes Cooke	
July 12	Joan Sheppard	**** See 6 July
July 12	Agnes Sheppard	****
July 13	Leonard Grove	
July 14	Richard Parker	

Date	Name	Remarks
July 15	Stephen Sheppard	****
July 15	Elizabeth Sheppard	****
July 15	Richard Gyles	
July 15	Amie [Anne?] Peirson	
July 19	Thomas Watson	
July 20	Ellen Styles	
July 24	Lucy Brooks	**
July 26	Richard Sheppard	****
July 28	William Parker	
July 28	Joan Presbury	
July 30	Ellen Raylston	
July 30	Mary Worrall	
Aug 3	Alice Clerke	
Aug 3	Elizabeth Clerke	
Aug 4	Lucy Dobbins	
Aug 5	Richard Sheppard	****
Aug 8	Elizabeth Castell	
Aug 9	Joan Brooks	**
Aug 11	Henry Brownsword	
Aug 11	Agnes Cannan	
Aug 13	Henry Skynner	
Aug 13	Margery Brownsword	
Aug 16	Thomas Dobbins	
Aug 16	Alice Dobbins	
Aug 20	Elizabeth Raylton	
Aug 21	Anne Castell	
Aug 21	Alice Castell	
Aug 30	Robert Bayley	
Sept 10	Elizabeth Cowper	
Sept 14	Agnes Tomlynson	
Sept 17	Richard Cowper	
Sept 25	Joan Smyth	
Sept 25	Bartholomew Cannan	
Sept 26	Ellen Shippie	Anno 3 Edward 6
Oct 13	Oliver Hurlocke	
Dec 6	Agnes Porter	Anno 3 Edward 6
Dec 30	Elizabeth Talbott	

1550

Date	Name	Remarks
Feb 12	Thomas, son of John White	Anno 3 Edwd 6(!)Baptised 6 Feb
Feb 17	Richard Birdsall	
Feb 22	Cicilie Burbage	
Feb 25	Alice, daur of John White	Anno 3 Edward 6(!) [Child]

Date	Name	Remarks
April 24	Mary, daur of Richard Skynner	Baptised 18 April
Aug 31	Dorothy, daur of Anthony Smyth	Baptised 17 Aug
Sept 19	John, son of John Ford	Baptised 12 Sept
Sept 21	Thomas, son of William Myller	Baptised 9 Sept
Oct 1	Bartholomew, son of Thomas Ragdall	
Oct 5	John, son of Geoffrey Brooks	** Baptised 14 July 1549
Nov 2	Thomas Wright	
Nov 24	Clement Talbott	

1551

Jan 13	Simon, son of John Ragdall	
Feb 18	John Bett	
Feb 25	John Ragdall	
March 1	Henry Boddymer	
July 21	Joan, daur of John Martyn	
July 22	Dorothy, wife of John Martyn	
Aug 31	Agnes, daur of Robert Houghton	Baptised 3 Jan 1550
Oct 6	Mary, daur of William Morgan	Baptised 25 Dec 1550
Nov 25	Nicholas Burton	

1552

Feb 7	Agnes Savage	
Feb 19	Amie, daur of Geoffrey Brooks	** Baptised 15 Feb 1552
March 13	Clement Sheppard	****
March 18	Richard Latham	
May 7	Margaret Hopkins, widow	
May 9	John, son of John Astell	
May 27	James, son of Mr Williamson	Baptised 17 May 1551
June 29	Thomas Wright, the elder	
July 12	William Tanner, a stranger	
July 15	William, son of Richard Nicholson	
July 17	Nicholas, son of Thomas Wylson	Baptised 11 Feb 1551
July 18	Thomas, son of Richard Skynner	
July 18	Anne, daur of John Norton	
July 20	John Cowper, the elder	
Aug 1	Agnes, daur of Nicholas Tedd	Baptised 28 July
Dec 28	Charity, daur of Nicholas Williamson	Baptised 22 Oct

1553

Jan 19	Thomas, son of John Hollis	Baptised 8 Jan
Jan 22	Thomas, son of John Hollis	?? - see Jan 19!
Jan 24	Alice Guy, widow	
Feb 4	Thomas, son of John Hollis	?? - see Jan 19!

Date	Name	Remarks
Feb 15	William, son of John Cowper	Baptised 28 Sept 1552
April 15	John Cox	
May 1	Agnes, daur of Ralph Birdsall	Baptised 12 April
July 24	John, son of William Myller	Baptised 15 July
Sept 14	William, son of Geoffrey Brooks	** Baptised 27 Aug
Oct 4	Mary, daur of Henry Bett	Baptised 11 July
Nov 15	Thomas, son of John Hurlocke	Baptised 5 Nov
1554		† No entries for these years.
1555		†
1556		†

SOURCES

Major sources of information
These include the following:
The Rev Serjeantson's 1904 book on the history of St Peter's church &c.
The Rev Glover's *Kingsthorpiana* of 1883, together with the other books cited in the Bibliography – particularly Bridges and Baker.
Vestry Meeting Books for 1808-1860 (NRO 189p/266/1) and for 1860-1958 (NRO 189p/267).
Churchwardens' Account Book 1781-1932: NRO 189p/263.

Walbeck Stream
Rev J C Fox: *Records of the Borough of Northampton*, ii 255.
Specification for works: NRO: FS 61/77.

The Manor
The following references are useful: VCH iv, 83. Baker, iv, p.39. Glover, p.1.
NRO: XYZ 1946. Glover, pp.10, 153. Legal documents: NRO: FHT 1, 2, & 14.
Rights of Warren: Details of the legal proceedings can be found in the records of the Star Chamber for the reign of Henry VIII at the Public Record Office: PRO catalogue ref: STAC 2/30/80, Bundle xxx.

Kingsthorpe Manor & Town Lands Charity
The appointment of Trustees on 24 January 1708/9: NRO: FHT 67.
Information regarding the Town Land: Glover, 1883; Kelly 1903; Baker, iv, p40.
Accounts of this charity: NRO 189p/289.
Papers relating to the footpath dispute: NRO: ZB/24/1-2, ZB/25/1-48 & ZB/26/1-18.

Land and Inclosure
Particularly useful sources in this area were:
Kingsthorpe Glebe Terriers (held at NRO).
The 1727 survey of the Kingsthorpe estates of John Robinson. NRO: ML 77.
A book of Rent Rolls relating to the Robinson estates. NRO: ML 62.
Poor Rate Assessments for 1833 and 1834. NRO: 189p/277-281.
The Crown Lease of 1747 to Sir John Robinson. NRO: ZA 6210.
The Kingsthorpe Inclosure Act was 6 Geo III c.80 Private. It is held at NRO: B (D) 703.

Other relevant NRO references are: Award: 189p/291. Inclosure Enrollment Volume B, pages 218ff. Inclosure Plan No 43, with good photostats in Map 2845.
The references to the inclosures in the North Field are from NRO: NPL 1019 and NPL 2419.
Regarding the Fremeaux/Thornton estates, see NRO documents: FHT 64 and ZA 6427; ZB 584/20-23 and Th 1997, 2000.

Local Government
Ordinances and statutes: Glover pp.38, 84.
Minutes of the Kingsthorpe Local Board and Urban District Council: NRO: Northampton Borough Records, Ref. 40/1-3.
Holy Trinity: NRO: 189p/232.

Problems of the Poor
Poor Levy Assessments: NRO: 189p/277/3.
The Poor Rate Assessment of 1786: NRO Ref: 189p/276.
Kingsthorpe Overseers' records: NRO Ref: 189p/270 to 274.
On the question of allotments, see Hammond, 103ff for details.
The minutes of the Select Vestry are in NRO: 189p/266/1.
Workhouse Inventory in NRO: 189p/272
Workhouse Regulations: NRO: 189p/285.

Charities for the Poor
Detail from the Order by the Charity Commissioners, 8 February 1683: NRO: XYZ 2061; also Glover, 1883: pp149-150.
Account Book of the Overseers of the Poor in 1690: NRO: 189p/270.
The details of the Will of Dame Sarah Prichard: Genealogical Memoranda, p.11.
The Kingsthorpe Bounty is mentioned in the VCH on p.88.

Overseers' records from the late 17th century
NRO references for documents quoted in the endnote: XYZ 2006; XYZ 2004; NPL 1019; XYZ 2005.

The workhouse
Deeds of property next to the workhouse: NRO: ZB 135/15/1-10.

Population Statistics
Hearth Tax Returns of 1674: Public Record Office: E 179/254/14.

SOURCES

'The Compton Census of 1676: A Critical Edition' Edited by Anne Whiteman. 1986, London. Page 388.
Militia List of 1777: Hatley, 178-9.
Bridges, p.413.

Epidemics
Cholera in 1638: State Papers; Domestic Series. Recorded in *Northamptonshire Notes & Queries*, Series I, Vol 6, page 168.

Occupations in 1777 and 1851
NRO documents referring to bakers and bakehouses: XYZ 2012; XYZ 2013; 189p/131/29 (Settlement); ZA 5097; ZA 5093 (abstract of title); YZ 7316.

Romance of the Mills
Windmill, Kingsthorpe North: NRO: ZB 584/20-23, FHT 64 and ZA 6427.
1574 Will of Robert Cooke: Archdeaconry of Northampton, 1st Series, T. 146.

The account books of Charles Fitzhugh
These are held under NRO references ZA 9042-9046.

The Coal Mine
Information extracted from Brooking, pp.27-8.

Education
For much of the detail of the history of the Free School and the National School I have made use of the excellent and detailed research carried out by G R Bispham for his thesis of 1970. (Northamptonshire Local Studies Room, Ref: 372: *The Kingsthorpe Schools*. Unpublished thesis for Dip. Ed., Univ. of Leicester, 1970.)
The inscription over the door of the Free School is from *Genealogical Memoranda* p.4.
Bridges, p.415, mentions the Free School master's salary.
For Philip Doddridge see Nuttall: letters 361, 421, 521, 1174, 1255, 1365, 1509. See also the chapter *Non-conformists in Kingsthorpe*.
Sale of the National Schoolmaster's House: NRO: Peterborough Diocesan records: PDBF 165.
Kingsthorpe School Managers' Minute Book, 20 Oct 1903 to 1 Feb 1949. NRO: ML 1675.

Hospital of St David or The Holy Trinity
For the history of this building up to the end of the 19th century I have relied heavily on C A Markham's text, as cited in the Bibliography. Stories about its conversion in the early years of the 20th century are from articles by Dickens in NRO: ZB 667/6/15 (12 April 1967) and ZB 667/6/19 (20 April 1967).

Sources for the four walks around old Kingsthorpe
Walk 1
Purchase of the Institute: Verbal communication by Rev A J Wolstenhulme, past Rector of Kingsthorpe.
Phyllis Collins's Thesis: *'Dovecotes, with particular reference to the dovecotes of Northamptonshire.'* (City of Leicester College of Education, Corby Annexe.) Northampton Public Library, Local Studies: Ref: 16979/1-120. This very interesting thesis covers the history, forms and uses of dovecotes from Roman times onwards. The author visited the majority of dovecotes in Northamptonshire, and provides a description of each including photographs.
1574 Will of Robert Cooke: Archdeaconry of Northampton, 1st Series, T. 146. The bills and receipts for the construction of Kingsthorpe Hall are at NRO: Th 2324-2479.
For more detail on the Lane family, see Baker, iv 41, and VCH, 83.
The information about the Kingsthorpe Bowling Club is contained in the five NRO documents CAM 1049-1053, which consist of record books kept by the Club between the years 1771 and 1852.
For information on the Kingsthorpe stone, see Diana Sutherland (2003) *Northamptonshire Stone* p.70.
Papers relating to the footpath dispute are at NRO: ZB/24/1-2, ZB/25/1-48 & ZB/26/1-18.
The Robinson estate Rent Rolls are at NRO: ML 62.
The Thornton Estate notebook is at NRO: FHT 61.
Charity Commissioners' Order: Glover, 1883: p.145

Walk 2
Mary Thornton's 1878 Diary: NRO: YZ 2166.
Thornton estate notebook: NRO: FHT 61.
Documents relating to *Green End Cottage*: NRO: ZB 584/12-16.
Details of *Church View*: NRO: ZA 5097; Particulars of sale, following the death of T J Trasler.
Faculty granted to Revd. Samuel Price Davies, Perpetual Curate of

Kingsthorpe, for taking down dilapidated buildings & erecting others in lieu thereof. Dilapidated barn, two stables & a cowshed, part of the Glebe Farm, standing near or adjoining his Parsonage house. NRO: 189p/252: 30 Aug 1855.
Witnesses to the footpath dispute: NRO: ZB 584/26/11 and ZB 584/25/1-48.

Walk 3
Collection of deeds relating No.1 The Green and its neighbours: NRO: ZB 135/15/1-10.
Description of the estate of Geo. Danes deceased: NRO: ZB/542/14/4.

The Church and its Rectors
Descriptions of the church that I have used are found in Serjeantson (1904), Wolstenhulme (1982), Thorneycroft (1998) and the VCH.
The church survey: NRO: Peterborough Diocese Church Survey Books, Vol. 5, in X2159.
Details of the patronage are in Serjeantson (1904), p.157 and footnote.
Rev H I Longden's book on the Clergy of Northamptonshire and Rutland from 1500 to 1900 is a mine of information.

Church Business
Early Churchwardens &c.: NRO: 189p/269/1.
Early Churchwardens' records: NRO: 189p/260, 261, & 262.

Foundation of new Parishes
Establishment of Kingsthorpe Parish: NRO: Peterborough Diocese Records, C 14.
St Paul's: NRO: 189p/228.
St Matthew's: NRO: 189p/231.
Brooking, p.50.

Nonconformists in Kingsthorpe
Meeting House registrations: NRO: ML 581-583.
Geoffrey F Nuttall's calendar of correspondence of Philip Doddridge (see the Bibliography).
Moments in Time: A brief history of College Street Baptist Church 1697-1997, by David Powell. (NRO Ref: ROP 2901).

Entertainments
The Mountjoy poster is in the NRO collection D(CA)501.

BIBLIOGRAPHY

Baker, G. (1822) *The History and Antiquities of the County of Northampton*. Part I. (London). [Kingsthorpe: Vol IV, 39].

Bispham, G. R. (1970) The Kingsthorpe Schools. Unpublished thesis for Dip. Ed., University of Leicester. Northampton Library Local Studies Room; ref: 372.

Bridges, J. (1791) *The History & Antiquities of Northamptonshire*, compiled from the manuscript collections of the late learned antiquary John Bridges Esq., by the Rev. Peter Whalley. (Oxford). [Kingsthorpe: Vol I, 413].

Brooking, A. (1967) *Kingsthorpe: From Village to Neighbourhood*, 1851-1967. (Unpublished) Northampton Library Local Studies Room: Closed access: KING 942.55.

De Wilde, G. J. (1872) *Rambles Roundabout and Poems*. (NRO Library 319.) The author was editor of the Northampton Mercury. His writings were edited posthumously by Edward Dicey and printed and published by Dicey & Co., Mercury Office, Parade, Northampton.

Dickens, L. W. *Scrapbooks* containing articles by this reporter in the Chronicle & Echo and Mercury & Herald in the 1960s and 1970s. NRO: ZB 667/[Book No.]/[Page or cutting No.]

Fox, Revd. J Charles (Ed.) (1898) The Records of the Borough of Northampton; volume ii. *Genealogical Memoranda relating to the Family of Cooke of Kingsthorpe*, Etc. (1873), privately printed, Mitchell & Hughes, London. Northamptonshire Studies Collection, Public Library, Northampton.

Glover, J.H. (1883) *Kingsthorpiana, or Researches in a Church Chest*. Being a calendar of old documents now existing in the Church Chest of Kingsthorpe, near Northampton, with a selection of the MSS. printed in full, and extracts from others. (London). NRO Library ref. 1501 (LC).

Hall, David. (1995) *The Open Fields of Northamptonshire* (NRS Vol XXXVIII).

Hammond J L & Hammond Barbara. (1978)
The Village Labourer. Edited, with general introduction and bibliographical note by G E Mingay. (London: Longman).

Hatley, Victor A. (1973) *Northamptonshire Militia Lists* 1777.

Northamptonshire Record Society.

Hollowell, Steven (2000) *Enclosure Records for Historians*. (Chichester). Phillimore & Co Ltd.

Hone, Wm. (1832)*The Year Book...*(London).

Longden, Rev. H I (1938-1943) *Northamptonshire and Rutland Clergy from 1500*. (Northampton: Archer & Goodman.) NRO Library.

Markham, C.A. FSA (1898) *The Hospital of St David, or the Holy Trinity, Kingsthorp, Northamptonshire*. (Architectural & Archaeological Societies Reports & Papers, Vol. XXIV, pp 162-174). NRO Library.

Noon, Frank E & Valentine, Peter (1973) *Kingsthorpe Baptist Church, Northampton: Ter Jubilee 1823-1973: A Brief History*. A copy can be found in the Northamptonshire Studies Collection.

Nuttall, Geoffrey F. (1979) *Calendar of the Correspondence of Philip Doddridge D.D. (1702-1751)*. Northamptonshire Record Society Vol. XXIX and Historical Monuments Commission JP 26. London. HMSO.

Richardson, J.   (1999) *The Local Historian's Encyclopedia*. (London, Historical Publications Ltd). ISBN 0 9503656 7 X

Serjeantson, Rev.R.M. MA FSA (1904)
A History of the Church of St Peter together with the Chapels of Kingsthorpe and Upton. (Northampton: W Mark, 27 The Drapery).

_____ (1913) *Sanctuary Seekers in Northamptonshire*. (Architectural & Archaeological Societies Reports & Papers, Vol. XXXII, pp 423-484). NRO Library.

_____ (1915) *The Leper Hospitals of Northampton*. Reprinted from the Journal of The Northamptonshire Natural History Society, Vol. XVIII, No: 141, March 1915.(NRS Pamphlet 708 in NRO Collection).

Sutherland, Diana S (2003) *Northamptonshire Stone*. (Wimborne, The Dovecote Press).

Thorneycroft, R J NDD MCSD (1998) *St John the Baptist Church Revealed*. Produced for the District Church Council and available at the church.

VCH.   *The Victoria County History of the Counties of England.* A History of the County of Northampton in 4 volumes. Vol I: 1902 edited by W Ryland D Adkins BA & R M Serjeantson MA. Vol. IV: 1937 edited by L.F Salzman MA

FSA. [Kingsthorpe: IV, 81].

Wolstenhulme, Rev A J (1982) *A History of the Church and Parish of St John the Baptist, Northampton.* (Ramsgate, The Church Publishers).

Wright, Suzanne 1997. *Kingsthorpe, village or suburb: a study of a Northamptonshire parish 1700-1931.* (Unpublished Thesis for MA in Local History). Northampton Library Local Studies Room.

INDEX

Blackstone, George John 136
Bland, Elizabeth 111
Bland, Samuel 49
Blennerhassett, Mr 283
Bletsoe 161
Board of Health 61
Boddington family 255, 260
Boddington, Harriet 30
Boddington, Harriott 255
Boddington, Maria Catharina 255
Boddington, Miss Frances 126, 136, 139, 255
Boddington, Misses 136, 138, 179, 255
Boddington, Mrs Frances 295
Boddington, Susannah 255
Boddington, Thomas 179, 255
Bond, Mr 270
Bone boiling 71
Borough Boundary Inquiry 1900 72
Borough of Northampton Extension Order 1900 73
Boswell, Mr 116
Boughton 1, 17, 31, 38, 46, 73, 125, 126, 161
Boughton Field 33
Boughton Green Fair 138
Boughton Green Road 3, 14, 44, 45, 50, 52, 57, 62, 64, 117, 123, 130, 164, 227, 229
Boughton Meere 266
Bovate xii
Bowker, Charlotte Frances 206
Bowker, James 189
Bowker, Mary 205
Bowling Green 44
Bowling Green Club 8, 300. See also Kingsthorpe Bowling Green Club
Boys, John 95
Bradshaw, Billing 66
Bradshaw, George 287
Bradshaw, John 87
Brampton 161, 213, 265

Brampton Station 129
Braunfield, William 121
Brazier, George 114, 115
Brazier, Henry 115
Bread Fund, The 92, 259, 273
Breast-shot waterwheel 118
Breeches makers 106
Bretch Lane 33
Bretteyn, William 213, 263, 267
Bretts Lane 44
Brick kiln 4
Briggs family 142
Briggs, William 85, 87, 95
Bright, Robert 263
Brixworth 105, 112
Brockhall 21, 48, 123, 148, 175, 177, 206
Brook Field 3, 4, 24, 27, 31, 32, 33, 34
Brookes family 142
Brookes, William 97
Brookfield Road 5
Brookhaven, Mr 27
Brookland Road 5
Broughton stone 257
Brown, John 29, 110
Brown, Rev J T 291
Brown, William Henry Freise 242
Browne, Mr E M 16, 273
Brownknave family 142
Bryan, Mark 114
Bubonic Plague 105
Buckler, John 59
Buckler, William 287
Bugbrooke 59
Bunker, William 113
Burdsall, Richard 263
Burial Register 102
Burials 78, 84, 272
Burials 1539 - 1553 326
Burleigh Road 4, 51
Burnell, Walter 91
Burton family 142

de Houton, John 262
de Leeke, John 263
de Morton, Thomas 263
de Novo Castro, Hugh 262
de Putron, Rev John Percy 186, 256, 264
de Wilde, George James 5, 7, 10, 162, 165, 174, 235
de Windsor, William 262
Denarii xi
Dickens, L W 180
Dickenson family 142
Dickenson, Richard 111
Dickson, Charles. See Dixon, Charles
Diconson, Peter 18
Dines, John 36, 287
Dines, Mr 277
Dines, William 38
Dining Club 297
Diphtheria 66, 68
Dissolution of the monasteries 56, 74, 161
Dix, John 114, 115
Dixon, Charles 205
Dixon, Mary 205
Doddridge, Philip 133, 286, 288, 335
Doddridge's Northampton Academy 133, 141
Dolphin Cottage 203
Domesday Survey 2, 11, 99, 117
Dove Houses 48, 170, 171, 173, 215, 336
Dovecote, The Old 170, 171
Dovehouse Close 26, 49, 53, 192. See Dovecote, The Old
Dowdeswell, Lucy 266
Dowdeswell, William 266
Dr Morgan's Close 33
Drapery, Northampton 112
Dressmakers 107
Drury Lane 120
Duck End 67, 188, 194

Duck Lane 188, 206
Dumbleton, Samuel 49
Dunkley family 142
Dunkley, George 30, 110, 112
Dunkley, Mary 206
Dunkley, Thomas 287
Dunkley, W 117
Dunkley, Wiliam 109
Dunkley's Lodge 229
Dunmore, Robert 113
Durant, G T 283
Dwarris, Fortunatus 179

E

Ealey, John 287
Earl (formerly known as Litchfield) 243
Earl of Halifax 288
Earl, Richard 86
Earls Barton 148
Earls of Upper Ossory 157
East Haddon 161
Easter Vestry 268
Eastern Avenue 52
Eastern Avenue South 51
Ecclesiastical Commissioners 285
Edmunds family 142
Edmunds, Widow 36
Edmunds's Farm 3, 32, 42, 44, 46
Education 131, 335
Education Bill 1833 135
Edward the Confessor 11
Electricity 71
Elliott, Robert 112
Ellis, Mr 38
Ellis, Rev Welbore 214, 263
Ellis, Richard 111, 121
Enteric fever 61
Enterprise Works 52
Epidemics 102, 335
Episcopal Registers 5
Erysipelas 67

Johnson, John 116, 211, 287
Johnson, John (Architect) 176
Johnson, Mary 78
Johnson, Mr 279
Johnson, Mrs Mathilda Ruth 114, 115
Johnson, Richard 287
Johnson, Samuel 287
Johnson, Thomas 95
Johnson, Widow 36
Johnson, William 277
Johnson's Lane 44, 45, 67, 227
Johnston, Rev. 156
Jubilee Well 185
Julian calendar xiii
Justice of the Peace 85, 90
Justices of the Peace 56

K

Kelsey, Mrs E 70
Kelsey, William 224
Kelseys Yard School Cottages 291
Kenning, Joseph 38
Kenning, Josiah 241
Kenning, Robert 241
Kenning, Ruth 242
Kerkdorp, Captain 153
Kettering 72
Kettering Road 3, 4, 44, 51
Kilborn, William 120
Killingbeck, Mr 62
Kinestrop 11
King Charles I 143
King Charles II 143, 156
King Edward 1, 2
King Edward III 267
King Edward VI 262
King Edward VII 280
King George III 278
King George V 262, 274, 281
King Henry III 267
King Henry IV 74

King Henry VI 11
King Henry VII 11
King Henry VIII 11, 19, 56, 99
King James I 12
King John 12
King Richard II 12
King William IV Public House 114, 185,
    193, 195, 207, 294
King, Miss Sarah Ann 139
King's Park 3
King's Survey 1548 249
Kingestorp 11
Kingham, Oxon 266
Kings Well 7, 63, 164, 165, 166, 183,
    185, 193, 217
Kingsley 32
Kingsley Park 1, 68, 69, 72
Kingsley Road 3, 44, 51
Kingsthorpe Baptist Church 134, 186,
    222, 226, 288, 289, 290, 292
    Manse 292
    organ 292
Kingsthorpe Bounty 94
Kingsthorpe Bowling Green Club 174,
    336
Kingsthorpe Church 245. See St John
    the Baptist Church
Kingsthorpe Clinic 235
Kingsthorpe Club 83, 96, 154
Kingsthorpe Equitable Friendly Society
    96
Kingsthorpe Golf Club 53
Kingsthorpe Golf Course 5
Kingsthorpe Grove 6, 10, 44, 51, 52,
    140, 162, 296
Kingsthorpe Hall 49, 108, 116, 126, 138,
    164, 167, 173, 175, 176, 177, 178,
    211, 217, 256, 293, 295, 296
    stables 180
Kingsthorpe Heath 3, 17, 45, 93
Kingsthorpe Hollow 4, 62, 175
Kingsthorpe Horticultural Show 295